Ezra Pound's *Cantos*

A CASEBOOK

D1556980

EZRA POUND'S
Cantos

◆　◆　◆

A CASEBOOK

Edited by
Peter Makin

OXFORD
UNIVERSITY PRESS

2006

OXFORD
UNIVERSITY PRESS

Oxford University Press, Inc., publishes works that further
Oxford University's objective of excellence
in research, scholarship, and education.

Oxford   New York
Auckland   Cape Town   Dar es Salaam   Hong Kong   Karachi
Kuala Lumpur   Madrid   Melbourne   Mexico City   Nairobi
New Delhi   Shanghai   Taipei   Toronto

With offices in
Argentina   Austria   Brazil   Chile   Czech Republic   France   Greece
Guatemala   Hungary   Italy   Japan   Poland   Portugal   Singapore
South Korea   Switzerland   Thailand   Turkey   Ukraine   Vietnam

Published by Oxford University Press, Inc.
198 Madison Avenue, New York, New York 10016

www.oup.com

Oxford is a registered trademark of Oxford University Press

Library of Congress Cataloging-in-Publication Data
Ezra Pound's Cantos: a casebook / edited by Peter Makin.
p. cm.—(Casebooks in criticism)
ISBN-13 978-0-19-517528-8; 978-0-19-517529-5 (pbk.)
ISBN 0-19-517528-X; 0-19-517529-8 (pbk.)
1. Pound, Ezra, 1885–1972. Cantos.   I. Makin, Peter.   II. Series.
PS3531.O82C28517 2006
811'.52—dc22   2005022298

1 3 5 7 9 8 6 4 2

Printed in the United States of America
on acid-free paper

For Sara
who opens paths

Credits

cuso, is reprinted from *Pound e la Cina* (Milan: Feltrinelli, 1974), pp. 89–116, by permission of the author.

"A Metaphysics of the State," by Peter Nicholls, copyright © 1984 by Peter Nicholls, is reprinted from *Ezra Pound: Politics, Economics and Writing* (London: Macmillan, 1984), pp. 104–106, 112–125, by permission of the author.

Preface

Each Canto citation in the introduction and the following chapters is accompanied by a Canto number, either in Arabic or in Roman numerals. Where this Canto number is followed by a page number, in whatever style (for example, LIV, p. 285; or XVII.76; or 20/89), the page number refers to the edition used by the author of that essay, which is listed in or with his notes.

Since a given Canto is rarely more than a few pages in length, the Canto number is sufficient to find a cited passage without difficulty.

(By now the number of *Cantos* editions with different paginations is large. There is little point in rewriting all the *Cantos* page references in these essays to conform to the latest edition; this would be of no help to the student in a library that did not hold that edition, or the student who had picked up secondhand an edition dated before 1995, or the student who had sought out a pre-1975 Faber edition because she had been told [correctly] that its text was superior to those currently available.)

Abbreviations for other texts used in individual essays are listed before the notes to those essays. Short titles refer to books that are listed in "Selected Further Readings" at the end of this book.

Acknowledgments

This work, like all my academic writing over the past two decades, has been made immeasurably easier by the skills as a librarian of John L. Makin, formerly of Nottingham Trent University. I wish to thank Massimo Bacigalupo of Genoa University for helpful suggestions. I thank my colleagues in the Faculty of Letters at Kansai University for providing the environment that has made this writing possible: most particularly Tetsuhiko Kamimura, friend and mentor for 22 years.

Contents

Ezra Pound's *Cantos*

A CASEBOOK

Introduction

PETER MAKIN

◆   ◆   ◆

P OUND'S MASTERPIECE *The Cantos* took him at least fifty years to write—from, say, 1915 to 1967—but, for the first 35 years of the long poem's life, there were no developing critical approaches to it, for the poem was not being read.[1] The poet himself had to provide theoretical frames for those few who tried to approach it. By the time these frames were discovered by the academic world, the poem had changed, and this has had consequences for *Cantos* criticism.

The Cantos had begun with a method that was *par excellence* impersonal and dogma-free. It had passed through a dogmatic phase; and it ended in a situation where the only strong connector between the parts was the speaker's "I." Put off the scent by Pound's hints, critics at first found only "holistic"[2] schemes of interpretation, organizing the whole long poem as one coherent work. Later *Cantos* criticism began to decode the language in which Pound had hidden some of his real concerns, and to see how deep were the breaks between the major segments of the poem and how much they were controlled by shifts in the writer's politics. And now that the whole wealth of manuscript documentation—drafts, letters, local and minor publications—in the archives Pound left has begun to be explored, we have reached a conception so fluid that it scarcely seems possible to talk of coherences. We see the groping vision that the writer had of the present moment in which he was writing; his recall of fading traces left by former versions of his own self, as they struggled with the political scenes they were confronted with; and sketch-maps—always growing less clear—for ways out of the thicket in which his attempts to "write Paradise" had entangled him. The great work does, indeed, support differing approaches, just because—partly from intention, and partly not—it changed.

Pound began to publish pieces of his great work in 1917, but by that time he was already moving into critical oblivion. In 1931, Iris Barry would look back at the great days of Pound's literary "vortex" during the First World War. She recalled the weekly meetings in a restaurant in Regent Street—Pound with his greenish cat-eyes, Ford Madox Ford back from the Front, the "tall, lean and hollow cheeked" T. S. Eliot—all described with immense respect and affection, as for Barry's own golden youth. But the whole account of Pound is already in the past tense. It concludes wistfully:

> The immensely larger-than-life-size head of Pound by Gaudier-Brzeska is presumably still sinking into the ground in Miss Hunt's garden. Pound himself is invisible and, save for his own poetry, comparatively inaudible nowadays. He pontificates rarely, has few disciples, as though with that immense effort of his from 1912 to 1919 he had done all that (had in truth done more than) could be expected of anyone and were glad of the years from thirty-five onwards to till his own plot.[3]

"Comparatively inaudible," says Barry, and—perhaps out of kindness—she adds "save for his own poetry. . . ." But the poetry, too, was inaudible: in 1931 no one was reading it.

Such had been the case since at least 1917. And such would remain the case until, let us say, 1947 or 1950. Robert Creeley described (in 1965) how he and Olson and their friends had rediscovered Pound:

> [I]t should . . . be remembered that during the forties, that time in which we came of age, Pound's situation was, in all senses, most depressed. To the young of that period he was often simply a traitor, an anti-semite, an obscurantist, a money crank—and such courses in universities and colleges as dealt with modern poetry frequently avoided all mention of the *Cantos*.[4]

For three decades the critical world was uninterested in reading Pound's offshore productions, let alone in developing any consensus as to how they worked.

Pound, of course, had done very well in literary London of the 1910s—still the center of the English-speaking literary world—while he was the flamboyant aesthete. London was fond of poets who wore long capes and ate the flowers from the dinner-table centerpiece: that was Wilde and Dowson. But the magazine *Blast* (first issue, 1914), which Pound helped Wyndham Lewis to produce, took aim at the British middle class's idea of itself and its privileged relation to Nature, to the empire, and to the late Queen Victoria. It named a great many names. People began to take offense; Pound was no longer fun. The functionaries of literature wanted to disown Pound, and he soon handed them more reasons.

He found a vehicle for his disgust in the works of the Roman poet Propertius, which he adapted to produce an oblique satire on London and its empire. But Pound's Latin, though often acute in catching the tone of an author where others had not, was of a fast-skimming kind, and this ironic quasi-translation of Propertius was full of obvious errors.[5] So he was now a charlatan: he had pretended to be a scholar and was not. His so-called translations of the Anglo-Saxon *Seafarer,* and the allegedly Greek scansion of "The Return," were likewise found to be fakes. He now conformed to one of the standard types of the American on British shores: loud, self-advertising, and empty.

The reality was that Pound was a good deal more professional than his attackers: he knew exactly what his poetry needed and worked to the utmost to acquire it. But he had attempted to break through "the hybrid social intellectual ring to something that is a matter purely of the imagination or intelligence," as Wyndham Lewis put it;[6] he had offended those fringes between the aristocracy and the upper middle classes which "ran things." They had their weapon of revenge, and used it; Pound was excluded.

Pound quit London in 1920, and ensconced himself in Paris. Since at least 1915, he been working on what he called his "forty-year epic," the *Cantos*. But he had not yet found a way to start it. Here and there he published his first attempts in groups of two or three Cantos, but they were stillborn drafts, fixed in a stilted pastiche-Romantic mode:

> And Louis, French King, was jealous of days unshared
> This pair had had together in years gone.[7]

He offered this in 1921 to a Paris–New York avant-garde dominated by Dada, by the mysteries of Gertrude Stein, and (in 1922) the severe architecture of Joyce. Pound's mode was clearly fustian. Finally (Massimo Bacigalupo, in chapter 6, below, vividly describes the turning-point), Pound discovered his method, his true tone, and his modernity. In 1925 commenced the long series of *Cantos* sections in books. But his critical audience was gone.

In this critical silence, Pound began to offer hints to the few friends and disciples interested in reading him. These hints make up what we can call the first stage in Pound criticism: the set of integrating principles on which, at the outset, his whole structure was intended to be built.

The first principle was the "ideogrammic method," which can be subtitled "concretenesses judge each other."[8] General terms, like "humanity," "freedom," "love," Pound would argue, are inherently vague: if you wish to communicate an understanding precisely, it is necessary to take complexes of *particulars*, and arrange them so that they interact, so that they "talk to each other." So, in the early Cantos, we get what Pound loved to call "blocks" of material adjoining each other. There is one, for example, in Canto XIII, where Confucius, amid humble rural scenes, speaks to his friends and disciples on the subject of scholarly honesty:

" . . . And even I can remember
A day when the historians left blanks in their writings,
I mean for things they didn't know,
But that time seems to be passing."

Next door there is Canto XIV, with its professors

sitting on piles of stone books,
obscuring the texts with philology,
hiding them under their persons,
the air without refuge of silence,
the drift of lice, teething,
and above it the mouthing of orators

One cannot *not* correlate these. There is something there, to begin with, about self-knowledge, and about its relation with self-advertisement. There is also . . . the reader can consult her own intelligence and experience; the matter will bear a good deal of thought; and in that sense, there is no limit to what this interaction of blocks "means." But between these blocks, in Pound's book, there is no explaining discourse: for any such discourse would blur, and at the same time simplify the relations between the blocks, and those relations are the meaning.

When Pound was finally rediscovered in the 1950s, this principle, planted here and there in Pound's critical writings and letters, was one of the first to be understood, and Hugh Kenner expounded it brilliantly in *The Poetry of Ezra Pound*:

> Anyone who has seen pots boiling on the ungainly black iron wood stove in the back of a farmhouse kitchen will know what is meant by taking it to typify, as distinguished from the enamelled gas-range, a 'way of life'. An attempt to explore his sense of this way of life further will yield remembered details like the oilcloth on the kitchen table, the beaten path to the root-house, the worn stair-boards, the cupboards filled with preserves, the rocker on the back porch. Even a casual visitor's knowledge of the 'feel' of American farmhouse life is perfectly real, though resistant to propositional formulation and derived from observed particulars that have no syllogistic connection with one another. These data do not lie about inscrutable in odd corners of the mind. The mind works upon them, relates them, draws from them real if not articulate knowledge. Hence the good poet or movie director knows exactly what glimpses to give us. An attempt to convey such knowledge leads back to the data. The knowledge resides in the particulars.[9]

It is the most "open" principle there could be, and also one of the most impersonal, for the author "says nothing."

This, then, was one of the master-plans offered by Pound, and eventually taken up decades later by *Cantos* criticism. But Pound offered it only indirectly, as part of his writing about literature in general, and he never showed how it would apply to the *Cantos*. Meanwhile his best allies floundered. W. B. Yeats had taken up winter residence alongside Pound in Rapallo, on the Italian Riviera, with its "thin line of broken mother-of-pearl along the water's edge." There Pound seems to have made a serious effort to explain the workings of his long poem. Yeats strove to pass on the scheme to his readers in *A Packet for Ezra Pound*, written in 1928; but it is clear that his real opinion was that Pound's scheme for the *Cantos* was no more than a mathematical game on mechanically Futurist principles.[10]

Pound was only beginning to describe the other aspect of his plan, which concerned the content. The "ideogrammic" principle showed how the "blocks" were supposed to interact, but it could not show why they were selected. Pound's answer to that involves an intersection between the moral and the metaphysical.[11]

On the moral plane, Pound wanted to show and compare a great series of human mental states, organized into three great clusters derived from

Dante: the Hellish, the Purgatorial, and the Paradisal. He wanted to educate his reader by highlighting distinctions between states of mind seen around him, in the present world—illustrated by constant juxtaposition with the past. This is a method for telling the reader, by illustration-and-comparison (ideogram), what a given mode of behavior really consists of: the horrible or admirable aspects of it that are usually hidden, and its consequences.

Pound had been working at this mode since his very first surviving attempts at a long poem, produced when he was eighteen or nineteen. In the most fully depicted circle of his early Hell he comes across figures who, his guide (Dante) tells him, are "the searchers for dogmas." They are seen

> some digging in the stony earth
> & others chipping at the larger pieces of yellow rock,
> and some peering with dulled eyes
> at empty slabs as one that readeth in a failing light
> & ever rattling in their dry throats, & all speaking together
> so that none heard what his neighbour said.[12]

That's the principle of the *contrappasso*, as Pound was to explain it in *The Spirit of Romance* (1910). It is a principle of justice: the punishment fits the crime by being an extension of that state of mind in which it was committed—which was itself hellish. This principle clearly still operates in the new Cantos published in 1925, with its bankers,

> the ranked presbyterians,
> Directors, dealers through holding companies,
> Deacons in churches, owning slum properties,
> *Alias* usurers in excelsis, . . .
> whining over their 20 p.c.
> and the hard times, . . .
> (XII.55[13])

For, like Dante, Pound "conceived the real Hell, Purgatory, and Paradise as states, and not places."[14]

But one key element of the Dantescan plan was missing—as Reed Way Dasenbrock argues cogently (chapter 4). In one of its meanings, Dante's great poem is a spiritual autobiography: it tells how he, personally, began lost ("in Hell"), but found enlightenment. But Pound in practice ignored this element: he described Dante's plot as merely "a walk upstairs"[15]—a walk by the hero, Dante, visiting all those planes that the damned and enlightened inhabited. In his own poem, at these early stages, any reference to the poet's self was almost invisible. The method was impersonal—as impersonal as the best Imagist poem.

By 1930, when *A Draft of XXX Cantos* was published, Pound had included elements that corresponded to the "top end" of Dante's *Purgatorio*, namely the "earthly paradise." Canto XVII is a locus of calm clear light, like the landscape backgrounds of Italian paintings of the 15th century:

> With the first pale-clear of the heaven
> And the cities set in their hills
>
> (XVII.76)

It is inhabited by nymphs, gods, and goddesses, but also by some of Pound's Renaissance heroes: Borso d'Este, the peacemaker, and Sigismondo Malatesta, the *condottiere* who built the great "temple" at Rimini. These, in Pound's scheme of things, are people who rise to some long-term constructive aim—like Pound's newer hero, Mussolini.[16]

But to understand the idea of his Paradise, we must switch to another mode: the metaphysical. In 1932 he answered a young questioner about the *Cantos* by saying, "There are only three main planes. . . . Best div[ision is] prob[ably] the permanent, the recurrent, the casual."[17]

Pound had a deep belief that some states of mind are always there, and that one could "enter" them, thus becoming that god or that goddess—for "A god is an eternal state of mind."[18] He also held that when one perceived or underwent what Ovid called "metamorphosis," or transformation—when a creature seemed to become a creature of an entirely other kind—one understood the permanent realities. In Ovid's story, the fisherman Glaucus eats a certain strange herb, plunges into the sea, and becomes a companion of Neptune. Dante picks up this story and uses it to explain the transformation that he himself underwent as he entered the realm of Paradise. Beatrice was gazing intently on the "eternal wheels" of the spheres; Dante gazed on her; and

> Gazing on her such I became within, as was Glaucus, tasting of the grass that made him the sea-fellow of the other gods.

And just in case we don't understand how total his transformation was in that moment, he tells us:

To pass beyond humanity may not be told in words, wherefore let the example satisfy him for whom grace reserveth the experience.[19]

Pound seized on this passage in his *Spirit of Romance*, when he tried to explain
why Dante surpassed both Wordsworth and Whitman in the expression of
pantheism: "The disciples of Whitman cry out concerning the "cosmic
sense," but Whitman . . . has never so perfectly expressed the perception of
cosmic consciousness as does Dante in the canto just quoted."[20] And this,
Pound explained in a letter to his father, in 1927, was one of the planes of
the *Cantos*: "The 'magic moment' or moment of metamorphosis, bust thru
from quotidien [daily life] into 'divine or permanent world.' Gods, etc."[21]

These hints, then, offered schemes for Pound's long poem. They suggested what the interactions of the "ideogrammic" principle might yield:
what kinds of understanding a reader might look for, for example, when
she moved from the god Dionysos in Canto II to the serene Confucius of
Canto XIII to the busy greed of Canto XIV and its

> air without refuge of silence,
> the drift of lice, teething

These were hints toward a "holistic" interpretation of the *Cantos*: one that
would explain how its main parts interrelated, how the subthemes supported these, how the whole was focused as one. But time was passing;
the author was changing.

It was always part of Pound's understanding of the relation between art
and life that one could not write the very greatest poetry unless he was
"up against it," like the hero-poet of the Anglo-Saxon *Wanderer*.[22] One could
not write about life from the outside. And he came from a New England
activist tradition. (Back in 1905 he had had to defend himself against his
mother's charges that he was a frivolous aesthete. His hero, Dante, he had
countered, "probably encountered much more personal Danger than Mr
Rooseveldt in Cuba. He held chief office in his city & that for clean politics
& government."[23]) It followed that Pound needed a crusade—a cause with
a leader. He had been finding one; and his identification with this leader,
Mussolini, would take him to places that changed his view of life, his tone
in writing, and his poetic method.

In the early 1920s, Pound said, "England was dead and the corpses were
lying about in the streets; . . . France was dead but had had the decency to
bury the dead; . . . Italy was the only Country of the three where any vital
activity was taking place." Italy's Fascism, in that phase, did not have the

reek that it would develop later. Mussolini was simply the rather heavy-handed young leader of a régime that had set out to shake up a decaying country, rather in the manner of a Hugo Chavez or a Che Guevara. Pound identified with the leader because of the charisma that attracted a good many visitors in those days, from the American ambassador to Winston Churchill. But there was another factor: Mussolini seemed to be open to Pound's ideas about economics: "About 1929, I had an interview with BENITO MUSSOLINI, who knew my book "GUIDO CAVALCANTI," which I had presented to him the year before. He expected me to talk about my book, but I took a very strong economic questionnaire to him."[24]

Pound identified with the Duce—the "Boss," as he called him—to an extraordinary degree, and Mussolini's career dragged Pound along in its wake. As the position of Italy grew more isolated, Pound stiffened. He changed from explorer to dogmatist, while the method of the *Cantos* moved from "ideogram" 's openness to the squeezing of slogans out of history read by program.

Pound had his "key" to the Hell of history, derived from economists such as C. H. Douglas and Silvio Gesell. Manipulations of money continuously enriched a whole class of lenders at the expense of the public, and government finances and an endless series of wars were arranged in order to feed this system. This was Pound's crusade: this was the wrong he wanted to put right. This was the theory he first tried to sell to Mussolini; who, by origin a socialist radical, was very inclined to make the sympathetic noises that would persuade Pound he had a convert.[25] The Duce's scorn for the Western democracies was enough to persuade his poet-disciple that Mussolini wanted Italy to break free from the secret rings of international finance.

The Wall Street Crash of 1929, quickly followed by the Depression, shook poets; some quit poetry, others turned Marxist. Pound already had his answer to the question why the Depression had happened, and his need to expound it became stronger. Meanwhile Hitler was rising out of the economic chaos created by the First World War and the Versailles Treaty, and Mussolini was becoming fascinated by the glamour of Hitler's militarism. In 1935 Mussolini invaded Ethiopia, and this was a crucial step in Pound's emotional shift. The League of Nations, dominated by the Western democracies, announced economic sanctions against Italy, and Pound's denunciation of the democracies rose to shriller heights.

Pound now routinely denounced all poets, including his friends and correspondents, who refused to plunge into the study of economics and be persuaded that Douglas's theories were the answer to the current ills.

The usual concerns of poetry were simply out of date. And so now the method of the *Cantos* had to change.

Where, before, the "ideogrammic" principle had let "blocks" of unlike things (as it were) talk to each other, openly, in a language to be understood, not by the rationalizing and categorizing mind, but by the whole intuiting sensibility, now Pound forced blocks of material, arranged historically, to say things to each other explicitly, in slogans, in black and white. Thus Canto L commemorates the defeat of the Austrians by Napoleon:

> 14th. June, 1800 MARENGO
> Mars meaning, in that case, order
> That day was Right with the victor
>   mass weight against wrong
>   (L.247)

Where "ideogram" had let the reader infer a complex truth from organized data, here the poet really gives no data: here is no picture, nothing seen. Instead the statement of an abstraction is glamorized by rhetoric (not "war," but "Mars"; not "on that day right was with . . . ," but "That day was Right with . . ."). As his material thins, Pound reverts to the archaism that, in 1912, he had striven to throw out along with the iambic pentameter:

> in their soul was usura
> and in their hand bloody oppression
>   (L.248)

And his matter thins toward that ancient simple polarity that has boxed in the mind of the West ever since Plato—a polarity where on one side is Light, Enlightenment, and the Mind, and on the other is Darkness and Moral Filth, and Matter. Thus Pound describes the "usurious" powers arrayed against Napoleon:

> S..t on the throne of England, s..t on the Austrian sofa
>   (L.248)

The excremental extreme always goes with the move toward dualism in Pound's mind.

This divide allows Pound to grow more and more hysterical in his rant against the Evil, for it is an Evil allied with Darkness, and Secrecy, and all that is alien, hidden, and unknown. In particular it allows him to develop his inhuman rant against Jews, for Pound's evil—financial corruption—was by definition hidden, an unrecognized conspiracy, and the darker turns of Western cultural history gave him a ready-made enemy to inhabit its secret spaces, in the form of the Jewish people. From the late nineteenth century there had been available the widespread myth of the international Jewish conspiracy to control the world, which Pound was to buy into entirely.[26]

The "ideogrammic" principle was supposed to save poetry from the crudity of "ideas," which lump phenomena together under labels with unreal boundaries between them and then form the basis for that futile form of juggling known as "reasoning" (or the syllogism). But Pound now had certain ideas that he wanted to sell, and sell quickly, to his reading public. There was the idea that "usury" (profiteering on the lending of money) corrupted culture, and also political culture, leading to the domination of lies and a succession of wars. This needed to be shown historically. So, from about 1930 onwards (as Reed Way Dasenbrock has argued), the material of the *Cantos* began to be arranged in a new kind of order: an order given by history.[27]

From Cantos XXXI to LI the poem is dominated by large sets of Cantos concerning one given historical period each. John Adams and Thomas Jefferson receive four Cantos, their spiritual "descendant" Martin Van Buren one, and Monte dei Paschi of Siena—the only good bank in history (according to Pound)—receives four. Then, suddenly, from 1937, this "historical unwinding" accelerates. At some point in 1937—the year that Italy signed up with Germany and Japan in the anti-Comintern pact—Pound obtained *The Works of John Adams*, and by 1938 he had decided that this, with a multi-volume pro-Confucian history of China, should be his sources for the next section. Working at frenetic speed, by March 1939 he had ready two whole new blocks of roughly ten Cantos each, covering the history of China from the beginning to (neatly) the year of Adams's birth, and from Adams's birth to the end of his life.

The only relation with "ideogram" that persisted was a changed idea of concreteness: Pound worked in little snippets from his sources that gave no context, but expected the reader to infer essential qualities from some glimpse of action or scene. To help the reader toward meanings that were now simply political, Pound fell back on various forms of slogan.[28]

The earlier Cantos had been a jungle, a kaleidoscope of interacting differences, because that was what their writer saw as a desirable condition of life: to be the free, quick-leaping spirit, relying on no more than mental powers that were developed because they had not been hemmed in by dread. Pound in his early days was essentially Ovidian, believing in the sudden vision:

> Lynx-purr, and heathery smell of beasts,
> > where tar smell had been,
> Sniff and pad-foot of beasts,
> > eye-glitter out of black air.
> > > (II.8)

Even as late as 1931, in Canto XXXI, the ideal statesman was Thomas Jefferson, a man of pure intuition, who embodied the ability to respond to circumstance by the force of genius: and this Jefferson, of course, was a figure of Mussolini as he admired him in those days. Now, in 1940, the ideal statesman was an Adams who pondered the history of human behavior, worked out institutional frameworks, and defined his terms.[29]

And here, in 1940, the *Cantos* stopped. Perhaps it makes little sense to say that, even if Europe not collapsed about his ears, Pound would have been stuck. But the reality seems to be that by 1940 the writing of the poem had reached a dead end. For "even after seventy-one cantos of his epic had been written," as Dasenbrock puts it, "Pound had not quite figured out how to write it."[30] And one of the things that he had not been able to handle was the relation between complex and fully felt experience, on the one hand, and the ideas that arose from his involvement (as a political writer) with the immediate situation of history. Deeply felt experience had moved well in the open anti-framework of the "ideogrammic" principle. It did not go well in a framework mainly designed to put over certain ideas.

Pound, then, had provided his readers, indirectly and belatedly, with a set of holistic principles ("ideogrammic," moral, and metaphysical) for reading the *Cantos* as one work, with parts variously supporting one overall shape. But by the early thirties those principles in fact were no longer applying. Already the long poem was at least two.

But Pound had a schedule, and he persisted with it. By the end of the 1930s he felt that he had finished expounding the human errors of hell and purgatory, and he set himself to "write Paradise."[31] In December 1941 came Pearl Harbor, and from that point until the end of the war Pound was in almost complete isolation from the English-speaking world—if we except the one-way non-communication of his ill-conceived radio broadcasts, cast in a hectoring cracker-barrel mode that Pound believed would make them accessible to Americans, but peppered with the shorthand references and cryptic economic slogans that made his letters incomprehensible even to his friends. He had not stopped trying to write the *Cantos*, but all he could produce was fragments, in Italian, of paradisal visions interwoven with myth.[32] That is, from spring 1940 to June 1944, Pound produced no Cantos and no material directly usable for Cantos: the longest break in their history. In June 1944, he set about writing two Cantos in Italian, essentially appeals to the courage and historical sense of Italians, calling on them to rally to the resurgence of the Fascist regime (by now in reality a puppet of the Nazis) against the advance of the Allies through north Italy.[33]

Then came the end of the war, and the *Pisan Cantos*, which amounted to another major break in the architecture of the long poem. But this break led to Pound's best poetry, and, finally, brought the attention of the literary world—thus starting critics' investigation of those plans and purposes that the whole work had begun with.

The shift in time between Pound as irate propagandist for an embattled Fascism and the Pound of the *Pisan Cantos*—broken poet of the self, of the lost companions, and of Nature—is very short. In April 1945 he was still sending items to his contact in Milan for broadcast by the radio of Mussolini's Salò Republic. By July he was imprisoned in the U.S. Army's camp for its dregs and criminals, had been through a kind of emotional collapse, and was starting to write.[34]

At the beginning of 1945, Pound seems to have seen his chief value to the world not as a poet but as a writer on politics. He was handed over to the U.S. Army interrogators in May 1945 under impending charges of treason for having supported the enemy in wartime. He then set out on a double effort. First, he aimed to clear himself of the charge of treason by persuading his captors that his politics would have been the right course for his country. Roosevelt, abetted by Churchill, had in fact betrayed the Constitution by ignoring the clause on the issuance of money; Pound had been carrying out his constitutional duty by telling hearers of these facts. Second, since the ultimate basis for his approach to politics was the ethics of Confucius, based on self-examination and integrity in administration, Pound felt it was his urgent duty to finish the translations of Confucius he had been working on, and this he now tried to do. So he labored—as the camp commandant observed—not to prepare a legal defense, but to finish his Confucius. His English typescript of the Confucian "Chung Yung" is dated 10 May 1945.

He seems to have thought that his message was persuading his young

interrogators; hence his total shock when he was told he would be taken
to a prison camp and was handcuffed to an MP and driven off. The camp
was the Disciplinary Training Camp outside Pisa, where 3,600 of the Army's
rapists, murderers, and thieves endured a 14-hour-a-day reform regime or
waited to be shipped off for execution in nearby Aversa. No one ever
escaped; an Army newspaper dated November 1945 noted that, from a
recent attempt, the count had been seven shot down and three recaptured.

Pound was put in one of the cells for those waiting to be executed,
specially reinforced with the sliced-steel strip used for the foundations of
runways, and there, as an important and dangerous prisoner, was kept
incommunicado. Neither prisoners nor guards were allowed to converse
with him. Overhead the only protection was a piece of tarpaper thrown
over the cage; there was no shelter from the hot wind in the day or from
the Klieg lights at night. Pound was by now almost 60. It became clear
that something was happening to him, and the doctors, who feared they
might be blamed, demanded that he be allowed to speak to someone.[35] He
was permitted to walk for an hour a day with the Catholic chaplain.
Finally, after three weeks, he was moved to the medical tents, having
undergone some kind of experience that he later described as a mental
"lesion."

The immediate trigger for the writing of the *Pisan Cantos* seems to have
been the execution of Pound's companion from the next cell:

> black that die in captivity
>   night green of his pupil, as grape flesh and sea wave
>   undying luminous and translucent
>
> (LXXIV.452)

From then on, between the beginning and the end of July, Pound impro-
vised his poem continuously, writing on a table built from a packing-case
by a sympathetic prisoner:

> "doan you tell no-one
>   I made you that table"
>
> (LXXIV.454)

And the result of this month-long improvisation, with perhaps one pair
of major additions, is the *Pisan Cantos* as we know them.

The *Pisan Cantos* are unprecedented in Pound's long poem (and in modern poetry), being a sort of recollection of the past, plus contemplation of

things seen, plus free meditation on all this. The poem sees what is in
front of it, or remembers things seen, with unequaled clarity. The particular phrasing of some haiku-like glimpse will bring in layers of meaning
from the classics or from myth. And always this vividness of observation
takes Pound back to his politics.

He watches a resting fellow prisoner—like the majority of those in the
Disciplinary Training Camp, an Afro-American, and therefore evoking
Pound's studies of Leo Frobenius and his interest in African masks:

> and Mr Edwards superb green and brown
> in ward No 4 a jacent benignity,
> of the Baluba mask: "doan you tell no one
> I made you that table"
> methenamine eases the urine
> and the greatest is charity
> to be found among those who have not observed
> regulations
> (LXXIV.454)

The word "superb" suggests the man's solidity and calmness (Latin *superbus*:
proud), as well as the fine color sense Pound finds in Africans; it goes with
this prisoner's benevolence in repose. But this is the man who—breaking
the rules—helped Pound by making him a writing table. The act of charity
is not some idealized vagueness, but as concrete as the drug that helps an
old man pee; and yet it is tied to one of Pound's motifs in the *Cantos*: the
wild unregulated figure who shows real kindness. (The main example up
to now has been Cunizza da Romano, who freed her slaves; now Pound
sees himself as one of the slaves.[36]) And so we move straight to a renewed
justification of Pound's politics:

> not of course that we advocate—
> and yet petty larceny
> in a regime based on grand larceny
> might rank as conformity nient' altro [and nothing more]

Since the Western democracies are based on theft, one can't blame those
at the bottom of the heap for imitating. Thus the long improvisation of
thought brings in many concerns, some from the earliest Cantos, some
from Pound's wartime involvement with Mussolini, some from what he
now sees.

This is undisputedly Pound's masterpiece, but it amounts to the second major collapse of his plans for the long poem. This is not juxtaposition of "blocks" any more. The unit of thought is a long wandering with a very uncertain ending. Sometimes the "ending" is a subtle shift, where secondary associations in something mentioned take over (unannounced) the dominant role of connector. Sometimes the "ending" is the crudest, most unpersuasive of fake transitions.[37] Where a new meander starts, it is no longer clearly distinct in time and place, as Confucius (in Canto XIII) had been from the minor racketeer Baldy Bacon (XII and XIII), or Siena from the Chinese Seven Lakes (XLIX and L). It is true that there are real continuities between these Cantos and what has gone before, in their concerns, often evoked by micro-allusions. But now the real and essential connector is not unstated relations between major blocks of material presented without comment, but, simply, the "I": the thought and experiences of the seeing writer in the then-and-now.

It was at this point in the lifetime of the *Cantos*, when they had changed radically for the second time, that they started to come within the horizons of literary criticism. Scandal made them of interest, and a bold critical act seemed to justify serious attention. They appeared in July 1948, and six months later their author received the Bollingen Prize, awarded by a committee set up under the auspices of the Library of Congress. Since Pound by this time had been arraigned in Washington of charges of treason, and had escaped trial only on a plea of insanity, this seemed to the media-led public to be rewarding Fascism and anti-Semitism. Pound and the committee were vilified. At this point the young Canadian academic Hugh Kenner intervened. He had been directed to Pound's works by his mentor, Marshall McLuhan, had visited Pound in the lunatic asylum, and having read through the major Pound works in prose that his publishers had limpingly kept in print, in three months he wrote *The Poetry of Ezra Pound* (1950), which was the starting point of all postwar critical interest in the *Cantos*.

Kenner constructed his starting point around those principles that he had found set out by Pound in his critical prose and his letters. They were those principles of coherence that I have described: the "ideogrammic method" and the distinctions between planes of moral and metaphysical being. Kenner removed the reader's terror by showing him that these methods were not new. "Ideogram" could be found working in Dickens, in Wordsworth; the ideas behind it, in Aristotle. Kenner laid great emphasis (for the same purpose) on Pound's concern with tradition, on learning from the artistic past.

This holistic approach was very persuasive. The principles themselves seemed valid, and yet fresh, and Kenner had an eye for the passages of poetry whose richness might show them working. Kenner had a program: as an ideological conservative, he wanted to use Pound as a great argument for renewal of cultural tradition, which would itself be a reflection of an underlying permanence in the nature of things. This was, essentially, a Platonism.

To some extent this program matched Pound's, especially as Pound was promoting it in the frantic literary activities he conducted from inside the walls of St. Elizabeths Hospital, where he was confined, as a legal lunatic, for twelve years. But it is remarkable how little either program limited the wider effect of Pound's *Cantos* or his literary criticism. Pound now became the real literary parent of two major related movements of the 1950s: the Beats and the Black Mountain poets. None of their writers would have subscribed to his politics or to the tradition-based view of culture that he was now espousing. They took Pound as a teacher because of the freshness of his approach to the art of writing, which aimed at real contact with experience and thought, and never at the borrowing of tokens and imitation of surfaces that made up the "well-made poem." Pound's writings had an overwhelming influence on Allen Ginsberg and Gary Snyder and many others of their generation: an influence rather similar to that of another father-figure, Kenneth Rexroth, who was at the opposite pole from Pound in any spectrum of politics.

Kenner's *Poetry of Ezra Pound* was followed by a generation of holistic critical approaches to the *Cantos*: Mancuso on "ideogram," Davenport on myth (for both of these, see below), Pearlman on the concept of the "sacred time" that human consciousness can break into, and Quinn on the principle of metamorphosis, to give a few notable examples.[38] Each of these studies tried to apply Poundian principles to the great Poundian work, taken as a whole.

But something in this was unreal. It ignored the fact that Pound had been, and was still, a Fascist and anti-Semite,[39] and that the poetry expressed these attitudes. It also ignored the fact that the poet and his poem had changed, and that these changes had a great deal to do with the politics. Several factors had caused this elision.

The poem obviously, in some way, "worked": the depth and freshness were there for all to see, and, as we have seen, they had their effect on young writers as much as on academic critics. Naturally enough, critics wanted to read the "rightness" of Pound's approach to writing into the rest of his attitudes. They succeeded in doing so: to read the analyses of

critics like Sister Bernetta Quinn one would think that Pound's views of
the world had been as innocent as Blake's. In certain ways Pound and
those who worked with him connived at this. His Italian Cantos—pure
Mussolinian ideology—were kept unpublished; initials ("H." and "M." for
Hitler and Mussolini) were used in certain passages of the *Cantos*; an edition
of his letters was produced that was revelatory, and had an immense influence on younger writers, but included none of the viciously anti-Semitic
passages that can be found in the archives of his correspondence. Meanwhile Pound's most virulently Fascist utterances lay unread in small
pre-war publications and in the articles he had written in Italian for the
propaganda effort of the Salò Republic. Pound himself would deny having
ever been a Fascist, though the center of Fascism is adherence to the single
Leader, and no Italian had outdone Pound in his willingness to serve Mussolini to the bitter end.[40]

The critics, having been led to some of the integrating principles behind
the *Cantos*, also wanted to believe that they governed the whole work.
Pound himself in a sense abetted this. His important criticism was all pre-
war; in it he explained the ideas that seemed to govern the *Cantos*; having
laid them out, he never retracted them, or gave a hint that they had
ceased to apply to the long work—perhaps because he did not want to
admit that they had.

By the 1980s, reader-response criticism seems to have made critics less
uneasy with the idea of a poem as a developing entity. And so "because
none of the static designs has proven generally persuasive," wrote Reed
Way Dasenbrock in 1988, "recent criticism has moved away from thinking
in terms of a grand structure towards a more dynamic and historical sense
of the poem. Pound always had a sense of the poem's design, but that
sense kept changing."[41] Such writers as Bacigalupo (1980), Peter Nicholls
(1984), and Dasenbrock (1984) documented these changes. Nicholls, for
example, argued that the Fascist-derived political vision of the Cantos of
the late thirties had moved toward an idea that the State was an ideal
structure, transcending any mere individualities that might be part of it;
this political Platonism underwrote the authoritarianism and fear of dis-
order Pound was now expressing. Even the tiny irreducible glimpses of
wasps and ants caught in Pound's discourse at Pisa were used, Nicholls
argued, as part of a rhetoric that claimed Pound's political stances had been
equally parts of a rock-bottom, indestructible reality.[42]

Increasingly these writers were opening up the unknown mass of
Pound's "collateral" writings in minor journals (English and Italian) and

correspondence. The next step was to correlate such writings with Pound's moves, step by step and month by month, in writing the individual Cantos themselves—moves recorded in the undestroyed drafts for those individual Cantos. Lawrence S. Rainey (1991), for instance, investigated the great wealth of materials about Pound's interest in the "Temple" built by Sigismondo Malatesta at Rimini. He showed how Pound had taken over views of that cultural artifact created for him by late nineteenth-century post-Romantic historiography; and he also showed how Pound had used this Romantic myth of the Temple—seen as Malatesta's act of worship to his mistress, Ixotta—to focus a piece of pro-Fascist myth-making about another Italian love-goddess who had sacrificed herself in the dying moments of Mussolini's Salò Republic. Later Rainey argued that a timely intervention by the local Fascist boss in Pound's Malatesta researches had a critical effect in turning Pound's sympathies in favor of the new regime.[43] In similar fashion Ronald Bush, collating the drafts for the *Pisan Cantos*, suggested that a specific event—the news of the death of a poet-friend—turned Pound's feelings away from whatever acceptance and humility he had attained, and impelled him to add, at the beginning and the end of the whole section, the harsh political statements that we now know.[44]

Such work is probably representative of where *Cantos* criticism has "got to" at present. Its value is evident, as long as it is used as a qualifier of what the poet in fact organized.

This recent critical work seeks to historicize the *Cantos*: to say that they subsist, not as a self-consistent artifact that obeys merely artistic laws, but as the record of needs to persuade—and self-persuade—impelling their author at specific moments, which is to say, at specific converging-points of cultural and social history. Much of this work is made possible by a peculiarly modern condition of things: the collecting and preserving of massive quantities of authorial scraps in university libraries. (No such study is possible for Shakespeare, whose scraps mainly fed the jakes, still less for the Anglo-Saxon *Seafarer.*) And Pound himself made it possible. He was always opening up some new field; he knew that any lode he had opened—the Fenollosa manuscripts, for example, or the Siena data—was left by him half-mined; and no doubt he hoped that one day he, or some disciple, might return to work further on it. So he rarely destroyed his notes. The effect on studies of his poetry might have struck him with some irony. He held that one of the main jobs of the writer was to clean up, to eliminate matter of low concentration, and thereby to focus attention on the better. Yet he has left enough material in the archives to distract readers permanently, for the tendency of the archival approach to criticism is to shift the reader's attention from what is on the page to what isn't.

Is there a significant difference between what is on the published page and what is not? There is no absolute difference: what the poet happens to declare "part of the poem" is no crystal, cut off from all circumstance and from all of its own drafts—still less so when the poet himself found it hard to decide which drafts to include, and which to leave out. But there is a difference of degree, to just the extent that what is on the published page of poetry is more concentrated. For "poetry is concentration"; that is its reason for existence.[45]

It is tempting to confuse the archive with the poem. But the archive is, in practice, limitless: it reaches not only to the parts of the sourcebook that Pound did underline but to those that he didn't; not only to what Pound wrote on his postcards but to what his correspondents were telling him at the time. And it has its own kinds of order (chronology, shelving, type of document), from which one can construct biography and argue from that to what the poem "ought to be saying."

And yet "its own order" is one of the elements in that concentration that poetry is supposed to have. This assembled fragment comes at the end of the "Seven Lakes" Canto (XLIX):

> Sun up; work
> sundown; to rest
> dig well and drink of the water
> dig field; eat of the grain
> Imperial power is? and to us what is it?
>
> The fourth; the dimension of stillness.
> And the power over wild beasts.

It matters that this piece should come here, and not elsewhere: the calm previously established by the whole portrayal of the lake scenes—

> Behind hill the monk's bell
> borne on the wind

—qualifies it. Without that, the first part of this fragment would merely be some jaunty, folksy assertion. But it matters also that this small assemblage has its own internal ordering. The acknowledgment of imperial power comes *after* those work-patterns ("Sun up; work"), so that we know the emotional locus from which the acknowledgment is made: a peasant sense of the immovable fact of labor. It matters down to the micro-level: "dig well and drink of the water" is followed, but not exactly paralleled by, the wording in "dig field; eat of the grain," which creates some sense of resistless ongoing rhythm—not a Popean jog-trot, and yet a rhythm. *Then*, and not before, come the lines about stillness and Dionysian power. Thus these two final lines themselves acquire tremendous power from the ordering of what has gone before—like the "Shantih, shantih," or "peace that passeth understanding," at the end of Eliot's *Waste Land*.

And though we can know that the whole little package was cooked up from assembled sources that can be identified, we also know that this particular macro- and micro-ordering is exactly what differentiates it from those sources, and what gives it different meanings. We need to be clear, then, what we are reading: this particular highly structured artifact (the Canto, or group of Cantos), with the meanings given by its structures, or the heap of papers it (in a certain sense) came from, whose orderings are likely to be very different.

If our aim is to get at the exact meanings of what the poet published, arguments from the background tend to be circular. A given quality or feature is either visible in the verse, or irrelevant. If deep fault lines are visible in *The Cantos* as published, then we can see them in what is written, without looking at biographical data to tell us they are there. If they are not visible, they can have no significance. The tension between Pound humbled, Pound accepting—even Pound seeking some kind of annihilation in the flow of things—on the one hand, and Pound the politically defiant, on the other, is there in the *Pisan Cantos*, and we can assume it was visible to intelligent readers from the start.

Creeley, Ginsberg, and Olson certainly had no illusions about the doctrines embodied in the *Cantos*.[46] The paradox, if it is one, is that these "extreme libertarians" (as one might call them) not only followed Pound's examples in the matter of writing but thought of him as anti-establishment, as a breaker of molds and an opener to new ways of thought. The solution to this paradox is that Pound's Fascism may not be the key to what the later *Cantos* in fact communicate. The nature of the medium that Pound created communicates on a deeper level.

The medium of the *Cantos* is open (more here, and less there); it prizes truth to experience; as a mode of communication, it allows the discourse to get "nearer to the knuckle" than perhaps any modern rival. As local messages, it includes the Platonism and the authoritarianism that critics have pointed out—hence the self-serving logic about Mussolini's "dream" in the *Pisan Cantos*. But the *Pisan Cantos* are also full of the teachings of Mencius, whose mental models are more contingent: the pooling of the water on the earth at one's feet (LXXXIII.550); the leaders who spread their corruption from the top downward (LXXIV.457). It is not the "ism" in the writer's mind that makes the writing's value, but the emotive qualities that the writing produces—and this it does by its modes of organizing sound, referent, movement of thought, and play of association. For these aspects of the *Cantos*, the earlier phases of criticism retain their usefulness.

It will be clear that criticism of the *Cantos* has opened up a range of approaches, and that there is room for plenty of controversy—in part because of the poem's fractured history. The essays included in this volume represent each of the major phases of *Cantos* criticism. For the holistic phase, Kenner's first essay is introductory to the whole project, while Davenport's essay on myth tries to show the functioning of this mode of thought in all parts of Pound's poem. D. S. Carne-Ross's subtle reading of the *Pisan Cantos* is one of the most convincing attempts to show that the necessary material of the poem is there in what is printed, if one watches the implications of the lines and makes the necessary connections between them. Donald Davie watches a later phase in the writing, where the nature of reference becomes more problematic. Likewise Girolamo Mancuso's essay, here published in English for the first time, takes a variant view of Pound's "ideogrammic method" by arguing that it persists throughout the long poem, its method mutating from section to section. Reed Way Dasenbrock shows the grave drawbacks in taking Dante as Pound's schematic model, but argues that the *Cantos* were planned as a moral map of interconnected world-pictures, put together essentially for the purpose of showing the ideal ruler (Mussolini) how to rule. Makin, Bacigalupo, Oderman, and Nicholls can be taken to represent the first "historicist turn," inasmuch as each tries to place the working of the *Cantos*, in successive sections, in the context of Pound's wider thought at the given period, seen in a documentation whose less attractive elements are no longer suppressed. Kenner's second essay examines the local fumblings with intertwined doctrine and philology that led Pound into his method of interpreting Chinese, which bulks so large on the page of the *Cantos*. Finally, Ronald Bush develops to its fullest extent the method of collating manuscripts and ancillary documents, to show how the final section of the long poem is the result of an emotional history and of external pressures that lead to questions, not only as to its consistency, but as to how far it will ever be possible to know what Pound wanted to publish and in what order.

Notes

1. The major exception is Wyndham Lewis's critique in *Time and Western Man* (1927). For a survey of prewar *Cantos* criticism, see Makin, *Pound's Cantos*, 310–313.

2. Reed Way Dasenbrock's term, in "Jefferson and/or Adams: A Shifting Mirror for Mussolini in the Middle Cantos," 505, *ELH* 55.2 (1988): 505–526.

3. Iris Barry, "The Ezra Pound Period," 171, *The Bookman* (October 1931), 159–171.

4. Robert Creeley, "A Note followed by a Selection of Letters from Ezra Pound," 11, *Agenda* 4.2 (October–November 1965), 11–21.

5. For this controversy see J. P. Sullivan, *Ezra Pound and Sextus Propertius: A Study in Creative Translation* (Austin: University of Texas Press, 1964), and Ezra Pound, *Omaggio a Sesto Properzio*, ed. Massimo Bacigalupo (Genoa: S. Marco dei Giustiniani, 1984).

6. Eric Homberger (ed.), *Ezra Pound: The Critical Heritage* (London: Routledge and Kegan Paul, 1972), 169.

7. *Poems 1918–21: Including Three Portraits and Four Cantos* (New York: Boni and Liveright, 1921), 83.

8. See also below, p. 65. Much critical ink has been expended on Pound's errors concerning the nature of the Chinese written character, or "ideogram," but since his theory concerns methods of writing in English (or any other language) these errors are hardly relevant. His concern with the "juxtaposition of concretenesses" clearly predates his concern with the Chinese character.

9. Kenner, *Poetry*, 83–84.

10. See W. B. Yeats, *A Vision* (London: Macmillan, 1962), 3–5.

11. For some of Pound's cues on this subject see Makin, *Pound's Cantos*, 63–77.

12. Ezra Pound, "It Befell That Wearied with Much Study," *Agenda* 34.3–4 (Autumn–Winter 1996/97), 83. See also A. David Moody, "Dante as the Young Pound's Virgil: Introduction to Some Early Drafts & Fragments," *Agenda* 34.3–4 (Autumn–Winter 1996/97), 65–74.

13. Pound, *The Cantos* (New York: New Directions, 1998). All citations of the *Cantos* in this introduction refer to this edition.

14. Pound, *The Spirit of Romance*, 128.

15. Stock, *Life*, 458.

16. "Mussolini . . . will end with Sigismondo and the men of order, not with the pus-sacks and destroyers." Pound, *Selected Letters*, 239.

17. Pound, *Selected Letters*, 239.

18. Pound, *Selected Prose*, 47.

19. Dante, *Paradiso*, 1.67–72. This translation is from the Temple Classics edition, which Pound used.

20. Pound, *The Spirit of Romance*, 155.

21. Pound, *Selected Letters*, 210.

22. See Pound, *Literary Essays*, 64.

23. Cited in Moody, "Dante as the Young Pound's Virgil," 68.

24. Ezra Pound and Dorothy Pound, *Letters in Captivity*, 59.

25. It is often asserted that Mussolini treated Pound as a joke, but Mussolini's recorded discourses suggest otherwise. See Yvon de Begnac, *Taccuini mussoliniani*, ed. Francesco Perfetti (Bologna: Il Mulino, 1990), esp. pp. 617–619.

26. See in particular Leon Surette, *Ezra Pound in Purgatory*, 234–238, 250–253.

27. Dasenbrock, *Literary Vorticism*, 203–213.

28. See for example LXII.350, on John Adams: "pater patriae / the man who at certain points / made us / . . . / by fairness, honesty and straight moving."

29. For the shift from Jefferson to Adams, see Dasenbrock, "Jefferson and/or Adams," passim.

30. Dasenbrock, *Literary Vorticism*, 212.

31. See Pound, *Selected Letters*, 331; the phrase is from the *Cantos*, "Notes for CXVII et seq.," 822.

32. See in particular Ronald Bush, "Towards Pisa: More from the Archives about Pound's Italian Cantos," *Agenda* 34.3–4 (Autumn–Winter 1996/97), 89–124.

33. See Massimo Bacigalupo, "Ezra Pound's Cantos 72 and 73: An Annotated Translation," *Paideuma* 20.1–2 (Spring–Fall 1991), 11–41.

34. For the background see in particular Pound and Dorothy Pound, *Letters in Captivity*, and Ezra Pound, *The Pisan Cantos*, ed. Richard Sieburth (New York: New Directions, 2003), ix–xliii.

35. Wendy Stallard Flory, "Confucius against Confusion: Ezra Pound and the Catholic Chaplain at Pisa," 148, in Zhaoming Qian, ed., *Ezra Pound and China* (Ann Arbor: University of Michigan Press, 2003), 143–162.

36. VI.22–23; XXIX.141–142; LXXIV.456.

37. See for instance the transition from death to cats, via "the odour of eucalyptus [with its cat-faced shape] or sea wrack," LXXX.518; and the quite arbitrary shift at LXXX.530, "or did they fall. . . ."

38. Daniel Pearlman, *The Barb of Time: On the Unity of Ezra Pound's Cantos* (New York: OUP, 1969); M. Bernetta Quinn, O.S.F., "The Metamorphoses of Ezra Pound," in Lewis Leary, ed., *Motive and Method in the Cantos of Ezra Pound* (New York: Columbia University Press, 1954).

39. For Pound's postwar views see *"I Cease Not to Yowl": Ezra Pound's Letters to Olivia*

Rossetti Agresti, ed. Demetres P. Tryphonopoulos and Leon Surette (Urbana: University of Illinois Press, 1998).

40. That Pound associated with dissidents from the regime, and interpreted its doctrines in his own ways, does not seem to detract from this point.

41. Dasenbrock, "Jefferson and/or Adams," 505.

42. See below, chapter 8, and Nicholls, *Ezra Pound*, 170–181.

43. Lawrence S. Rainey, " 'All I Want You to Do Is to Follow the Orders': History, Faith, and Fascism in the Early Cantos," in Rainey, ed., *A Poem Containing History: Textual Studies in the Cantos* (Ann Arbor: University of Michigan Press, 1997), 63–114.

44. Ronald Bush, " 'Quiet, Not Scornful'? The Composition of *The Pisan Cantos*," in Rainey, ed., *A Poem Containing History*, 169–211. See also the response by Massimo Bacigalupo, "Pound's *Pisan Cantos* in Process," *Paideuma* 27.2–3 (Fall–Winter 1998), 93–106.

45. Cf. Pound, *ABC of Reading*, 36. This passage explains that poetry intensifies meaning by drawing on image, sound, and diction-play; to which I would add the ordering of main referents, or "sequence of thought."

46. See, for instance, Creeley, "A Note followed by a Selection of Letters"; the interview with Allen Ginsberg recorded in Carpenter, *A Serious Character*, 897–899; *Charles Olson & Ezra Pound: An Encounter at St. Elizabeths*, ed. Catherine Seelye (New York: Grossman, 1975).

Ezra Pound

HUGH KENNER

◆ ◆ ◆

I

Homer L. Pound was deputy assayer at the mint in Philadelphia; his wife Isabel believed in high decorum. Their house in Wyncote, Pennsylvania, had a stained-glass window. Growing up surrounded by studied gentility, their son Ezra (born in 1885) experienced day by day a comfortable culture of fervid blankness. Its rationale is well described by Peter Makin:

> At a certain point the *raison d'être* for the whole economic structure was the Sunday-afternoon tea and chat, this being the ideal end of the consumer chain: for this heavy industry fed light industry, that ultimately some might sit among the latter's products and chat, and that others might aspire to.[1]

Spelled out, some unthinking assumptions sound parodic. Thus the purpose of two light industries, painting pictures and framing them, was to decorate the spaces where tea was taken. Thus Michelangelo had existed that in rooms so ornamented women might come and go and chat of him. Thus the University, yet another light industry, was valued for equipping the sons of the more favored with qualifications easy chat could allude to. T. S. Eliot's first subject would be the suffocation induced by such a world, and the first bond between him and Pound, when they met in London in 1914, would be the way they had both put distance between it and themselves.

And the poet? The role of the poet could only be to fill awkward spaces in *The Atlantic* and other magazines with rhythmic accolades to the refinement of the browser's soul. Pound would remember a time when he had supposed that appearing in *The Atlantic* was an honor to aspire to. He went to a good school where he was taught Latin so well he would read Latin verse at sight for the rest of his life, and at fifteen he was duly enrolled in the University of Pennsylvania, to study what we now call comparative literature, though the phrase was yet to be coined. In those years the four percent of college-age youths who went to college might be understood to be fulfilling their families' aspirations. A boy learning Provençal was a boy to be proud of!

It was college that freed Pound from those aspirations, though he was never estranged from the mother and father who held them; one thing we can hear behind his lifelong didacticism is the effort to bring them along, to explain himself to them.[2] Talent and fortune had brought him a vocation. In classrooms at Penn and Hamilton, and through the languages he picked up there, he glimpsed what he aspired to join—the world community of poets, the sons of Homer.

II

Homer drew on unrecorded bards. Vergil read and emulated Homer. Dante, twelve centuries later, shut off from Greek, read Vergil, to visit the dead as Aeneas had and as before him had Odysseus. A poet using English centuries later had better be familiar with all three. So much would have come as no surprise to Tennyson, who praised Vergil, and envied Dante the Italian vowels, and even Englished a few vignettes of Homer's.

But the generation of Pound and Eliot had access to a new way of thinking about languages and their masters, rooted in studies that had come to fruition long after the great Victorians' minds were formed. It was possible to ignore the national literatures, to conceive poetry as international and interlingual, and to imagine poetry in English as intertwined with poetry in Greek, Latin, Italian, French, in much the way those languages were themselves intertwined. By 1900, the affiliations of languages stood documented and comprehended. The literature of Europe, like its speech, could be conceived as one rich organism, and the study of poetry be seen as inextricable from the study of philology.

In the classrooms where Pound developed this sense of tradition, the nineteenth century's chief intellectual adventure still quickened. That was the vast cooperative effort that had ordered the lore of the Indo-European languages, a subject unsuspected before 1788, when Sir William Jones announced his great discovery that Sanskrit held the key to the kinship of the tongues of Europe. (So, in *The Waste Land* [1922], T. S. Eliot's quester after lost origins would hear an Indo-European root, *DA;* uttered by thunder near the Ganges.)

By the mid-nineteenth century it had grown clear that dictionaries wanted organizing on historical principles, not starting from current usage but ending with it. So old texts needed faithful old-spelling editing for dictionaries to cite, and decade after decade lexicography and textual scholarship went hand in hand. Manuscripts were transcribed, collated, arranged by families; principles of emendation were arrived at; scholars devised fine-print apparatus to record intricate webs with economy. Something like Ugo Canello's edition of Arnaut Daniel (only twenty years old when Ezra Pound used it in W. P. Shepard's seminar) was in effect a new kind of book, neatly compressing into notes and appendices the cross talk of dozens of scholars. Much detail was understood to be not yet settled, and all this information was meant to assist further thought. One lesson for Pound was the way light came incrementally as minds grappled with minutiae; that foreshadows the role into which he would maneuver the reader of his *Cantos.* He himself shirked no detail. For help with one word on which Canello was unpersuasive, he was to seek out the lexicographer Emil Levy in Freiburg; the story is told in Canto XX. And Sweet's *Anglo-Saxon Reader,* which he'd used in college, went with him to London. It's arresting, that glimpse of old textbooks claiming space in a poet's luggage.

Whoever retraces Pound's dealings with a source will be struck by the extent of his engagement with its notes and appendices. It was always to the apparatus that he turned, in a scholarly book. Fred Robinson[3] has beautifully documented his engagement with Sweet's notes as he worked on the Anglo-Saxon "Seafarer," making textual decisions as he went. (They have passed for guesses and misreadings, and are often, to say the least, debatable; but they were demonstrably *pondered.*) That was in 1911. By a decade later he was incorporating fragments of academic fact into the very page he showed his reader. Thus in Canto xxv we confront the committee minutes that enabled the slow creation of the Ducal Palace in Venice:

1335. 3 lire 15 groats to stone for making a lion.
1340. Council of the lords noble, Marc Erizio
Nic. Speranzo, Tomasso Gradonico:
                                    that the hall
be new built over the room of the night watch
and over the columns toward the canal where the walk is . . .

because of the stink of the dungeons. 1344.
1409 . . . since the most serene Doge can scarce
stand upright in his bedroom . . .
                        vadit pars, two gross lire
stone stair, 1415, for pulchritude of the palace

                        254 da parte
                        de non 23
                        4 non sincere
Which is to say: they built out over the arches
and the palace hangs there in the dawn, the mist,
in that dimness,
or as one rows in from past the murazzi
the barge slow after moon-rise
and the voice sounding under the sail.

                                    (C, XXV. 117⁴)

The first part of this is the poetry of the footnote, disclosing the minute particulars of research. "Which is to say" introduces a transition, into the poetry of sonorous evocation. Pound's mastery of sonorous evocation has never been doubted, but the poetry of the footnote was his major discovery, a flashing of "gists and piths."

(And though the five sonorous lines make a formal sentence, the gists and piths that precede it—fourteen lines—consist of discrete phrases and clauses, implying structures of surrounding syntax but never spelling them out. Increasingly, the economy of such a procedure would enter Pound's system of poetic and discursive habits, until there were times when he resembled a lecturer who disdains to comment on the slides he is showing. We'll return to this theme.)

He came to define the epic as "a poem including history" and thought that there was no other worthy subject. History, ideas of history, dominated the century that discovered evolution and made it a regnant metaphor. The very word "Renaissance" was a nineteenth-century coinage. And the very idea of an interlingual community of poets cohered with the great idea that languages were siblings, that a creating urgency flowed across their (miscalled) boundaries. "Provençal, Italian, Spanish, French, Portuguese, Catalan, Roumanian and Romansch," so Pound told the readers of his first prose book, were at first simply "ways of speaking Latin somewhat more corruptly than the Roman merchants and legionaries spoke it."[5] A commonplace by 1985, that truth in 1910 had the power to excite imagination. Latin was not a dead language. There are no dead languages, nor dead poets save the nonpoets who were always dead.

We may pause to notice the two conceptions of history involved here. If like a nineteenth-century scholar you attended to the process by which Latin got "corrupted" into several Romance tongues, then you were thinking of something irreversible, related to the theme of entropy that was occupying scientific imaginations. After some centuries, Latin is simply *gone*. French, Italian, Spanish, Portuguese have replaced it, no doubt to be supplanted in their turn by future derivations (though the printing press to be sure has slowed the rate of change). Even Renaissance Latin is a specialist's tongue, newly emerged and, despite all efforts at elegance, never to be confused with the Latin they spoke without effort in a culture long since vanished from the earth. So runs an evolutionary reading of history, dominated by the sense of the past's irretrievability that underlies much of the ache of Romanticism.

The Romantic nostalgia set at a hopeless distance whole ages, customs, cultures; and that was a new way to think of the past. True, a Horace may seem a poet of nostalgia: "Eheu, fugaces . . ." he writes; "labuntur anni. . . ." Alas, the years slip by, unbiddable. But what Horace laments is personal aging. That we cannot expect a second Regulus, a second Hercules even, was a different theme that did not enter his head. For Horace the better times gone were, yes, reclaimable; "et veteris revocavit artes," he wrote of Caesar Augustus: he has brought back our former way of life, the old way that made us glorious.

We need not think that Horace, or any pre-Romantic, had a special sense of history, different from ours, any more than painters who lived before perspective was invented had a special sense of space. Pictorial space was an invention of the Renaissance, ineluctable history an invention of the Romantics. But with their invention came the option of denying them, electing with Picasso a special sense of space, or with Ezra Pound a special sense of time.

For if, in the twentieth century, you perceived with a poet's x-ray eye the Latin language, for instance, still durable under shifting guises—if you could say, as Pound said in 1940, "Rome is where they speak LATIN"—then you were extolling the durability of tough patterns beneath recorded mutability. To that sense of history the past is always reclaimable, and whatever was possible once remains possible now. Circumstance continues to present similar dilemmas, similar options. So we study history to learn from recorded experience which courses of action are favorable, which foolhardy. Though "labuntur anni" remains a human constant, though all men age and die ("Thy work in set space of years, not over an hundred" [*C,* XLII.210]), yet the quality of human experience alters little, and the relevance of what we can learn from the past.

It was toward this latter sense of history that Pound tended, and in turning to it he allied himself with a disused tradition that ran from Plutarch's time clear to Pope's. Plutarch's parallel *Lives* offer patterns of good and bad judgment in situations we are to regard as comparable, both with one another and with what we ourselves may expect to confront. A Venetian painter of the sixteenth century could depict the troops before Troy in sixteenth-century Italian costume, so little, to minds of his era, had anything really changed. And for English Augustans the moral decline of Rome was a cautionary tale, modern men having left semibarbarism behind much as the Romans had and having climbed to a comparable plateau only to hear the same voices that tempted Rome with luxury, idleness, avarice, rootless novelty.

That way of perceiving the past survived in odd places. As late as 1896, his mind on the fiscal crises of his own decade, Brooks Adams in the first chapter of *The Law of Civilization and Decay* was examining anew and in new detail the lesson of Rome's misfortune, inextricable from Roman mismanagement of monetized wealth. "The stronger type exterminated the weaker; the money-lender killed out the husbandman; the race of soldiers vanished, and the farms, whereon they had flourished, were left desolate."[6] Pound was past fifty when he heard about Adams's book, but he instantly found it congenial. It read the past, in his own way, into the present. . . .

III

. . . At the threshold of *The Cantos,* it's worth surveying the resources he had developed on their behalf.

1. He had a repertoire of voices. Unlike, say, Wallace Stevens, who always sounds like himself, Pound in sounding like himself could sound like people as disparate as the "Seafarer" bard, the Roman ironist, and the

Chinese connoisseur of light rain falling on the light dust. The adoption of a range of voices—he called them "personae," masks—was from the very first intrinsic to his method.

2. Out of his passion for condensed fact of the kind that gets tucked into footnotes, and his impatience with such long words as end in "-ation," he'd developed an eloquence of the isolate phrase—

> A wet leaf that clings to the threshold
> (P, 108)

—that names something and with rhythmic assistance surrounds the thing it names with auras of emotion. At one stage (1912–13) this got theorized as "Imagism." Later, talking of "the ideogrammic method," he would draw on an imperfect analogy with the components of the Chinese written character to indicate what happens when several such concretions are placed in each other's company. It is like what happens when five sharp words come together:

> Air hath no petals now
> (C, XCIII. 630)

—with which compare,

> *Poikilothron' athanat' Aphrodita*

—every word of Sappho's a surprise, or

> IN A STATION OF THE METRO
>
> The apparition of these faces in the crowd;
> Petals on a wet, black bough.
> (P, 109)

—the second image not only unforeseeable, but a new way to view the first one.

Such writing puts a premium on concreteness, definition, concision. There is little metaphor in Pound's language; he came to shun metaphor as a *mis*calling, and to value the short definite words at the core of the language:

> Hay new cut on hill slope,
> And the water there in the cut
> Between the two lower meadows; sound,
> The sound, as I have said, a nightingale
> Too far off to be heard.
>
> (C, XX. 90)

Such concreteness moves the poem easily to its "visionary" episodes:

> or Anchises that laid hold of her flanks of air
> drawing her to him
> *Cythera potens, Kuthera deina*
> no cloud, but the crystal body
> the tangent formed in the hand's cup
> as live wind in the beech grove
> as strong air amid cypress.
>
> (C, LXXVI. 456–57)

It also conduced to what could be an unfortunate mannerism, when the withdrawal of syntactic support leaves us at a loss what to make of floating elements whose context is not the visionary imagination but some book we haven't read or some historic nexus we haven't grasped. Here one reader's trenchant condensation is another's hopeless obscurity; that was a risk *The Cantos* always ran. Pound's belief that poetry inheres in condensation, that nothing damps it more than unnecessary words, especially words that do niggling syntactic chores, shaped alike the poem's most and least successful passages.

3. An incomparable melodic sense, innate and his lifelong resource. "Ere the season died a-cold" (*C*, 519) runs as if effortlessly up the scale of the vowels A, E, I, O. And such a detail as

> Behind hill the monk's bell
> borne on the wind.
> Sail passed here in April; may return in October
> Boat fades in silver; slowly;
> Sun blaze alone on the river
>
> (C, XLIX. 244)

draws its authority from its pauses and stops, its alliterations, its intertwining of vowels and liquids. That all sounds pedantic till you let yourself experience it. Experiencing the sound of words is for most modern readers the awful daring of a moment's surrender. We've been taught to abstract, abstract, to sniff after "meaning." For Ezra Pound speech was always physical, bodied. And the words were *these* very words, not lexical substitutes: hence his tags of French, Latin, Greek, at moments when the very phonemes mattered.

4. The sense of the past's steady relevance we've already glanced at; now combined with

5. a new set of convictions, and these need particularizing. During the war years he frequented the *New Age* circle, and there one day he met Major Charles H. Douglas, who had noticed something about how currency flows. It was Douglas's conclusion that the books never balance, no factory ever distributing enough wages for its workers to buy back its product. That is because of "finance charges," and there is consequently a perpetual shortage of purchasing power, coped with in the short term either by starting wars to gain markets or by issuing new currency as interest-bearing debt (the so-called deficit). So War and Want inhere in a bookkeeping system, and for Pound this had the importance of a scientific discovery. His villains became the international bankers, the present system's sole beneficiaries. His hero would be whoever should put the insights of Douglas into practice. History suggested that scientific discoveries were normally in practice within a generation or so (Clerk Maxwell's equations, 1873; Marconi's radio, 1896). The hero he elected was Mussolini, in whom people as diverse as Winston Churchill and Secretary Mellon at one time also discerned a positive force.[7]

6. Finally, there was the accumulation of his own published prose, in effect a growing body of commentary. During the war years especially, he had kept himself fed and clothed in London by ceaseless intellectual journalism; for 1917 alone his bibliographer lists 117 items. The best of these (which turned out to be the ones for which he'd been paid the least, or not paid at all) were gathered into books. So a reader of Canto I, wanting help with the name "Andreas Divus" and finding none in the *Encyclopaedia Britannica,* might turn to Pound's 1920 *Instigations,* which reprinted his *Little Review* articles on Renaissance translators of Greek, and exhibited as a sample of Divus's Latin *Odyssey* (1538) the identical pages the first Canto draws on. Later collections extracted the gists of the early ones; in the thirties "Translators of Greek" reappeared in *Make It New,* and since 1960 it has been in print in *Literary Essays.*

As over the years *The Cantos* grew to unforeseen length (802 pages in the complete edition), the ancillary prose grew too. By now there is scarcely a sentence Pound wrote anywhere that has no bearing at all on the poem. Even collections of his private letters abound in rewards for the student. This reflects in part the way the poem came to express his whole mind; in part, too, his loss of touch, over forty years, with any definable body of readers. In Rapallo (1926–40) he fell insensibly into the assumption that his own energies were creating and educating the poem's audience. And in Washington (1946–58) the friends and correspondents who sustained his alertness were the readers he could assume would follow its thought.

IV

A Draft of XVI. Cantos for the Beginning of a Poem of Some Length appeared in 1925 in a sumptuous limited edition. That volume has one evident unity. It begins in prehistory and ends in the twentieth century, and as *Cathay* was built around three war poems, so this section of *The Cantos* is built around three wars. It starts with Odysseus sailing home from the war at Troy, it ends amid the confusions of the 1914–18 war, and at its center we find a fifteenth-century Italian free-lance. Human history, then, has moved from war to war, its most recent war its most horrible and anticlimactic. And the pretexts for warfare have altered. Greeks fought Trojans over the beauty of Helen. Sigismundo Malatesta's various employers had less noble but intelligible incentives (and his purpose in taking their money was to build his Tempio). But what so many died for in our time will remain obscure until Canto XLV waxes explicit about usury, and Canto XLVI about banks.

But more important than wars at this stage of the poem is the complex laying down of themes; Canto I is an especially rich instance. The poem begins not only *in medias res* but as it were in midsentence, with the word "And":

> And then went down to the ship,
> Set keel to breakers, forth on the godly sea, and
> We set up mast and sail on that swart ship,
> Bore sheep aboard her, and our bodies also
> Heavy with weeping, and winds from sternward
> Bore us out onward with bellying canvas,
> Circe's this craft, the trim-coifed goddess.
> Then sat we amidships, wind jamming the tiller,
> Thus with stretched sail, we went over sea till day's end.
>
> (C, I.3)

We have entered the *Odyssey* at Book XI. If we look back before "and" we
see the preceding books, then beyond them in time the matter of the *Iliad,*
and beyond that, unrecorded darkness. But if Homer's predecessors are lost
they are not quite obliterated. In the Mediterranean way, he built with old
stones, and Pound thought the narrative of Book XI, the *Nekuia,* the journey down to the realm of the dead, was manifestly "*older* than the rest . . .
hinter-time."[8] Thus the oldest verse we have in a Western language is
celebrating the oldest of human concerns: rites to keep us in touch with
our dead.

And what this Canto does is open communications with dead masters;
Homer for one, and for another the "Seafarer" poet whose strong alliter-
ative line,

> We set up mast and sail on that swart ship

is audible throughout, the oldest Greek sounding through the oldest English. The Canto has other archaic qualities. Its rush of narrative is pre-
syntactic; the first verb has no subject, the first adverb ("forth") works like
a verb, and no Flaubertian subordinations conceal the simplest narrative
connective, "and." Contrast the Loeb translator's more formal sentence:

> But when we had come down to the ship and to the sea, first of all we
> drew the ship down to the bright sea, and set the mast and sail in the
> black ship, and took the sheep and put them aboard, and ourselves
> embarked, sorrowing and shedding big tears.

Though "correct," this makes both tidy and naive the utterance of a bard
whose strong units were phrasal and metrical.

In the underworld they fill a pit with sheep's blood. And the shades
gather, frantic for blood such as once made them feel alive.

> Souls out of Erebus, cadaverous dead, of brides
> Of youths and of the old who had borne much;
> Souls stained with recent tears, girls tender,
> Men many, mauled with bronze lance heads,
> Battle spoil, bearing yet dreory arms,
> These many crowded about me; with shouting,
> Pallor upon me, cried to my men for more beasts;
> Slaughtered the herds, sheep slain of bronze;
> Poured ointment, cried to the gods,

> To Pluto the strong, and praised Proserpine;
> Unsheathed the narrow sword,
> I sat to keep off the impetuous impotent dead,
> Till I should hear Tiresias.

Impetuous, impotent . . . these are all the people who have ever lived. One man confronts the whole past of the world: that is one meaning of this episode in *The Cantos.* And his confrontation will one day, in another land, inspire the sixth book of the *Aeneid,* the author of which will in turn guide Dante on a like journey through three realms of the Christian underworld. When. this Canto that began with "And" makes its end with an open-ended "So that:" the *Divina Commedia* is one term we can append to the colon.

When Tiresias speaks, it is with the aid of the blood Odysseus brought.

> "Stand from the fosse, leave me my bloody bever
> "For soothsay."
>   And I stepped back,
> And he, strong with the blood, said then: "Odysseus
> "Shalt return through spiteful Neptune, over dark seas,
> "Lose all companions."

In reducing to twelve words the thirty-eight lines Homer gave Tiresias, Pound makes us attend to the transaction with the blood. For the dead speak only thanks to blood we bring them; Odysseus and Homer and the Seafarer-poet are speaking now, enabled by the blood of a live man, Ezra Pound. The drunk blood is a communion, the act of translating by implication a sacrament. We should recall that Chaucer was esteemed as *le grand translateur* before "originality" came into esteem. We may also ponder a story Robert Fitzgerald tells.

Fitzgerald before translating the *Odyssey* made a ritual visit to Pound, as it were to Tiresias, for benediction. He said he intended to do only the high spots, and was told: "Oh no, don't do that. Let him say everything he wanted to say."[9] A successful translation, this means, is less a feather for its maker's cap than a new opportunity offered to the dead. Two things at least we owe them: voices, and a hearing. Before this long poem is over the dead will have spoken in hundreds.

And among the ghosts in the Canto there's an un-Homeric ghost, whom a voice new to the poem suddenly addresses:

Lie quiet, Divus.

And as if aware that we're disoriented, this modern voice supplies information, embedding the poem's first footnote in the text itself:

I mean, that is Andreas Divus,
In officina Wecheli, 1538, out of Homer.

For, Pound's Latin being superior to his Greek, he's been working from a sixteenth-century Latin version he'd found about 1909 at a Paris bookstall. (That, by the way, is why the sea is "godly"; for Homer's *dian,* bright, Divus had *divum,* divine.) It's indicative of the poem's increasingly austere criteria for relevance, that the incident of the Paris bookstall was present in early published drafts, to hint at a parallel with Browning's *The Ring and the Book,* but later got pruned and now must be retrieved from Pound's *Literary Essays.* That happened when he decided to attenuate the Browning theme, to state it openly only in four lines of Canto II and diminish it to a single quoted phrase in Canto III. It's arguable that the poem gains in distracting us less with early indications of its author's successorship to Browning. It's equally true that such artistic decisions have had the side effect of erasing seamarks we might wish were in the text.

What Divus had made was no ornate "rendering" of Greek but a serviceable pocket-size crib, meant to match, page for page and line for line, the Aldine octavo *Odyssey.* Before Aldus there'd been folio Homers, but folios are for venerating; a pocketable octavo is meant for *use,* and by a busy man away from home.

So here, superimposed on Homer (the beginning of Greek) and on The Seafarer (the beginning of English), is yet another beginning: the unquenchable romance of the Renaissance, when western Europe rediscovered Greek and discovered printing almost simultaneously. In Canto I we may perceive in triumphant embodiment the young Pound's classroom vision of European poetry, a rich multilingual organism which develops in time but keeps all times simultaneous, and is preserved for us in strings of printed letters.

The presence of the Renaissance, here and throughout the first thirty Cantos, should detain us a little, since men's historical interests are guided by their deep concerns. In the eighteenth or "Augustan" century the most applicable part of the past was the story of Rome and what happened to it; Gibbon's work could be read as a cautionary tale. Early in the nineteenth century, the invention of the word "Renaissance" marks a need for an updated paradigm. Things were beginning anew; three revolutions, American, French, and Industrial, helped prompt new scrutiny of Europe's last time of new beginnings. Soon the Renaissance was a happy hunting ground for enthusiasts. Browning's imagination returned to it repeatedly, and so did Pound's. It was Jacob Burckhardt's *Die Kultur der Renaissance in Italien* (1860; English translation, 1878) that supplied, in a chapter title, "The State as a Work of Art," the romantic metaphor by which Pound would fatefully misjudge Mussolini. He was always prepared for yet one more new beginning—to resolve the world's fiscal mess there *had* to be one—and how the first Renaissance had succeeded and failed was to engage him much of his life.

But that is a later story; we are still in Canto I. It ends with an evocation of Aphrodite, who shimmers through a mosaic of Latin phrases Pound took from the *Hymni Deorum* appended to Divus's book. Gold and copper (later to be coin-stuff) ornament her. And one recurrent ritual of *The Cantos* is established: after a fabulous journey, a vision of a goddess.

"So that:" concludes it. From "And . . . and . . . and" to "So That:" from succession to causality: come to think of it, the progression of Greek thought.

V

Such is a partial engagement with any Canto; an encounter, first, with the authority of its local rhetoric; consideration, next, of any prior documents it refracts;[10] and always, attention to minutiae. Gradually, we collect a sense of the poem's rituals. Its first cats attend an apparition of Dionysios; any cat thereafter will always precede a theophany. Its first drink is blood, its first eating (in Canto IV) a human heart; eating and drinking will thenceforward be sacramental acts: sometimes profaned, as when the Emperor Tçin Ou "ended his days as a gourmet" (*C*, LIV.282). And the way China makes its first appearance in Canto XIII, right after the first Canto to be situated in America, prepares us for the way the two countries will invariably be juxtaposed (as they were in the fortunes of Columbus, who encountered the one while seeking the other). The successive volumes in which the work appeared constitute structural units, most often units of eleven; from the moment of its launching with Book XI of *The Odyssey*, eleven was to be the poem's magic number. Names recur, lines recur, verbal motifs recur, while different Muses preside over different parts.

In 1940, the year of Cantos LI–LXXI (ten China Cantos, ten John Adams Cantos), the poem was still proceeding more or less according to plan, much though chance might have altered the plan's details. But the *Pisan Cantos* (published in 1948) reflected an unforeseen emergency. Writing in an American army stockade near Pisa in the summer and autumn of 1945, a poet who confronted the wreckage of all his hopes was thrown back on monologue and reminiscence. And the remaining sections—a third of the poem's pages—came from a Washington hospital to which friends brought the needed books: mostly books of which the man who wrote the first two-thirds had not suspected the existence. Their convention is marginalium, commentary, cross-light, excerpt: the Poetry of the Footnote, indeed.

Getting familiar with it all can take years, a consideration that has inspired charges of charlatanry. But until quite late in history, when the Easy Book was devised, it was normal to assume that major works of literature lent themselves to lifelong study. Milton did not expect to be skimmed. If his "story" yields itself quickly, little else does. (His first readers even had trouble with the story, which is why the second edition of *Paradise Lost* was equipped with prose summaries.) Our "desire to make the poem add up to something quickly"[11] comes from reading habits formed on texts of contrived simplicity, and we need to acknowledge that Pound set out systematically to frustrate any such appetite. One intention of *The Cantos,* Margaret Dickie has argued, is to restore the old art of "slow reading": creative reading: such a reading as (Fred Robinson has shown) Pound gave the Anglo-Saxon "Seafarer," when he scrutinized the credentials of each word. The poem demands, and also offers to train, "the attention usually reserved for partially destroyed Renaissance documents." "If reading were simply a copying of the palimpsest, or if reading were only an affirmation of the figure in the carpet, it would be a task easily assignable to clerks or to particularly sensitive geometricians. But reading is something beyond this passive copying and active affirming, as Pound himself had discovered in a lifetime."[12]

Lest we fear, with the frontier warrior in *Cathay,* that "hard fight gets no reward," jewels lie scattered for the picking up. They include historical curiosities like the Jefferson letter—

> "Could you," wrote Mr. Jefferson,
> "Find me a gardener
> Who can play the french horn?"
> (C, XXI. 97)

(as he did: in June 1778); also the lyric interludes and the matchless evocations of landscape:

> From Val Cabrere, were two miles of roofs to San Bertrand
> so that a cat need not set foot in the road,
> where now is an inn, and bare rafters,
> where they scratch six feet deep to reach pavement
> where now is wheat field, and a milestone,
> an altar to Terminus, with arms crossed
> back of the stone
> Where sun cuts light against evening,
> where light shaves grass into emerald . . .
>
> (C, XLVIII. 243)

A former generation of readers tended to deem these the successful parts
of the poem, from which the rest fell away into incoherence. But the
poem is a continuum, and everywhere it is anchored in factuality. We note
that it cites the Jefferson letter by date, and tells us where to find the altar
to Terminus. The library contains the one, southwest France the other.
One learns to trust the surface indications. No poet since Wordsworth (an
analogy that would have surprised him) has been so tenacious in fidelity
to fact. "Mount Taishan at Pisa" designates the one mountain on the
skyline in question that looks indisputably oriental, as you'll see if you go
there. Much obscurity dissipates as one begins to take the literal sense on
trust.

And the place of entry which every passage affords is its most accessible
one: its verbal surface, its locally contrived "style." There is no more dramatic event in the early Cantos than the turn of the page that discloses
prose documents frankly offered as prose: the contents of Sigismundo Malatesta's mailbag (C, IX. 37–40). Browning, Pound's predecessor in the use
of Renaissance documents, had transformed everything in *The Ring and the
Book* into blank verse, postulating that there is a poem, and also a domain
of language outside the poem, and that to merit inclusion in the former
the latter needs transforming into "poetry." But Pound's Poetry of the
Footnote acknowledges no sharp boundary between verse and prose, or
between fact and imagination; only an ineluctable boundary between live
writing and dead:

> Perspicax qui excolit se ipsum,
> Their writings wither because they have no curiosity,

This "leader," gouged pumpkin
                that they hoist on a pole.

                                        (C, LXXXV. 545)

VI

The Cantos were never finished. About 1959, aged seventy-four, Pound simply felt unable to write any more. Nine years later he published the *Drafts and Fragments* into which the end of the poem had dissipated. Some are of unparalleled limpidity:

A blown husk that is finished
                but the light sings eternal
a pale flare over marshes
                where the salt hay whispers to tide's change.

                                        (C, CXV. 794)

Nothing to paraphrase there, nothing to footnote. Something autumnal to see, caught in a few common words, with embedded in their solemn rhythm that trope of the singing light. He might have wished that more of the poem could have been made of details so simply turned, but learning the way of them had taken long, and "There is no substitute for a lifetime" (*C, XCVIII. 691*).

He died in Venice on November 1, 1972, two days after his eighty-seventh birthday.

I have said nothing about the political controversies that stormed round the last third of Pound's life: the rant of the wartime broadcasts, the indictment, the imprisonment near Pisa and in a Washington madhouse. The emphasis belongs where I keep it, on the continuities of the life of the mind and on the pleasures of his craggy texts. "These are the Alps," wrote his friend Basil Bunting in a poem called "On the Flyleaf of Pound's Cantos." It ends,

Fools! Sit down and wait for them to crumble.

Notes

1. Peter Makin, *Pound's Cantos* (Baltimore, MD: Johns Hopkins UP, 1992), 1–2.
2. Thus his most general statement about *The Cantos* is a 1927 letter to Homer

L. Pound: "Dear Dad: . . ." D. D. Paige, ed., *The Letters of Ezra Pound 1907–1941* (New York: New Directions, 1950 1st edition, 1971), 210.

3. Fred C. Robinson, "Pound's Anglo-Saxon Studies," *Yale Review* Vol. 71, No. 2 (Winter 1982): 199–224.

4. *C*, XXV. 117 refers to page 117 of *The Cantos of Ezra Pound* (New York: New Directions, 1970). All Canto references will appear in the text of this chapter in this form.

5. Ezra Pound, *The Spirit of Romance: An Attempt to Define Somewhat the Charm of the Pre-Renaissance Literature of Latin Europe* (London: J. M. Dent & Sons, Ltd., 1910), 2.

6. Brooks Adams, *The Law of Civilization and Decay* (New York: Knopf, 1951), 89.

7. For an excellent brief exposition, see Makin, *Pound's Cantos,* 105–14 [below, chapter 5].

8. In a 1935 letter to W. H. D. Rouse, Paige, *Letters,* 274.

9. "Interview with Robert Fitzgerald," *The Paris Review* 94 (Winter 1984): 51.

10. Locating these is greatly facilitated by Carroll F. Terrell's *Companion to the Cantos of Ezra Pound,* 2 vols. (Berkeley: University of California Press, 1980–84).

11. From Margaret Dickie's fine essay, "*The Cantos:* Slow Reading," *ELH* 51.4 (Winter 1984): 819–35.

12. Ibid., 823, 833.

Persephone's Ezra

GUY DAVENPORT

❖ ❖ ❖

I: *The Flowered Tree as Koré*

Of the twenty-three poems in Ezra Pound's first book of verse, the unpublished *Hilda's Book* now in Houghton Library at Harvard, written between
1905 and 1907 for Hilda Doolittle in whose possession it was during most
of her lifetime, only "Donzella Beata," "Li Bel Chasteus," and "The Tree"
were salvaged for *A Lume Spento* in 1908. "Donzella Beata" prefers a live girl
to a Blessed Damozel waiting in heaven, and "Li Bel Chasteus" depicts
Tristram and Iseult high above the common world in their rock haven.
"The Tree" however, begins a theme that has remained in Pound's poetry
for sixty years. It is the first poem of the *Personae* canon, and is echoed as
late as Canto CX ("Laurel bark sheathing the fugitive"). It is a poem under
the spell of Yeats, kin to "The Song of Wandering Aengus" and other
evocations of an enchanted wood. The Pre-Raphaelite Yeats is everywhere
in *Hilda's Book*.

> Autumn is over the long leaves that love us,
> And over the mice in the barley sheaves;
> Yellow the leaves of the rowan above us,
> And yellow the wet wild-strawberry leaves

begins Yeat's "The Falling of the Leaves" (*Crossways,* 1889). The first poem of *Hilda's Book* opens with a hint of Whitman but proceeds as if by Yeats:

> Child of the grass
> The years pass Above us
> Shadows of air All these shall love us
> Winds for our fellows
> The browns and the yellows
> Of autumn our colors

But Celtic twilight and Yeatsian diction are but part of the strange beauty of "The Tree." That a tree can be a persona at all is startling. Joyce, years later, will have a tree speak in his poem "Tilly" (*Pomes Penyeach,* 1927). Pound's poem trembles between the imitative and a strong originality. It is as precious as the early Yeats while having the masculine boldness of William Morris. It is both Ovidian and Thoreauvian. It is seed-rich in matters that will occupy Pound for years: the theme of metamorphosis and the mimetic act of assuming a mask and insisting on the most strenuous empathy. Daphne and the figures of Baucis and Philemon will appear throughout *The Cantos.* The most fructive theme, however, is that of chthonic nature as a mystery, the Eleusinian theme. To understand "many a new thing. . . . That was rank folly to my head before" is to find a mode of perception other than one's own. *Omniformis omnis intellectus est,* Psellus says in *The Cantos,* quoting Porphyry. But why begin with the nymph's supernatural, intranatural sense of things? The question is a large one, for trees are everywhere in Pound's poetry, and become symbols of extraordinary power and beauty in *Rock-Drill, Thrones,* and the cantos now in draft form for the poem's conclusion.

Hilda's Book is green with trees, poem after poem. "*Dulce myrtii floribus,*" we read; "sweeter than all orchards breath"; "She swayeth as a poplar tree"; "the moss-grown kindly trees"; "some treeborn spirit of the wood / About her." *A Lume Spento* was originally titled *La Fraisne,* the ash tree; and the poem of that name is a variant of "The Tree," as is "A Girl" in *Ripostes.*

In 1960 Pound chose for the translator Alfredo Rizzardi a selection of his poems to be published in Arnoldo Mondadori's *Poeti dello Specchio* series. From the twenty-three poems of *Ripostes* as that book is preserved in the *Personae* canon, he chose "N.Y.," that charmingly ironic-romantic poem in which he persists in having the New York of "a million people surly with traffic" appear as a girl praised by Solomon, "a maid with no breasts, / . . . slender as a silver reed"; "A Girl" ("The tree has entered my hands"); "The

Cloak," a poem about the claims of love and death and a paraphrase of Sappho's poem reminding a girl who refused her gift of roses that death is long and loveless (Fragment 55, Lobel and Page); Δώρια, another poem of love and death ("The shadowy flowers of Orcus / Remember thee."); and "Apparuit," a ghostly and splendid evocation of Persephone, in sapphics and with the touch of Sappho more finely upon it than any translation yet of Sappho into English. A glance at *Ripostes*—a book dedicated to William Carlos Williams, with the Propertian tag *Quos ego Persephonae maxima dona feram,* to which Williams replied in his *Kora in Hell* (1920)—will show that Pound selected for his Italian translator only those poems that contained the theme of Persephone as the sign of youth radiant before its doom or as the indwelling spirit of springtime. Conversely, Pound chose from the early *Personae* volumes (1908–1910) only those poems that are about Aidonian Persephone whose beauty is destructive, Helen and Iseult, the figure that will become Circe in *The Cantos.*

Pound was not without clues as to how to move from the neurasthenic dark of the nineteenth century Circe-world and its Hell-like *cul de sac;* he has acknowledged his debt to Whitman and Whistler. He had the end of the thread when he wrote "The Tree." But he preferred to go back to the very beginning of literature, to see its growth from sensibility to sensibility, and to arrive, if possible, with its masters who knew the art best. We find him instinctively turning toward robustness and clarity. There are many ways of studying Pound's evolution; his own criticism will probably remain the surest record. But everywhere we turn in his poetry there is the clear emergence of Persephone and her springtime as a persistent image and symbol. The first great search concentrated on the springtime of styles and cultures; with what sureness does he introduce the archaic Minoan undulations and Cretan basketwork braids into the Edwardian fog of *Mauberley!* (and he was working, except for the *Illustrated London News* and Sir Arthur Evans's *Mycenaean Tree and Pillar Cult* of 1901, well ahead of the world's knowledge of Knossan art; *Mauberley* was published a year before Evans's *The Palace of Minos*).

As if Persephone were his guide toward the light he sought, as if she, the power of renewal, had chosen him and not he her (as in the conceit in Canto LXXVI where we have "Dafne's Sandro," the fleet laurel nymph choosing Botticelli as her painter rather than the other way round), his eye went to the master poets whose manner is limpid, sharp, clear, and simple: Homer, Ovid, Dante, and Chaucer. So carefully did he study each that one can plausibly trace Pound's style wholly to Homer, or wholly to Dante, as it would seem; what we would be looking at is the unbroken tradition of the Homeric phrase in western literature, clear equally of metric, sound, image, and thought. We would also be looking at a special propensity to find conjunctions of trees and radiant girls, reminiscent of the Cretan and Mycenaean assimilation of pillar and tree as the goddess's sign. It is an atmosphere that can best be described as Botticellian or Ovidian. In Arnaut Daniel,

> Ges rams floritz
> De floretas envoutas
> Cui fan tremblar auzelhon ab lurs becs
> Non es plus frescs,

in Cavalcanti,

> Avete in voi li fiori, e la verdura,

in Dante,

> Tu mi fai rimembrar dove e qual era
> Proserpina nel tempo che perdette
> la madre lei, ed ella primavera,

in Li Po,

> While my hair was still cut straight across my forehead
> I played about the front gate, pulling flowers,

he found a mode of poetry that moved him with a force that is easier to illustrate than to attempt a theory versatile enough to encompass all its dimensions. In "The Alchemist" he brings such illustrious women as Odysseus saw at Persephone's request in Hades in conjunction with American trees, "under the larches of Paradise / . . . the red gold of the maple, / . . . the light of the birch tree in autumn. . . ." The heart of the poem is a prayer to Persephone ("Queen of Cypress") in her other kingdom, the world under earth or ocean:

> From the power of grass,
> From the white, alive in the seed,
> From the heat of the bud,
> From the copper of the leaf in autumn,

From the bronze of the maple, from the sap in the bough;
Lianor, Ioanna, Loica,
By the stir of the fin,
By the trout asleep in the gray-green of water;
Vanna, Mandetta, Viera, Alodetta, Picarda, Manuela
From the red gleam of copper,
Ysaut, Ydone, slight rustling of leaves,
Vierna, Jocelynn, daring of spirits,
By the mirror of burnished copper,
   O Queen of Cypress,
Out of Erebus, the flat-lying breath,
Breath that is stretched out beneath the world:
Out of Erebus, out of the flat waste of air,
  lying beneath the world;
Out of the brown leaf-brown colourless
    Bring the imperceptible cool.

Apart from the satires and the studies of the forces counter to Persephone, such as the Hell cantos, which are about the abuses of nature, and the great "Sestina: Altaforte," in which Bertran de Born welcomes Easter as good weather for a military campaign, there is little in Pound that is far away from Persephone and her trees.

It is curious that Michael Ventris was born when Pound was drafting the first canto. A man with *The Cantos* in his head sees this correlation of *periploi*—Odyssean voyages—as being within the *numen* that Pound, more than any man of our time unless it be Picasso and his Ovidian eyes, has recovered and charged with meaning. Canto I, set in Persephone's kingdom which is not the dead past but the communicable spirit of being, metamorphosed from the temporal to the eternal, is Homer's most archaic matter, his deepest plumbing of "rite and foretime" (in David Jones's resonant phrase). It is the hero's necessary recognition of his life's roots in the powers that sustain him.

  Poured ointment, cried to the gods,
  To Pluto the strong, and praised Proserpine

These words contain strata, like a geological cross-section, or, to take an even more pertinent image, like the rings of growth in a tree, for they are Homer's words (first discernible date: the beginning of Mediterranean literature), Andreas Divus's words,

Excoriantes comburere: supplicare autem Diis,
Fortique Plutoni, et laudatae Proserpinae,

(second date: the Renaissance), cast in the Anglo-Saxon rhythms of *The Seafarer* (third date: the Renaissance of 1910, the linguistic renovations of which are still not understood, but which grow out of Morris's and Doughty's new sense of the genius of English), and they are words written with the intuition that their chthonic matter would continue to speak, as Ventris, Chadwick, and Palmer found Persephone and Demeter in the Linear B tablets; Frobenius, "the car of Persephone in a German barrow" (*Kulchur,* 244).

Persephone weathered the decline of antiquity, and survived the Middle Ages to emerge in the Renaissance. Ovid and Vergil had kept her in Italian tradition. Chaucer brought her to the north, "Proserpyne, / That quene ys of the derke pyne." Arthur Golding's Ovid of 1567 (when Ovid still, as for Chaucer, meant the *Metamorphoses*) renders her myth with particular beauty; she is made accessible to the age as far more than a bit of classical iconography around which to shore up emblematic patterns (as in Francesco Colonna's *Hypnerotomachia* of 1499). Ovid's plastic terseness becomes an English narrative voice of lively extravagance:

By chaunce she let her lap slip downe, and out the flowres went.
And such a sillie simplenesse her childish age yet beares,
That even the very losse of them did move hir more to tears.

Milton's typological mind began the impressive baroque flourish that foreshadows Eve's temptation with an evocation of Persephone:

Not that faire field
Of *Enna,* where *Proserpin* gathring flours
Her self a fairer Floure by gloomie *Dis*
Was gatherd

And Shakespeare, enchanted by flowers, gave Perdita the speech that outdoes Poliziano in the imitation of Ovid's floral imagery:

O *Proserpina,*
For the Flowres now, that (frighted) thou let'st fall
From *Dysses* Waggon: Daffadils,
That come before the Swallow dares, and take

> The windes of March with beauty: Violets (dim,
> But sweeter then the lids of *Juno's* eyes

Thereafter she is everywhere, as firmly within English poetry as Latin or Greek. But as the Renaissance fades, she disappears from poetry. Neither the eighteenth century nor the early nineteenth thinks it sees anything in her myth, except to reflect the subterranean existence of her *Paradis artificiel* in such figures as La Motte Fouqué's *Undine* or Poe's *Ligeia*. Then all at once she is again in the open air, whether awakened by Sir James Frazer's *Golden Bough* or the new, charismatic interest in natural beauty that begins with scientific eyes (Humboldt, Agassiz, Darwin, Hugh Miller, Gosse) and is rapidly taken up by poetic ones (Thoreau, W. H. Hudson, Ruskin), or because of the new and pervasive interest in myth generated by archaeology, new texts, and folklore.

Like Sappho and Chaucer, Ruskin wrote about girls as if they were flowers, about flowers as if they were girls (so that his botanical treatise called *Proserpina* has more of an archaic Greek flavor than any of the period's translations), and Lewis Carroll's Alice is a kind of Persephone. There is Tennyson's sombre, Vergilian "Demeter and Persephone," Swinburne's "The Garden of Proserpine" and "Hymn to Proserpine." The young Pound grew up in an ambience congenial to myth; the power it had over the minds of his generation can be seen in Frederic Manning's "Koré," to which Pound wrote a reply that T. S. Eliot kept in the Faber *Selected Poems* but which Pound cancelled in the *Personae* canon.

Persephone enters Pound's poetry early and remains, and she is always there in an Ovidian sense, embodied in a girl or flower or tree, so that his most famous *haiku* is like a face Odysseus sees in Hades, reminding him of the springtime above in an image combining tree and girl: *petals on a wet, black bough.* In "Heather"

> The milk-white girls
> Unbend from the holly-trees

"O Nathat-Ikanaie, 'Tree-at-the-river,' " we read in "Dance Figure" and in "The Spring" (that subtle mistranslation of Ibykos), "Cydonian Spring with her attendant train, / Maelids and water-girls. . . ." Her most poignant epiphany is as a ghost, Persephone bound in hell awaiting the spring.

> Les yeux d'une morte
> M'ont salué,

begins "Dans un Omnibus de Londres," where the *frisson* depends on our recognizing Persephone by her Ovidian swans, which Pound has given Plutonian colors (Neare *Enna* walls [as Golding puts it] there stands a lake *Pergusa* is the name. Cayster heareth not mo songs of Swannes than doth the same.):

> Je vis les cygnes noirs,
> Japonais,
> Leurs ailes
> Teintées de couleur sang-de-dragon,
> Et toutes les fleurs
> D'Armenonville.
>
> Les yeux d'une morte
> M'ont salué.

These are the eyes of Jacopo's Venus in "The Picture" and its pendant, "Of Jacopo del Sellaio," that belonged to a model long dead and are now pure vision,

> The eyes of this dead lady speak to me.

They are the eyes at the end of *Mauberley,* that do not know they are dead. They are the ghostly eyes of the *Pisan Cantos,* where they stand in relation to a continuum of images that reaches back to the

> Souls out of Erebus, cadaverous dead, of brides
> Of youths and of the old who had borne much:
> Souls stained with recent tears, girls tender

of Canto I, the murdered bride Inez de Castro of Canto III, the Ione and "Eyes floating in dry, dark air" of Canto VII. These eyes in Hades are one of the concomitants of Persephone's theme. Another is the alignment of girl and tree, as in

> And Sulpicia
> green shoot now, and the wood
> white under new cortex
> [Canto XXXV]

or the appearance of Nausicaa, a type of Persephone, in a canto about women whose souls are chaotic, establishing a contrast between neurosis and health, confusion and clarity:

> Beauty on an ass-cart
> Sitting on five sacks of laundry
> That wd. have been the road by Perugia
> That leads out to San Piero. Eyes brown topaz,
> Brookwater over brown sand,
> The white hounds on the slope,
> Glide of water, lights and the prore,
> Silver beaks out of night,
> Stone, bough over bough,
>   lamps fluid in water,
> Pine by the black trunk of its shadow
> And on hill black trunks of the shadow
> The trees melted in air.
>
>   [Canto XXIX]

This theme prepares itself in the first thirty cantos, recurs less frequently but rhythmically through the American and Chinese cantos (XXXVI: woman radiant, a *ric pensamen* to the mind, *inluminatio coitu* to the heart; XXXIX: Circe, the richly dark, chthonic nature of woman—the two cantos form a diptych, and are brought together in XLVII, which is about the harmonizing of intelligence and the fixed order of nature: "First must thou go the road / to hell / And to the bower of Ceres' daughter Proserpine"), and becomes in the *Rock-Drill* and *Thrones* sections a synergetic presence.

Beyond the poem's beginning in her underworld, Persephone is apt to be just off-stage, or invisibly contained. She is the spirit of natural metamorphosis; in the first thirty cantos her absence is as significant as her presence. In Canto XXI she, Pallas, and Pan, Titania, and Phaetusa, Aetna's nymph at the entrance to the under-realm, are set in contrast to Midas, Plutus, and gold: the power to grow toward renewal, to think, to reproduce—against greed and ungrowing matter. At the end of XXI her rape is staged like Icarus's fall in Brueghel's painting, unnoticed, its implications unsuspected:

> Dis caught her up.
> And the old man went on there
>   beating his mule with an asphodel.

The loss of form through aimlessness, through moral slither, through the continued use of form without content, or by influences hostile to the organic nature of a form is a metamorphosis that is seedless, a stasis.

> Life to make mock of motion:
> For the husks, before me, move
> [Canto VII]

One can follow throughout *The Cantos* the force that reclaims lost form, lost spirit, Persephone's transformation back to virginity. As Homer shows us a chastened and chaste Helen in the *Odyssey,* so the first thirty cantos end with the moral regeneration of Lucrezia Borgia, that archetype of the Circe-world of the late nineteenth century from which every major artist of the time had to extricate himself in order to discover the moral nature of reality. She appears with the drunken gaiety of Botticelli's Primavera, Dea Flora, and the Graces, "foot like a flowery branch," "Madame ῩΛΗ," a woman obedient to all of nature's appetites, but with the balance and rhythm of nature's seed-cycle regeneration.

Through the *Pisan Cantos* Persephone is the promise of rebirth from the dark, an Ariadne in the labyrinth. "When night is spent," ends the Pisan group, in which Persephone was prayed to throughout. Pisa parallels the Homeric episode of Odysseus captured by the Cyclops (of whom the brute violence of war is an example), and the evocations of Persephone are under the sign of Δημήτηρ δακρύων, nature impotent and dying.

> with a smoky torch thru the unending
>   labyrinth of the souterrain
> or remembering Carleton let him celebrate Christ in the grain
> and if the corn cat be beaten
>   Demeter has lain in my furrow
> [Canto LXXX]

But faith in all that Persephone has meant in the poem is unwavering.

> Elysium, though it were in the halls of hell,
> What thou lovest well is thy true heritage
> What thou lovest well shall not be reft from thee
> [Canto LXXXI]

In watching a baby wasp, born in a nest in the corner of Pound's tent at Pisa, the poet brings the theme to one of its most resonant statements:

> When the mind swings by a grass-blade
>   an ant's forefoot shall save you
> the clover leaf smells and tastes as its flower
>
> The infant has descended,
> from mud on the tent roof to Tellus,
> like to like colour he goes amid grass-blades
>   greeting them that dwell under **XTHONOS** *XΘONOΣ*
> *OI XΘONIOI*, to carry our news
> εἰς χθονιους to them that dwell under the earth,
> begotten of air, that shall sing in the bower
>   of Kore,   *Περσεφόνεια*
> and have speech with Tiresias, Thebae
>
>   [Canto LXXXIII]

"Man, earth," says Canto LXXXII, "two halves of the tally." Man is under Fortuna, the Pisan cantos say repeatedly, and the DTC at Pisa is "a magna NOX animae" (Canto LXXIV), a very dark night of the soul, a hell out of which some spiritual recovery like the earth's from winter must happen.

The placing of events in time is a romantic act; the *tremendum* is in the distance. There are no dates in the myths; from when to when did Heracles stride the earth? In a century obsessed with time, with archaeological dating, with the psychological recovery of time (Proust, Freud), Pound has written as if time were unreal, has, in fact, treated it as if it were space. William Blake preceded him here, insisting on the irreality of clock time, sensing the dislocations caused by time (a God remote in time easily became remote in space, an absentee landlord) and proceeding, in his enthusiastic way, to dine with Isaiah—one way of suggesting that Isaiah's mind is not a phenomenon fixed between 742 and 687 B.C. Pound's mind has to be seen for the extraordinary shape it has given itself. To say that *The Cantos* is "a voyage in time" is to be blind to the poem altogether. We miss immediately the achievement upon which the success of the poem depends, its rendering time transparent and negligible, its dismissing the supposed corridors and perspectives *down* which the historian invites us to look. Pound canceled in his own mind the dissociations that had been isolating fact from fact for four centuries. To have closed the gap between mythology and botany is but one movement of the process; one way to read the cantos is to go through noting the restorations of relationships now thought to be discrete—the ideogrammatic method was invented for just this purpose. In Pound's spatial sense of time the past is here, now; its invisibility is our blindness, not its absence. The nineteenth century had put everything against the scale of time and discovered that all behavior within time's monolinear progress was evolutionary. The past was a grave-yard, a museum. It was Pound's determination to obliterate such a config-uration of time and history, to treat what had become a world of ghosts as a world eternally present.

Whatever the passions and predilections that we detect in *The Cantos,* they are dispositions of mind that Pound is reflecting, not programs he is advocating, not even matters on which he has passed judgment. The bot-anist may have a preference for conifers but he does not therefore omit mushrooms from his textbook. Pound's understanding of the world is always directed toward making us share the understanding he has found in other minds; we hear St Ambrose and John Adams condemn usury, not Pound; Confucius speaks for rectitude and probity; a good thousand voices speak. It was Pound's skill, the duty he assumed, to keep us from imagining that we are listening to ghosts, or that we are hearing dimly over vast time, or that the voices are meaningless.

Persephone, as a word, was, in the historical account of things, current among certain Greeks, Cretans, Sicilians, and Romans between such-and-such a year and such-and-such a year. Ethnology can also tell us that she is also known as Koré (The Girl), Flora, Persephatta, Persephoneia, and Proserpina. Any actual modern reference to her, in, say, the Greek hills, is a quaint bit of folklore, like the Cretans' still placing in the corpse's hand some token for Charon. The springtime, however, is eternal, though man's emotional response to it depends upon his sensibilities and educa-tion. And everything we call civilization depends upon that response. Man is aware of or blind to the order in which he lives by keeping or losing the tone of that response. From the beginning Pound was intuitively drawn to speaking of women and trees as if the one transparently showed some-thing of the beauty of the other. From poem to poem this image grew; it is possible to point to where this or that detail was added in the enrich-ment, until coming across a late passage such as

> The purifications
> are snow, rain, artemisia,
> also dew, oak, and the juniper

And in thy mind beauty, O Artemis,
    as of mountain lakes in the dawn.
Foam and silk are thy fingers,
        Kuanon,
and the long suavity of her moving,
    willow and olive reflected
        [Canto CX]

we find the ideogram to be a focus for meanings (the purpose of the ideogram in the first place) rather than a surface from which the eye uneducated by all that has come before it in the poem can discern anything beyond the beauty of the words.

For these words are not primarily lyric; nor are they a detail of memory, as they would be in Wordsworth, nor the epiphany of a visionary state, as they would be in Yeats. They are lines from an epic poem, their muse is Calliope, and their concern is with men in action. Calliope is The Muse with the Beautiful Eyes, and her business is to have looked and seen.

Tell me of that man, Musa, who took the uneasy turn
At all the crossroads, who came homeward in disaster
From the plundering of the holy acropolis of Troia;
Many towns has he seen, known the minds of many men,

begins the *Odyssey*, a poem about a man who thought trees were as beautiful as girls, girls as beautiful as trees, whose patrimony was an orchard and vineyard, whose peace, given him by Athena, is permanently before him and his children in the signature of the olive tree, who in the darkest trope of his wandering was sent by the witch-master of the lore of flowers and leaves, Circe, to the dwelling of Persephone, whose mystery is the power of eternal regeneration, in order that he find his way home.

In *Thrones* Persephone's tragedy is over: she has returned; her trees are in blossom. The voices that speak of her are easy, colloquial, at peace:

And was her daughter like that;
Black as Demeter's gown,
        eyes, hair?
Dis' bride, Queen over Phlegethon,
    girls faint as mist about her?

The strength of men is in grain.
        [Canto CVI]

She is the power of moving from dark to light, from formlessness to form, from Circe, whose inhuman mind is instructive but tangential to the life of man, to Penelope, whose virtues are domestic, an unwavering continuum.

> this is the grain rite
> near Enna, at Nyssa:
> Circe, Persephone
> so different is sea from glen that
> the juniper is her holy bush

In 1958, after the thirteen Odyssean years in a fastness that had been an arboretum (and has kept its trees) before it became a prison, Ezra Pound, a free man, went first to the sea whose greatest poet he is in our time, and second to a particular apple tree in Wyncote, Pennsylvania, in whose boughs he read the lines of Yeats's that moved him to write "The Tree" that stands foremost in his poems:

> I have been a hazel tree and they hung
> The Pilot Star and the Crooked Plough
> Among my leaves in times out of mind

The stars by which Odysseus navigated!

II: *The Tree as Temple Pillar or Demeter*

. . . The nineteenth century was obsessed with visions of paradises and utopias: Blake's Jerusalem, Coleridge's Xanadu, Shelley's Bosch-like lands of the spiritually cleansed, Rimbaud's and Henri Rousseau's jungle gardens. Two poles of attraction, we have seen, seemed to control these visions. One was Arcadian and natural, with some of its roots in Christian thought, and was a node for those Romantics who were seeking a world order consonant with nature (Wordsworth, Ruskin, the Transcendentalists). The other was deliberately artificial, arcane, symbolic. Novalis's *Heinrich von Ofterdingen* searching for his blue flower, des Esseintes immured among his bibelots and curios, Yeats longing to be refined into a mechanical nightingale in a Byzantium under the spell of faery—Baudelaire (the spiritual heir of Novalis, Hoffman, and Poe) gives a name to the century's predilection for a counterfeit world, *les paradis artificiels,* a phrase that Pound saw as the ultimate etiolation of Villon's *Paradis paint, où sont harpes et lus.* Baudelaire was principally concerned to contrast the healthy mind with the drugged one, natural vision with that induced by opium. Helplessly he preferred the natural, but as the drunkard commends sobriety. He was committed to his *"nouveauté sublime et monstrueuse"* (as Guillaume Apollinaire called it). Practically all its practitioners saw the Décadence as a religious force, specifically an inverted, mirror-like parody of Christianity; Baudelaire, especially, saw *Les Fleurs du mal* as a kind of hymnal or missal. It contains litanies, prayers, meditations.

> Ô vierges, ô démons, ô monstres, ô martyres,
> De la réalité grand esprits contempteurs,
> Chercheuses d'infini, dévotes et satyres,
> Vous que dans votre enfer mon âme a poursuivies.
>
> [*Femmes damnées*]

What, to Pound's mind, the century was doing was imagining Persephone's reign in hell. And the artist is a prophet. He shows the first symptoms of what will become contagion. Persephone's hell is one of nature's modes—the dwarf world, as folklorists know it, a world with phosphorus for light, with strange parodies of growing nature (geode for fig, gems for flowers, crystal for water). Image after image betrays an unconscious longing to be released from the sterility of this gorgeously artificial Hades, though its evil consists solely in one's mistaking it for reality's wholeness. Poe symbolized its psychology by placing his demon raven atop a bust of Pallas: the irrational dominating the intellect. Rossetti's paintings became an endless series of portraits of Persephone in hell. The "Veronica Veronese" of 1872 shows a young lady in plush (Miss Alice Wilding, the model) in a room hung with heavy cloth. She is reproducing on a violin the notes of her caged canary. Flowers made of jewels hang from her wrist; shells of ivory, gold, and pearl figure in her necklace. Once Pound had perceived that the major artists of the late nineteenth century had, for the most part unconsciously, taken Persephone grieving for another world as a dominant symbol, he was in a position to write both *Hugh Selwyn Mauberley* and the first thirty cantos. He had identified the chthonic Persephone with Circe, and the mirror-world in which nineteenth-century art had locked itself as a counterfeit paradise, a *paradis artificiel.* One of his responses was to write "An Idyll for Glaucus," casting the problem of increasingly arcane subjectivity as that of a girl trying to communicate with the metamorphosed Glaucus (he has eaten a magic herb and become a sea creature).

Three English writers began almost simultaneously to transmute this precious, ungrowing world of the imagination (reflecting what malady of the soul practically every artist of the twentieth century has tried to say) into visions of growth and organic fulfillment, to find again the ancient conjunction of flower and stone, underworld, world, and empyrean ("Topaz, God can sit on," Canto CIV). All three, Joyce, Eliot, and Pound, were close students of Dante, and all three, however differently, were involved in the recovery of the Mediterranean past by archaeology and anthropology. In Dantesque terms, Eliot managed an *Inferno* (*The Waste Land*) and fragments of a *Purgatorio* (*Ash Wednesday, The Four Quartets*). Joyce constructed in *Ulysses* the century's *Inferno* and in *Finnegans Wake* a *Purgatorio*—a cyclic *Purgatorio* from which one cannot escape. Pound has attempted a *Paradiso*, a vision of the world's splendor encompassing, as he configures the design, both of Persephone's kingdoms, "the germinal universe of wood alive, of stone alive" (*Spirit of Romance*, p. 72). It is in religion eclectic and is as interested in justice and piety as reflected in collective human behavior as in the fulfillment of the soul's inwardness. Eliot's and Joyce's city is unquestionably hell. Pound chose to traverse the dark vision completely and posit the city as the one clear conquest of civilization.

Each of the first thirty cantos either ends with the image of a city wall or tower or contains such an image; even the comic Canto XII ends with the word "Stambouli." The darkest of these images are of ruin (III, IV, XVIII, XX) or treachery (V, VI, VII, XXVIII). The brightest are of Aphrodite's copper walls, Danaë's tower, Sigismundo's Rimini, Chinese dynastic temples, and Florence, Venice, and Ferrara at their height. Yet everything in *The Cantos* is seen in tragic deterioration up until Pound discloses in the Pisan group the enveloping idea of the past as a symbol alive in the present and holding within it the seeds of the future. It is here that he brings in the city "now in the mind indestructible" and the oldest myth in the entire poem, that of Wagadu in Africa, a Soninke legend of a city, Wagadu, that was lost as a reality but remained in men's hearts.

> Four times Wagadu stood there in her splendour. Four times Wagadu disappeared and was lost to human sight: once through vanity, once through falsehood, once through greed, and once through dissension. Four times Wagadu changed her name. First she was called Dierra, then Agada, then Ganna, then Silla.... Wagadu, whenever men have seen her, has always had four gates, one to the north, one to the west, one to the east, and one to the south. These are the directions from whence the strength of Wagadu comes, the strength in which she endures no

matter whether she be built of stone, wood, or earth, or lives but as a shadow in the mind and longing of her children. For, really, Wagadu is the strength which lives in the hearts of men and is sometimes visible because eyes see her and ears hear the clash of swords and ring of shields, and is sometimes invisible because the indomitability of men has over-tired her, so that she sleeps. . . . Should Wagadu ever be found for the fifth time, then she will live so forcefully in the minds of men that she will never be lost again, so forcefully that vanity, falsehood, greed, and dissension will never be able to harm her.[1]

In Canto XVI, emerging from the hell of the decivilizers, we have as a countervision:

> entered the quiet air
> 　　　　the new sky,
> 　the light as after a sun-set,
> 　　　and by their fountains, the heroes,
> Sigismundo, and Malatesta Novello,
> 　　　and founders, gazing at the mounts of their cities.

In Canto XVII: "and the cities set in their hills." In Canto XXVI there is a Jerusalem painted by Carpaccio, which was also a city foursquare, many times lost and now a vision in the mind, as it (or she) was in the time of Isaiah and Jeremiah, in whose pages the myth of Wagadu would be per-fectly at home. In the figure of the city that has become a throne—a spiritual power of greatest force—Pound sees the one inclusive symbol of civilization. Here the odysseys of men come to rest and cohere with the Penelope-work at the still centre. By Canto CVII Demeter has become Queen of Akragas, and the cities through whose histories *The Cantos* have moved become temples containing light, and the processes of architecture the music by which Amphion lifted the enchanted stones into place to ring Thebes with a wall.

> 　　Amphion not for museums
> 　　　but for her mind
> 　　　　like the underwave
> 　　　　　[Canto CVII]

The museum, twentieth-century parody of a temple, is all that we have, physically, of the past; and Joyce begins *Finnegans Wake* in a museum. The early interpreters of *The Cantos* tended to see the poem as a study of the man of willed and directed action, as a persona of Odysseus. It is now clear that the poem rests most firmly in a deeper, stiller sense of humanity, the city and its continuity, symbolized by the goddess of field and citadel wearing the sanctuary of her people as a crown.

Note

1. Leo Frobenius and Douglas C. Fox, *African Genesis,* London 1938, pp. 109–110.

The Ideogrammic Method in *The Cantos*

GIROLAMO MANCUSO

TRANSLATED BY PETER MAKIN

❖ ❖ ❖

Editor's Introductory Note

[Pound became interested in the Chinese ideogram—the written character—when he read a manuscript essay by the late orientalist Ernest Fenollosa, which he then edited in 1919 as *The Chinese Written Character as a
Medium for Poetry*.

Spurred by this essay and by his own curiosity, Pound noted that Chinese poetry is extraordinarily visual. The classical Chinese language often
juxtaposes characters with little or no grammatical indication, so that the
reader must infer meanings by considering the relations between what the
characters represent. The characters themselves often originated as pictures, and many of them show their own etymology, in that the meaning
of the whole character is the relations between the picture elements it is
made up of. Pound had already been stimulated by the Japanese haiku to
develop the new Imagist structure for short poems, where the complex
meaning of the whole poem amounted to the relations between two or
more images, juxtaposed without explanation. This, however, appeared to
him a dead end.

Mancuso's book argues that the very "sense of totality" of this haiku-
like complex of meaning meant that you could not develop it into a longer

poem. It was like two atoms combined into a molecule in such a way as
to satisfy all their respective valences. Then, he says, came Pound's studies
of Fenollosa and of the ideogram. Mancuso argues that Pound never clearly
explained the difference between the Imagist method and the ideogrammic
method: we have to infer it, by examining the poetry he wrote under the
ideogrammic banner. In that poetry, we find that the core is still juxtaposition of concrete data, without abstract explanation, but now these
quasi-Imagist concentrations break out of their limits by the device of
networking repetition. Mancuso distinguishes internal repetition, either of
whole passages or of single "cues"; external repetition, which is in fact
quotation from sources outside Pound's poem; and what he calls repetition
"in an extended sense," as in Pound's phrase "eyes of Picasso," which is
not a verbal quotation but evokes a whole visuality. Using such devices,
Pound, in *The Cantos*, wove his Images into a structure like that of a fugue.]

THE BEST APPROACH TO A DEFINITION OF THE ideogrammic method
is an analysis of *The Cantos*. In a certain sense, one is thus applying the
method to the problem of defining the method itself: instead of making a
discourse *about* the ideogrammic method, we shall show it in its concrete
operation. Certain significant elements can be found by bringing together
the original version of the first *Cantos* and their final version. Let us consider
the end of Canto I, after the long quotation-translation from the *Odyssey*:

> Lie quiet Divus. I mean, that is Andreas Divus,
> In officina Wecheli, 1538, out of Homer.
> And he sailed, by Sirens and thence outward and away
> And unto Circe.
> > Venerandam,
> In the Cretan's phrase, with the golden crown, Aphrodite,
> Cypri munimenta sortita est, mirthful, orichalchi, with golden
> Girdles and breast bands, thou with dark eyelids
> Bearing the golden bough of Argicida. So that:

> > > > (I.5)

In the *Ur-Cantos* [i.e., the early versions published in *Lustra*, 1917], the
corresponding passage is at the end of Canto III:

> Lie quiet Divus. Then had he news of many faded women,
> Tyro, Alcmena, Chloris,

Heard out their tales by that dark fosse, and sailed
By sirens and thence outward and away,
And unto Circe. Buried Elpenor's corpse.
Lie quiet Divus, plucked from a Paris stall
With a certain Cretan's "Hymni Deorum";
The thin clear Tuscan stuff
Gives way before the florid mellow phrase,
Take we the goddess, Venerandam
Auream coronam habentem, pulchram . . .
Cypri munimenta sortita est, maritime,
Light on the foam, breathed on by Zephyrs
And air-tending Hours, mirthful, orichalchi, with golden
Girdles and breast bands, thou with dark eyelids,
Bearing the golden bough of Argicida.

In rewriting this passage for the final version, Pound has made cuts and substitutions. In particular, he has brought in a bibliographical note about the Latin translation of the *Odyssey* by Andreas Divus (used in the preceding passage). He has inserted this instead of the information that he acquired this translation from a bookstall in Paris, and that it contained, besides the *Odyssey*, the *Homeric Hymns* in the translation by Georgius Dartona Cretensis (source of the quotations about Aphrodite that form the end of the Canto).

The information that he has dropped had served, in a certain way, to justify the connecting of the preceding passage (the *Nekuia*) with the one that follows. Suppressing it amounts to eliminating a logical connector, so that, in the final version, the two passages appear simply to be juxtaposed, apparently without reason. But in fact the biographical information, now dropped, gave a connection that was (though immediately comprehensible) merely external and accidental. Meanwhile, the "reasonless" juxtaposition shows up a connection, at a much deeper and more significant level, between the masculine theme of Odysseus and the feminine theme of Aphrodite. We would be tempted to say, "between the *yang* and *yin* principles," if it were not that Aphrodite is described here as "golden," and therefore appears in her luminous and solar aspect. Further, eliminating the whole passage from "Circe" to "Venerandam" places in direct contact—and therefore in connection—Aphrodite and Circe, and Circe too is a "daughter of the Sun" (see the chapters "The Witch" and "The Golden One" in Kerényi, 1944).

One might give another example by setting the first lines of Canto I (in the original version) side by side with the first lines of Canto II (final version). The *Ur-Cantos* began with an imaginary dialogue between the poet and the author of *Sordello*, Robert Browning:

> Hang it all, there can be but the one "Sordello,"
> But say I want to, say I take your whole bag of tricks,
> Let in your quirks and tweeks, and say the thing's an art-form,
> Your "Sordello," and that the "modern world"
> Needs such a rag-bag to stuff all its thought in;
> Say that I dump my catch, shiny and silvery
> As fresh sardines flapping and slipping on the marginal cobbles?
> I stand before the booth (the speech), but the truth
> Is inside this discourse: this booth is full of the marrow of wisdom.
> Give up the intaglio method?
> Tower by tower,
> Red-brown the rounded bases, and the plan
> Follows the builder's whim; Beaucaire's slim gray
> Leaps from the stubby base of Altaforte—

In the final version, this passage is radically transformed and shifted to the beginning of Canto II:

> Hang it all, Robert Browning,
> there can be but the one "Sordello."
> But Sordello, and my Sordello?
> Lo Sordels si fo di Mantovana.
> So-shu churned in the sea.
> Seal sports in the spray-whited circles of cliff-wash,
> Sleek head, daughter of Lir,
>   eyes of Picasso
> Under black fur-hood, lithe daughter of Ocean;
> And the wave runs in the beach-groove:
> "Eleanor, *helenaus* and *heleptolis!*"
>
>   (II.6) [romanized]

In this version, the laborious and prolix "discourse about a discourse" has been replaced with a rapid succession of marine images. (The sea is Aphrodite's native element.) But the more important point is that the convention of the imaginary dialogue, which acted as a unifier in the original version, has been eliminated. Even the *Ur-Cantos* were in fact constructed by juxtaposing images, but Pound still thought it necessary to find an external justification for this.

This artificiality does not disappear entirely from *The Cantos*. We find it, for example, in Canto XX, which Pound explained to his father (*Letters*, 224) as a flow of visions and memories in the mind of Niccolò d'Este in a kind of delirium after the execution of Parisina and Ugo. But the dominant tendency now is to find a justification within the discourse itself. Beyond the surface similarities, this is the main difference between Pound's ideogrammic technique and Joyce's technique of the interior monologue. Think, for example, of the episode of Stephen/Telemachus's walk on the beach, an episode which is dominated by the sea, as Canto II is. What Joyce tries to register is the uninterrupted flux of the interior discourse of the character, which proceeds by association of ideas. Pound, by contrast, tends to eliminate the psychological, interior dimension: "The key to Pound's method throughout *The Cantos* is his conviction that the things the poet sees in the sea of events are really there" (Kenner, 1954: 14). The connecting of one image and another does not take place in the mind of a character, or of the author, but in reality itself. Obviously such a connection does not actually exist in reality, and only occurs in the mind of the author—in the *formato locho dove sta memora*—but this mind is imagined as a mirror which reflects the flow of events, and by doing so transforms them into the fixity of crystal, like the perfect form of Venus Anadyomene, "emerging" from the sea. (The theme of water or the sea solidifying into stone, announced in Canto II, recurs in *The Cantos*.) This is no longer a literary *convention*, used to unify material, but a profound *conviction* in the poet's mind, concerning the nature of reality and also the nature of ideogrammic language. (Fenollosa had written: "When we read Chinese, we are not moving around mental dice: we watch *things* evolve their fate.") In this perspective, every literary or verbal artifice that seeks to justify the enchaining of images from the outside and a posteriori is redundant.

The elimination of these external justifications is effected also, and above all, by eliminating transitional elements and logical-discursive connectors. The nature of these can vary with the different levels on which the ideogrammic technique operates. At the end of Canto I, in its present version, the connector that has been suppressed (when we compare it with the original version) is the whole passage from "plucked from a Paris stall" to "take we the goddess." These suppressed connectors coincide with the grammatical connectors only in those rare cases where the ideogrammic method is used at the level of single words. Besides the "Moon, cloud, tower" [of LXXIX.504], other examples can be found (though the grammatical connectors in them are not eliminated entirely):

> above which, the lotus, white nenuphar
> Kuanon, the mythologies
>
> (LXXVII.492)

> cat-faced, croce di Malta, figura del sol
> to each tree its own mouth and savour
> *"Hot   hole   hep   cat"*
>
> (LXXX.518)

> 3 on 3
> chiacchierona   the yellow bird
> to rest   3 months in bottle
> (auctor)
>
> (LXXIX.507)

There is a good example of juxtaposition at the level of the phrase at the beginning of Canto II. The link between "Hang it all, Robert Browning, / there can be but the one 'Sordello' " and "But Sordello, and my Sordello?" can still be interpreted within the frame of an imaginary dialogue, but the next line ("Lo Sordels si fo di Mantovana") already goes outside this schema, and the passage from "So-shu churned in the sea" has no external justification at all. (It would be hard to imagine what transitional element *could* mediate between this line and the ones that precede it.)

And one shouldn't exaggerate the "incomprehensibility" that this technique produces. It functions also in passages like the celebrated Canto XLV ("With Usura"), which does not seem to be considered incomprehensible, to judge at least by the frequency with which it appears in anthologies. Canto XLV (like the parallel Canto LI) is in fact made up of a series of enunciations that are not connected with each other by a logical development (Alvarez, 1958); "The principle of organization is that of the tableau: the commanding figure of Usury, like the figure of Death in the medieval tableaux, appears in one scene after another" (Dekker, 1963: 175). In other cases, the difficulties of comprehension lie in the difficulty in identifying a unifying principle, and/or in the impossibility of finding a parallel in a procedure more familiar to our cultural tradition, which might give us, in some way, a key to reading. The use of the ideogrammic technique, on the other hand, does not exclude the use of more conventional techniques, which tend essentially toward the same goal. One example is the montage of fragmentary quotations from the letters found in the postbag of Sigismondo Malatesta (Canto IX), a technique modeled on *A Bundle of Letters* by Henry James and reused in Canto XXXI (the letters of Jefferson and Adams).

Quite frequently, the application of the ideogrammic method tends to fall to a lower level, and this is seen in the use of broken phrases, fragmentary quotations, and sentences left in suspense. Elsewhere, one finds the reverse of this, where the units constructed by juxtaposition are of a higher order than that of the phrase. At a still higher level, one may note that a single Canto is often made up of a number of "blocks," between which there is no apparent logical consequence. At this level, Pound often proceeds by parallelism or by contrast. In certain cases, the parallelism between two blocks reinforces and clarifies the sense of juxtaposition created within each block: thus in Canto IV the juxtaposition of Ytis and Cabestan has a parallel in the juxtaposition of Actaeon and Vidal in the following block, and by this parallel both become more transparent.

The technique of ideogrammic juxtaposition is finally applied to the link between one Canto and another. In the first Cantos, the logical jump from one Canto to the next is sometimes made more obvious by the use of "false connectors." Canto I ends with a "So that:" which seems to suggest a sense of consequence that is immediately denied. Canto II ends with "And . . .", while Canto III begins with a phrase that seems to have nothing to do with the argument of the preceding Canto (yet that argument is taken up again immediately afterward). Canto IV ends with a sentence left in suspense: "And we sit here . . . / there in the arena . . . ," which is not taken up again till Canto XII: "And we sit here / under the wall, / Arena romana."

At this level, we have reached a point at which the argument about the structure of *The Cantos* as a whole comes up again. The hypothesis of a fugal structure (theme, response, countertheme) is clearly the most convincing. It is also the metaphor best adapted to the ideogrammic method, which implies a break with Aristotelian schemes of any kind, and therefore with all "closed" forms. Pound himself, implicitly referring to the plan of the *Divine Comedy*, denies having any "Thomist map" ("I haven't an Aquinas-map; Aquinas *not* valid now": *Letters*, 355). Cross-references of the "arena" kind amount to a series of indications that help us to identify themes used in counterpoint, or to identify external devices, which are sometimes used partially, but remain always superficial and do not concern the real structure of *The Cantos*. Even at this level, the organizing principle is to be sought in the ideogrammic method, and not outside it.

We have seen how repetition is part of this organizing principle, either within the text (recurrent themes) or as a repetition of matter from outside it (quotations). An analysis of *The Cantos* from this angle must therefore include, as a first step, an careful examination of these repeated elements.

Recurring themes and quotations too are found at different levels. On the one hand, they concern units of discourse of varying size. A quotation may be limited to a single word (like the *remir* of Canto XX: 90), or it may be extended to the paraphrasing of a hundred lines or more (like the quotation from Book XI of the *Odyssey*, which occupies most of Canto I). Similarly, internal repetition may concern a whole Canto (like XLV, which is repeated with variations in LI) or one single thematic word (like "sapphire" or "crystal"). But on the other hand, and independently of the length of the expressions in which they appear, it is necessary to distinguish between the "major" themes (like usury, the *nostos*, metamorphosis, etc.) and "minor" thematic units (like the themes of Leucothea, of Tammuz, of Ecbatan, and so on). On the level of expression, the major themes are characteristically *diffuse*, while the thematic units are *compact*. From another angle, one may note that the thematic units are contained in the major themes, and sometimes in more than one major theme: for example, the theme of Leucothea constitutes part of the *nostos* theme as well as that of metamorphosis. All this suggests that it is best to start by identifying the thematic units, rather than the major themes, and to see exactly how these units are organized in relation to each other.

By analogy with the Chinese written character, we could say that the thematic units are the primitive signs (pictograms or elementary signs) which, by combination, form the compound characters. Clearly, then, it is useful to have available, at the outset, a listing of these elementary signs. Another reason for proceeding in this way is that, at this level, it is not necessary to make a distinction between quotations and recurrent themes—a distinction which, among other things, would oblige us to bring in a third category: recurrent quotations. And in most cases, it is not necessary even to locate the source of the quotation.

In an analysis of this kind, expressions in foreign languages take on a particular importance. Very often, they are quotations in the strict sense of the word, and quite often they are also quotations in the extended sense that we have given this term. Boris de Rachewiltz (1965: 10) has noted that the expressions in ancient languages have in *The Cantos* a value analogous to that of the *nomina arcana* and the *asema onomata* of the magical texts. Cook (1969: 357) meanwhile observes that the quotations attain the status of images, of things seen. In a certain sense, they are used as "linguistic objects," important as signs even more than as things signified. Pound himself seems to hint at something similar: "The quotes are all either explained at once by repeat or they are definitely *of* the things indicated. If reader don't know what an elefant IS, then the word is obscure" (*Letters*, 270). He also says, "I believe that when finished *all* foreign words in the Cantos, Gk., etc., will be underlinings, not necessary to the sense, in one way. . . . [T]he Greek, ideograms, etc., will indicate a duration from whence or since when" (*Letters*, 355). And this seems to confirm the value as magical "fulcrums" that de Rachewiltz attributes to the visual elements used in *The Cantos*, and in particular to the Chinese characters. Indeed, among the expressions in foreign languages, the Chinese quotations have a particular importance. They take on three distinct functions: that of quotations, that of images (of things seen), and that of ideograms (Cook, *loc. cit.*). One may add a fourth. Espey points out

the catalytic function played in Pound's mind by certain phrases and certain ideas: they precipitate or arrange other phrases and ideas about themselves. The most interesting instance of this in *Mauberley* is the way in which the orchid and iris of the Fenollosa notes attract to themselves the entire elaborate pattern of the second "Mauberley" poem. (Espey, 1955: 112)

In the same sense, Kenner (1972: 118) writes that sometimes a "single word . . . governs concentric fields" and that this "is characteristic of alien words in the *Cantos*." This is particularly true of those Chinese characters that Pound uses as visual pivot points, and around which words dispose themselves like "the rose in the steel dust" around a magnet. Often these characters are accentuated and distinguished from the others also by their massiveness and manner of writing, like the ideogram LING in Cantos LXXXV and XCVII, or the character CHEN in Cantos LXXXVI and XCVI:

> non coelum non in medio
> but man is under Fortuna
> ? that is a forced translation?
> La donna che volgo

Man under Fortune,

CHÊN

(LXXXVI.586)

With eyes pervanche,

all under the Moon is under

Fortuna

 CHEN

e che permutasse.

(XCVI.676)

In both these contexts the Dante quotation "under Fortuna" recurs, and this prompts us to look for other contexts in which it is repeated. We find them thus:

> All neath the moon, under Fortuna,
>   splendor' mondan',
> beata gode, hidden as eel in sedge,
>   all neath the moon, under Fortuna
> hoc signo 貞 chen (*four*), hoc signo
> with eyes pervanche,
>   three generations, San Vio
> darker than pervanche?
>   Pale sea-green, I saw eyes once,
> and Raleigh remarked, on Genova's loans non-productive,
>   that they had only their usury left

(XCVII.696)

and, a little further on:

> Earth under Fortuna,
>   each sphere hath its Lord,
> with ever-shifting change, sempre biasmata,
>   gode,
>   "Not difficult to make"
>   said Brancusi
> "mais *nous*, de nous mettre en état DE les faire."
> "Je peux commencer une chose tous les jours,
> mais fi—nir!'

(XCVII.697)

and:

>   Even Aquinas could not demote her, Fortuna,
>   violet, pervanche, deep iris,
>   beat' è, e gode,
>   the dry pod could not demote her, plenilune,
>   phase over phase.

>   (XCVII.698)

and finally:

>   Arab coins found in mounds in Sweden
>   under Fortuna
>   Raleigh noted that Genova's loans were not productive
>   "all they have left is their usury"

>   (CIII.756)

In these passages appear very clearly other recurrent themes, for each of which one could repeat the same procedure as we have followed for "under Fortuna": checking whether they recur in other contexts, and whether these have other recurrent themes, which could in turn be put through the same process, and so on, until the interconnected thematic units were exhausted. At that point, one could compile a listing of the recurrent themes identified in this way, and lay out a graphic scheme of their interconnections, thus obtaining a scheme of the fugal structure of *The Cantos*. A rough and incomplete draft of this prodecure will be found [later], where the point of departure will be the character HSIEN. For the moment, we prefer to halt the process at this initial phase and make a number of points about it.

The Dante quotation that is one of the most frequently repeated themes in these passages is given in a very fragmentary, and usually modified, form. The whole passage goes thus (with Pound's phrases in italics):

>   Or puoi veder, figliuol, la corta buffa
>   Dei ben che son connessi a la *Fortuna,*
>   Per che l'umana gente si rabbuffa:
>   Ché tutto l'oro ch'è *sotto la Luna*
>   E che già fu di quest'anime stanche
>   Non potrebbe farne posar una.
>   "Maestro" diss'io lui "or mi dì anche:
>   Questa *Fortuna* di che tu mi tocche,
>   Che è, che i ben del mondo ha sì tra branche?"

Ed egli, a me: "Oh creature sciocche,
   Quanta ignoranza è quella che v'offende!
   Or vo' che tu mia sentenza ne imbocche.
Colui lo cui saver tutto trascende
   Fece *li cieli e diè lor chi conduce*
   Sì che ogni parte ad ogni parte splende,
Distribuendo igualmente la luce.
   Similemente a li *splendor mondani*
   Ordinò general ministra e duce
Che permutasse a tempo li ben vani
   Di gente in gente e d'uno in altro sangue
   Oltre la difension de' senni umani;
Per che una gente impera ed altra langue
   Seguendo lo giudicio di costei,
   Che è *occulto come in erba l'angue.*
Vostro saver non ha contrasto a lei:
   Questa provede, giudica e persegue
   Suo regno come il loro gli altri dei.
Le sue permutazion non hanno tregue;
   Necessità la fa esser veloce;
   Sì spesso vien che vicenda consegue.
Questa è colei ch'è tanto posta in croce
   Pur da color che le dovrien dar lode,
   Dandole biasmo a torto e mala voce.
Ma ella *s'è beata* e ciò non ode:
   Con l'altre prime creature lieta
   Volve sua spera, e beata si gode.

                         (*Inferno*, VII, 61–96)

    This form of quotation by fragments is typical in the ideogrammic technique, which often condenses a long passage in a single thematic word. With it, Pound obtains two results: that of "charging" the words with meaning "to the utmost possible degree," and that of proceeding by variations. These two procedures are also used for the internal repetitions, which rarely recur in the same form, and which are often extremely condensed. We therefore have to make a distinction between *theme-type* and *theme-recurrence* (analogously with *sign-type* and *sign-token*)—that is, between the *theme*, considered as a constant, and the *variants* in which one identical theme is manifested (some of which are *condensed variants*). Though in general, for this kind of analysis, it is not necessary to identify the sources of the quotations, that information is sometimes necessary, not so much to grasp the *meaning* of the quotation, as to grasp the *identity* of the theme, through (and in spite of) all the variants in which it appears. From this arises the usefulness of listing all the interconnected themes, and their variants, as a preliminary phase of the analytic procedure offered here.

As we have said, the final phase should consist of a summary diagram of all the interconnected themes, in which their respective connections, too, would be shown graphically. Since these connections are of an ideo-grammic nature—that is, the various thematic units are connected by juxtaposition—we shall call the ensemble of the interconnected themes an *ideogrammic constellation*. The analysis of the ideogrammic constellations and the construction of their maps has the double aim of bringing out the "fine structure" of *The Cantos* and of showing in concrete form the functioning of the ideogrammic technique. There are two ways in which one could carry out this analysis. One could first compile a list of all the recurring themes in *The Cantos* and then group them in constellations on the basis of a study of their interconnections, or one could follow the procedure already shown for the character CHEN, that is, to start from a recurrent theme, identify the themes connected with that, and repeat the procedure for each of the themes as they are identified in this way. This second procedure has the double advantage that it is easier to follow and that one may limit it to the study of a single constellation. The search for thematic units is made easier by the fact that they are often condensed into a single word or expression, usually in a foreign language, and that nevertheless they contain expressions which, just as Pound says, act as underlinings. This is particularly evident with the Chinese characters or other visual elements used in *The Cantos*. And so it turns out that just those elements which, at first sight, seemed to offer a difficulty for the under-standing of the text are in fact the ones that, from our point of view, make it easier to read.

[Mancuso now constructs a map of the "ideogrammic constellation" that centers on the Chinese character HSIEN 顯: see figure 1. He observes that it means "to manifest," "to be illustrious," "evident," "visible," "to appear." He goes on:]

In the modern graphic form, HSIEN is made up of SUN (at the top on the left), SILK THREADS (bottom left) and HEAD (on the right). . . . Both in the translation of the *Doctrine of the Mean* and in the *Cantos*, Pound takes note only of the left-hand part of the compound: SUN over SILK THREADS (and hence his interpretation: "tensile light"). . . .

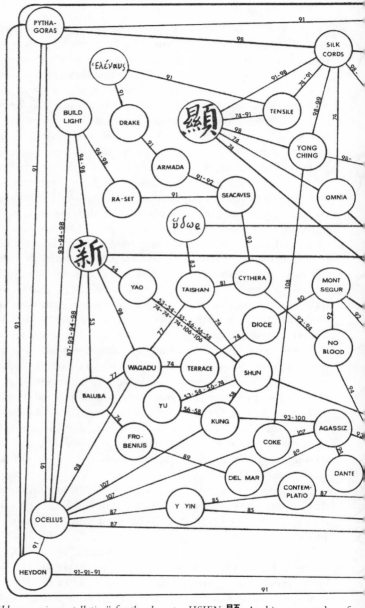

"Ideogrammic constellation" for the character HSIEN 顯. Arabic numerals refer to Canto numbers.

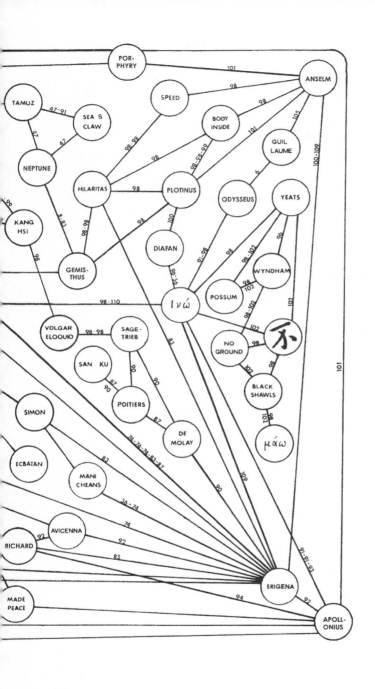

Bibliography

Alvarez, A. (1958). *The Shaping Spirit.* London.

Cook, A. (1969). "Rhythm and Person in the Cantos." In Eva Hesse, ed., *New Approaches to Ezra Pound.* London.

Dekker, G. (1963). *Sailing after Knowledge: The Cantos of Ezra Pound.* London.

Espey, J. J. (1955). *Ezra Pound's Mauberley: A Study in Composition.* Berkeley, California.

Kenner, H. (1954). "The Broken Mirrors and the Mirror of Memory." In Lewis Leary, ed., *Motive and Method in the Cantos of Ezra Pound.* London, 1969.

Kenner, H. (1972). *The Pound Era.* London.

Kerényi, K. (1944). *Figlie del Sole.* Turin.

Pound, E. (1998). *The Cantos.* New York: New Directions.

Rachewiltz, B. de (1965). *L'elemento magico in Ezra Pound.* Milan.

Why the *Commedia* Is Not the Model for *The Cantos* and What Is

REED WAY DASENBROCK

◆   ◆   ◆

ONE OF THE MOST IMPORTANT—perhaps the most important—critical frames we have used to read *The Cantos* is to see it as a modern *Commedia*. Pound's admiration for and extensive knowledge of Dante is on display everywhere in his work, and since he himself drew a number of comparisons between the *Commedia* and *The Cantos,* there has descended a critical tradition still with some life in it that sees Pound's poem in these terms.[1] What I want to try to explain here is both what is wrong with this approach to the poem and why this has been such a long-lived understanding of *The Cantos.*

Certainly, at first glance *The Cantos* do not resemble the *Commedia* in a number of important respects. To start out with some extremely obvious points, *The Cantos* do not form a single integrated narrative in the way the *Commedia* does. As *The Cantos* go on, they increasingly resemble nothing remotely narrative, but even in the earlier sections of the poem which contain narratives, these narratives are not linked into a coherent whole. Another way of putting this is that *The Cantos* have no integrating characters such as Dante, Vergil, and Beatrice. Pound makes a gesture at the very beginning of the poem toward using Odysseus as a unifying figure, a Dante without a Vergil or a Beatrice as it were, but there are only vestigial traces of this plan throughout the remainder of the poem.

This failure to resemble the *Commedia* in terms of its narrative hasn't escaped critics, and so most of the critics finding a resemblance between the *Commedia* and *The Cantos* have focused not on the narrative of the *Commedia* but on its form or design, its division into three symmetrical canticles. From the very beginning of the critical discussion of *The Cantos,* critics have looked for and claimed to find a structural resemblance between the *Commedia* and *The Cantos.* In this view, *The Cantos* divide into an *Inferno,* a *Purgatorio,* and a *Paradiso,* and the poem—though not unified at a narrative level— finds its unity in this "orderly Dantescan rising," to quote a famous phrase from Canto 74.[2] However, the full phrase—quoted less often—is "By no means an orderly Dantescan rising," and surely this is closer to the poem as it stands. *The Cantos* simply do not divide neatly (or even awkwardly) into an *Inferno,* a *Purgatorio,* and a *Paradiso;* the problem is that the critics have attempted to use the *Inferno/Purgatorio/Paradiso* scheme as a device to impose order on *The Cantos* rather than finding such an order in it. No one has satisfactorily found such a structural resemblance between the *Commedia* and *The Cantos,* and my sense is that this approach to *The Cantos* has been tried often enough that we can declare it a failure by now.

So *The Cantos* are not an integrated narrative; they contain no integrating characters; and they do not have the symmetrical form of the *Commedia.* Just to mention quickly some of the other respects in which they differ from their supposed model, the poet is only sporadically a figure in the poem, not the consistent presence Dante is in his poem. The vast majority of the material presented in *The Cantos* is historical material, considered by the poet to be historical truth, in contrast to the fiction or dream vision of the *Commedia.* The plethora of different historical moments depicted in *The Cantos* is in remarkable contrast to the explicit setting of the *Commedia* in the present, in 1300. Analogously, in the *Commedia,* virtually everyone speaks Dante's Italian, whereas in the babble of tongues that comprise *The Cantos,* virtually everyone is presented, at least partially, in his or her own language. A list of the languages found in Pound's poem would include English, Chinese, Italian, French, Greek, Spanish, German, Arabic, Japanese, and Egyptian hieroglyphics; nothing comparable is found in Dante, who has deliberately chosen to write in the *volgare* despite the fact that Pound's multilingualism was more characteristic of Dante's epoch than his own.

So obvious are these differences as I list them that we must ask why critics have ever sought to establish parallels between the two. The answer is a simple one: Pound kept making such comparisons himself, and critics assume rightly that he had some reason for so doing. However, the comparisons he drew were always slightly different, often contradictory, and in many cases revised the *Commedia* as he compared it to his own work. My favorite of these is this: "For forty years I have schooled myself, not to write an economic history of the U.S. or any other country, but to write an epic poem which begins 'In the Dark Forest' crosses the Purgatory of human error, and ends in the light, and 'fra i maestri di color che sanno,'" (*Selected Prose*, p. 167). This seems to present *The Cantos* as a careful imitation of the *Commedia* in just the way the critics have done; however, the closest thing in Dante's poem to Pound's "il maestro di color che sanno," Aristotle, is not in paradise at the poem's end, of course, but is in limbo at the very beginning of the poem. Even when Pound is asserting a structural resemblance between his poem and the *Commedia,* he reshapes his model in the process. The very moments at which Pound explicitly acknowledges or asserts an indebtedness to Dante tend also to be moments when he tacitly acknowledges or asserts his difference from Dante. And this suggests that we need to consider other ways in which Dante and his work may be relevant to the project of *The Cantos* besides having the *Commedia* serve as a structural model for Pound's epic. If we take the signs of an epic to be integrated narrative coherence, then the *Commedia* is a successful epic and *The Cantos* is either a botch of an epic or something else entirely. And those are the terms that have largely governed the critical tradition. However, the Italian culture of the Renaissance which was so decisive for Pound provides us—and provided Pound—with a very different way of thinking about epic, and it is instructive to think about *The Cantos* in terms provided by that tradition.

Renaissance theories of poetry were highly rhetorical theories: the lyric was seen, for example, as primarily praise of the beloved and thus falling under Aristotle's category of epideictic rhetoric.[3] Comparably, theories of epic underwent a rhetorical transformation in the Renaissance.[4] Aristotle's criteria of coherence and narrative integrity as outlined in the *Poetics* which are central for our received way of thinking about the epic were not known directly until the Cinquecento. And even in the heyday of Cinquecento Aristotelianism, these criteria were less important than an understanding of the epic as a kind of epideictic rhetoric oriented toward praise (of great men and their accomplishments) and blame (of unworthy men and their failures or malign accomplishments). The confident distinction between lyric and epic we might draw today is therefore blurred in one sense, since both draw on common rhetorical strategies and purposes, but a distinction in terms of domain is crystal clear. The inscribed audience of lyric is female,

its space is private (or at least courtly), and the aim of the praise is ultimately seduction. The audience of epic is male and its space is clearly
public, but what is its aim? Here, the central humanist notion of exemplarity needs to be introduced: the poet figures forth images of perfection
from the past in order to inspire a desire for imitation on the part of the
hearer or reader. If literature is, in Horatian terms, to instruct as well as
delight, the instruction consists in depicting exemplars of virtue from the
past who inspire feats of emulation on the part of the contemporary
reader.[5]

This notion of epic is very broadly diffused in the Renaissance. Sir Philip
Sidney's *Defense of Poesie* gives us perhaps the most familiar version of this
notion of epic in English language criticism: "For as the image of each
action stirreth and instructeth the mind, so the lofty image of such wor-
thies most inflameth the mind with desire to be worthy, and informs you
with counsel how to be worthy. Only let Aeneas be worn in the tablet of
your memory" (Gilbert, p. 434). Pound, of course, would have known this
tradition, as Sidney did, less from its currency in translation than from its
original sources in the Italian Renaissance. Tasso's *Discorsi* represents a convenient codification of this tradition: "There are two modes of teaching by
example, one that of inciting to good works by showing the reward of the
noblest virtue and of well-nigh divine valor, the other that of frightening
us from evil with a punishment. The first is that of epic, the second is
that of tragedy, which for that reason is less beneficial and also causes less
delight" (Gilbert, p. 503).

What is the place of the *Commedia* in this tradition of thinking about
epic? At once central and oblique. One of the great critical debates in the
Cinquecento, of course, was over the status of the *Commedia,* and an important line of defense of the *Commedia*—found particularly in Benedetto
Varchi and Jacopo Mazzoni—was to stress an epideictic reading of the
Commedia. In fact, these two noted defenders of Dante are the critics who
give us the fullest statement of the exemplary notion of epic which we
are tracing, and I would suspect that it is through this tradition of Dante
criticism—not through reading Sidney or other English-language sources—
that Pound encountered this view. Pound owned a beautiful edition of
Varchi's *Storia fiorentina,* and in J. E. Spingarn's *Literary Criticism in the Renaissance*—the standard treatment of this material when Pound was in graduate
school—Varchi is the first critic treated who has good things to say about
Dante. His general theory of literature is epideictic: "The end of all arts
and sciences is to make human life perfect and happy; but they differ in
their modes of producing this result. . . . Poetry attains this end more per-

fectly than any of the other arts and sciences, because it does so, not by
means of precept, but by means of example. There are various ways of
making men virtuous,—by teaching them what vice is and what virtue is,
which is the province of ethics; by actually chastising vices and rewarding
virtues, which is the province of law; or by example, that is, by the rep-
resentation of virtuous men receiving suitable rewards for their virtue, and
of vicious men receiving suitable punishments, which is the province of
poetry" (Spingarn, pp. 50–51). This sounds very much as if the *Commedia*
were the perfect embodiment of his theory of poetry, and indeed Spingarn
goes on in his summary of Varchi to say that "This twofold moral object
of poetry—the removal of vices, which is passive, and the incitement to
virtue, which is active—is admirably attained, for example, by Dante in
his *Divina Commedia*" (p. 51).

Yet in general it is the *Aeneid*, not the *Commedia*, which is the central
work for this vision of epic as a form of epideictic exemplarity.[6] Perhaps
the best way to put it is that this epideictic vision of poetry is used to
defend the *Commedia*, but it is almost always explained in terms of the *Aeneid*.
There are a couple of reasons why, and both are relevant to *The Cantos*.
First is that among the Cinquecento humanists and literary critics, the
largely Christian system of the *Commedia* has been displaced by a Humanist
return to the classical sense of virtue. This is one reason why the exemplars
found in Renaissance texts tend to be figures from classical culture, not
figures from the present or the immediate Italian past. The return to Vergil
as exemplar of the epic is of course a perfect example of this. Second,
though the *Commedia* is a deeply political epic, its politics have been replaced
by a politics of the court. The formal mark of this shift is a shift in the
intended audience of the epic: the audience for Renaissance epic is the
prince or king. Here, Vergil's relation to Augustus and the intended connection between Aeneas as hero and Augustus as audience is admired by
the humanist critical theorists and reduplicated by the Renaissance epic
poets. Tasso writes to Duke Alfonso, Camoens to King Sebastian, and Spenser to Queen Elizabeth; Dante addresses every one.

I have two central theses for this essay, of which the second is more
important. First, because of Pound's saturation in Italian Renaissance culture, he reads Dante through this epideictic tradition and therefore his
sense of Dante's achievement in the *Commedia* is significantly different from
our own. Second, *The Cantos* should be understood as an epic in this tradition, as an epideictic epic intended to establish exemplars of excellence
for its audience. The actualities of *The Cantos* correspond much more closely
to the prescriptions of this critical tradition than they do to the actualities

of any of the epics Pound admired, and a good deal that is problematic about *The Cantos* comes into focus when it is understood in this tradition.

To start with the vexed question of the narrativity of *The Cantos,* exemplarity is created by, yet is in significant tension with, narrativity. It is hard for a continuous narrative to yield a continuous flow of *exempla,* above all because a narrative tends to produce a more rounded picture of any character than the didactic aims of exemplarity require. This is perhaps the key respect why Renaissance descriptions of classical epics in terms of their exemplarity found in Spenser, Sidney, and Tasso seem so reductive. Surely there is more to Aeneas than *sum pius Aeneas,* and great violence is done to Homer's characters when they are fitted into such a scheme, as Plato recognized long ago. But there is a formal dimension to this as well: *exempla* tend to be short. If Vergil were indeed setting out just to model the perfect epic hero, a good deal of the *Aeneid* could be cut and indeed should be cut. The way the *Commedia* works, with its flow of circumscribed scenes or tableaux, is closer to the terms of the epideictic tradition than the epics this tradition values most highly. If one could imagine the *Commedia* without its integrating narrative of Dante's quest, in which portraits of negative exemplars were followed by positive ones and so on, one would be reasonably close to the kind of poem one imagines the classical epic to be while reading these descriptions and theories.

That's a useful way of thinking about *The Cantos.* Pound's poem is narrative for stretches but never forms a continuous narrative, precisely because Pound shifts from example to example after he has made the point he intends to make about them. When he takes over received narratives and chronicles, his impulse is always to cut away excess detail to get to the significant moment, the luminous detail, and this involves precisely a shift from an elaborated narrative to using narrative as a vehicle for exemplarity. This is easiest to see—and perhaps most true in—the Middle Cantos, which give us a montage of good rulers and good banks juxtaposed with less sustained images of bad rulers and bad banks.[7] We have never made much sense of Pound's concern with compiling images of virtuous and vicious political and economic behavior because we haven't understood the genre in which Pound was working. It is precisely an epideictic epic in the Renaissance sense, concerned with establishing images of virtue and vice. Our closest approach to this has been the comparison with Dante, to see that both—in James J. Wilhelm's useful phrase—are writing epics of judgment.[8] But Pound's practice is closer to the theory and practice of Renaissance writers than it is to Dante, in precisely the two crucial respects—their sense of virtue and their sense of their audience—in which the *Commedia,* though defended by exemplary theorists, is not their central poem. The virtues and vices Pound praises and condemns are entirely public, social in their nature; Pound has none of Dante's interest in psychology or—to put it in the way T. S. Eliot would have—Pound has no sense of sin. His virtues are Aristotle's, not Augustine's, and in this he reflects the classicism of Renaissance Humanist culture.

This is another reason why he would have found the exemplary model exemplary for his poetics, since it assigns such a strong public or social role to poetry. Jacopo Mazzoni, in his "Discourse in Defense of the Comedy," makes the remarkable (and thoroughly Poundian) assertion that Aristotle's "*Poetics* is the ninth book of the *Politics*" as both speak of "the management of the civil faculty" (Gilbert, pp. 374, 375).[9] Poetry is essential to a well-governed state because it can present images of the good and inspire imitations of them. Reading becomes a central activity for this tradition or, to be more precise, readers become central because the condition of the reader is something to be overcome. Timothy Hampton's recent work on "the rhetoric of exemplarity" in Renaissance literature is helpful here: "The evocation of the exemplary ancient in a Renaissance text is distinct from other rhetorical gestures of citation and allegation in that the exemplar makes a claim on the reader's action in the world" (p. 3). "Exemplarity aims at exhorting the reader to move from words to deeds, from language to action" (p. 29). This focus on the transforming power of poetry, on how poetry fails unless it moves its reader to action, is deeply Poundian. But who is the reader who is supposed to act, who is supposed to imitate the exemplar advanced by the poet? As Timothy Hampton has argued, "the Humanist writes to a privileged reader of history—the prince himself" (p. 32). It is the prince who is to be roused to emulate the epic hero of the poem. Camoens explicitly ends *Os Lusiadas* with an appeal to King Sebastian, urging him to continue the work begun by Vasco da Gama, Albuquerque, and others. Tasso comparably crafts his epic to appeal to Duke Alfonso II. As Hampton concludes his discussion of the exemplary nature of the *Gerusalemme Liberata,* "the fiction of the poem, then, is that Alfonso is to imitate both Goffredo and Rinaldo" (p. 98). These addresses to rulers have sometimes been read as fairly superficial gestures of flattery, but though such an appeal reflects the courtly setting of these poems, it is also inexorably a part of the epic of exemplarity. One depicts praiseworthy images precisely so as to stimulate someone else to emulate them. Dante wouldn't have disagreed with this aim in general, but the highly focused nature of the exemplary project of these dynastic epics is quite foreign to the *Commedia.* Dante's epistle to Henry worked (or tried to work) a comparable effect on a ruler, but he had a broader target in the *Commedia.*

But this is not at all foreign to *The Cantos,* and situating Pound in this genre or tradition helps us understand the aspect of Pound's poem that continues to give us most trouble, his commitment to Italian Fascism and his cult of Benito Mussolini. Criticism of *The Cantos* in recent years has come to a much better understanding of the role Mussolini plays in the poem,[10] and one way of defining that role is that it is exactly the same as the one Tasso imagines Duke Alfonso playing in his epic. Mussolini is the ideal reader of the poem in a number of crucial respects. He is the one who should learn from the array of exemplars Pound presents in the poem, who should be guided by them in his action in the present. If it is the fiction of *Gerusalemme Liberata* that Alfonso is to imitate Goffredo and Rinaldo, it is no particular fiction of *The Cantos* (though of course it remained very much a fiction of Pound's) that Mussolini is to imitate Thomas Jefferson, John Adams, and the Confucian Great Emperors depicted in the Chinese History Cantos. This has been seen clearly enough by critics, but we have taken this ambition of Pound to project his poem's images outward into history as an image of his eccentricity and madness. On the contrary: once we understand the tradition in which Pound is working, it is really not eccentric at all. I have elsewhere called Pound the last Ghibelline; in this context, it might be more appropriate to call him the last Renaissance Humanist or perhaps the last courtier poet.

In this respect, which is a crucial one for Pound's project, Pound's model is less Dante than Tasso, and *The Cantos* resembles the *Commedia* less closely than it resembles the Renaissance epics of Tasso and Camoens. I don't mean this merely as a conceit even though Pound expressed nothing but contempt for Tasso and Camoens.[11] Of the three great critical issues in the discussion on epic in the Cinquecento, Pound is on Dante's side on none of them: with Tasso, he chooses historical truth over fiction; with Tasso, he chooses representing the past over the present. Only in the debate over unity versus variety is his practice opposed to Tasso, but here he joins not Dante but Ariosto (someone else he has rude things to say about), as Dante is clearly an apostle of narrative unity just as Tasso is. Unfortunately, the life of an exemplary epic poet is a hard one: Pound is also with Tasso the only major epic poet to be confined to a madhouse. And it is not too farfetched to connect the vicissitudes of their lives to their theories of epic: exemplary epic poets tie the fate of their epic projects to their effect on a particular reader, and Mussolini proved to be just as unworthy a reader as his fellow *Romagnolo,* Duke Alfonso. The more focused project of the exemplary epic leaves the poet with little room to maneuver if words don't lead to action in the hoped-for manner. Pound staked the coherence of his poem on Mussolini's proving worthy of the role Pound had assigned him, whereas Dante kept his (equally ill-fated) hope that Henry VII was the Lamb of God out of the *Commedia.* In this as in other ways, Dante proves shrewder than the poets who followed him, which should occasion no surprise: in poetic history, he casts a very long shadow, which is one reason why we remain preoccupied with the question of how modern poets such as Pound positioned themselves with respect to his work.

Notes

1. Key texts here are Pearlman, the two studies by Wilhelm, and—most recently—Sicari.

2. Sicari is probably the only critic of those cited who centers his argument on the issue of narrative coherence rather than structural resemblance.

3. Hardison provides perhaps the best summary of these views.

4. See Vickers and Kallendorf.

5. I cite Horace here because this tradition is where ideas inherited from Aristotelian rhetoric intersect with the Horatian tradition in literary theory. See Weinberg, vol. I, pp. 71–249, and Hathaway, pp. 144–158. For two recent studies of the notion of exemplarity in the Renaissance, see Hampton and Lyons.

6. See Kallendorf for an excellent study of how the Renaissance viewed Vergil in these terms.

7. See my *Literary Vorticism* for a discussion of the Middle Cantos in these terms.

8. The only exception to this is a tantalizing aside in Michael André Bernstein's *The Tale of the Tribe:* "one general principle, formulated by Torquato Tasso in his *Discorso Primo,* is crucial for an understanding of Pound's treatment of history in *The Cantos.* Tasso insists upon what is basically an affective or intentional distinction between the epic and tragedy; in his view, the principal emotion aroused by an epic should be admiration for some distinguished achievement, or noble character-trait, rather than pity or fear" (p. 12). My purpose in this paper is to develop this insight.

9. I've found no direct evidence that Pound knew Mazzoni's *Defense,* though he was certainly learned enough in Dante criticism and in the Italian Renaissance to have encountered his work. But it is worth pointing out that Pound was a good deal more interested in Aristotle's *Politics* and *Ethics* than in the *Poetics.* A

detailed study of Pound's copies of Aristotle (now at the Harry Ransom Humanities Research Center at the University of Texas at Austin) would shed a good deal of light on Pound's work.

10. See Rainey, Redman, Casillo, and my own *Imitating the Italians.*

11. His comments on Tasso focus mostly on Tasso's language; he spends a good deal of *The Spirit of Romance* criticizing Camoens; for a book-length study responding to this, see Andrews.

Works Cited

Andrews, Norwood. *The Case against Camoens: A Seldom Considered Chapter from Ezra Pound's Campaign to Discredit Rhetorical Poetry.* New York: Peter Lang, 1988.

Bernstein, Michael André. *The Tale of the Tribe: Ezra Pound and the Modern Verse Epic.* Princeton, NJ: Princeton UP, 1980.

Casillo, Robert. *The Genealogy of Demons: Ezra Pound, Fascism, and Anti-Semitism,* Evanston, IL: Northwestern UP, 1988.

Dasenbrock, Reed Way. *Imitating the Italians: Wyatt, Spenser, Synge, Pound, Joyce.* Baltimore: Johns Hopkins UP, 1991.

———. *The Literary Vorticism of Ezra Pound and Wyndham Lewis: Towards the Condition of Painting.* Baltimore: Johns Hopkins UP, 1985.

Gilbert, Allan H., ed. *Literary Criticism: Plato to Dryden.* 1940; rpt. Detroit: Wayne State UP, 1962.

Hampton, Timothy. *Writing from History: The Rhetoric of Exemplarity in Renaissance Literature.* Ithaca, NY: Cornell UP, 1990.

Hardison, O. B., Jr., *The Enduring Monument: A Study of the Idea of Praise in Renaissance Literary Theory and Practice.* 1962; rpt. Westport, CT: Greenwood, 1973.

Hathaway, Baxter. *The Age of Criticism: The Later Renaissance in Italy.* Ithaca, NY: Cornell UP, 1962.

Kallendorf, Craig. *In Praise of Aeneas: Virgil and Epideictic Rhetoric in the Early Italian Renaissance.* Hanover, NH: UP of New England, 1989.

Lyons, John D. *Exemplum: The Rhetoric of Example in Early Modern France and Italy.* Princeton, NJ: Princeton UP, 1989.

Pearlman, Daniel D. *The Barb of Time: On the Unity of Ezra Pound's* Cantos. New York: Oxford UP, 1969.

Pound, Ezra. *Selected Prose, 1909–1965.* Ed. William Cookson. New York: New Directions, 1973.

Rainey, Lawrence S. *Ezra Pound and the Monument of Culture: Text, History, and the Malatesta Cantos.* Chicago: U of Chicago P, 1991.

Redman, Tim. *Ezra Pound and Italian Fascism.* Cambridge: Cambridge UP, 1991.

Sicari, Stephen. *Pound's Epic Ambition: Dante and the Modern World.* Albany: SUNY P, 1991.

Spenser, Edmund. *Poetical Works.* Ed. J. C. Smith & Ernest de Selincourt. 1912; rpt. London: Oxford UP, 1970.

Vickers, Brian. "Epideictic and Epic in the Renaissance." *New Literary History* 14 (1982–1983): 497–537.

Weinberg, Bernard. *A History of Literary Criticism in the Italian Renaissance.* 2 vols. 1961; rpt. Chicago: U of Chicago P, 1963.

Wilhelm, James J. *Dante and Pound: The Epic of Judgement.* Orono: U of Maine P, 1974.

———. *The Later Cantos of Ezra Pound.* New York: Walker & Co., 1977.

History and Money, Fact and Hysteria

PETER MAKIN

◆ ◆ ◆

THE HISTORICAL MATERIAL IN *THE CANTOS* as a whole
offers a thesis about history, which of course Pound did not arrive at
at the outset. Emersonian predispositions would have suggested to him
that spiritual enlightenment was not compatible with inhumanity toward
one's fellows; but Pound's own social and economic position seems to have
appeared to him, at first, essentially normal.

In the same year that Ford shook up his ideas about over-evanescent
verse, Pound became a contributor on literary subjects to the *New Age*,
edited by A. R. Orage. This was one of the few journals in British cultural
history to incorporate successfully both political and artistic concerns.[1] It
took in debates about literary realism (between such contributors as Shaw,
Bennett, Wells, and Chesterton); about Imagism and Vorticism, and socialism; it reproduced painting by Sickert, and the cartoon for Jacob Ep-
stein's "Rock Drill"; Lawrence, Ford, Harold Monro, Wyndham Lewis, T. S.
Eliot read it. After the war had started, one of the signs of a new restlessness was an intensified debate in the *New Age* about socialism. Certain
contributors began to attack what they called "Collectivist Socialism," fear-
ing that it would merely replace capitalist despotism with bureaucratic
despotism. Socialists seemed to conceive a perpetuation of the worker-as-

herd, directed in mass toward tasks in themselves of merely wealth-producing significance, and given no direct responsibility for the choice or development of their particular functions. The only change under this socialism was to be a reapportionment of wealth. The result would be nonresponsibility in attitude both toward the object produced and toward society. Like William Morris and like Marx, these *New Age* writers conceived that alienation in the process of production was the root problem. Like both of these predecessors they turned to the Middle Ages for a model of nonalienation. Unlike Morris, they did not fantasize a return to cottage industry, but "Guild Socialism," which amounted to monopoly control of a given industry by its workers, chartered by the government. Guild Socialism became a political movement between 1913 and 1915. The idea attracted Pound very strongly; he was to believe eventually that it had been made a reality in Italy's professional corporations under Mussolini. Images of it crop up in very late Cantos projecting spiritual and economic Paradise (for example in XCI, p. 613, and CIV, p. 741).

When the First World War began, Pound already feared it was merely the collision of an atavism with a corrupt mediocrity (*L*, 46). His eyes were opened to its realities the sooner because he was in contact with *New Age* circles. Then in 1919 occurred an important encounter in the *New Age* office: Pound met C. H. Douglas, who in that year published in the journal his new analysis of the economic problem.[2] Douglas wished to foster the fluidity and independence found in small-scale capitalism. He proposed that the seed of friction and war was not the capitalist mode of production, but systems of accountancy and, above all, credit. He argued that there were certain inbuilt leaks in the production-consumption cycle—one of them being the cost of credit. These drained away purchasing power, so that there was never sufficient demand for goods produced at the time of their production. Demand was often made up by finding new markets: hence colonialism, fierce competition, and conflict. Meanwhile the sources of credit controlled the producers. Hence centralization, the enslavement of the whole of society to high-speed turnover, and industrial sabotage. Decentralized local authorities should take away the administering of credit from private interests; and the state should create and distribute purchasing power to make up inevitable deficiencies.

These theories gave Pound a distinction between social health and un-health, around which he could organize a fundamental dissociation and grouping of values; for they so evidently went back to personal, emotional, "spiritual" values. The distinction was: the leech, parasite and distorter of values versus the responsible maker. And these theories gave him a program for action, with, as corollary, the sense of present resistance to it; he probably needed these to generate enough emotional pressure in himself to clarify and present those values. But there was lacking one important ingredient: the sense of crime. In Orage's writing, and Douglas's, there is no strong sense that any particular group of persons is criminally responsible for having arranged past or present injustices; it is felt, rather, that the system is in error (though many have profited from the fact), and must be changed. Pound, however, paid more and more attention to investigators who laid bare particular riggings of the system for the benefit of private interests. After the Wall Street Crash of 1929 and the coming of the Depression, these writers multiplied. Pound was most impressed by writers like Christopher Hollis, who sought out more ancient roots for the evil. Hollis's *Two Nations* (1935) took the present crime inherent in the credit-creating system back to a source at a particular historical moment (the founding of the Bank of England in 1694), and tried to show that there had existed throughout the subsequent centuries a hidden party or interest group, persistently at work corrupting the nation economically and politically.

In an interview broadcast in 1959, Pound said of the Cantos

> There is a turning point in the poem toward the middle. Up to that point it is a sort of detective story, and one is looking for the crime. (Int., 172)

Canto XLVI in particular (published in November 1936) has the rhetorical form of a prosecutor's address: it gives the damage inflicted by the economic crime (fetid brickwork; mass unemployment), the steps by which the investigator was led to track the crime down, and the documentation as to the time and the place where it was perpetrated. Said the founder of the Bank of England in 1694 (according to Hollis): the Bank

Hath benefit of interest on all
the moneys which it, the bank, creates out of nothing.
[XLVI, p. 233]

And similarly

> Said Mr RothSchild, hell knows which Roth-schild
> 1861, '64 or there sometime, 'Very few people
> 'will understand this. Those who do will be occupied

'getting profits. The general public will probably not
'see it's against their interest.'
                  Seventeen years on the case; here
Gents, is/are the confession.
                                    [XLVI, p. 233]

The prospectus of the Bank of England (then a private company) announced to shareholders that it, the Bank, would create money from
nothing, and draw interest on it. This seemed to Pound the key to all later
banking.

The historical thesis could thus be presented as formula by the mid-
1930s. Pound had come to believe that the reason for starvation, gross
inequality of wealth, and resultant conflict was a permanent undeclared
tax on most economic activity. This tax concentrated power where it was
used to bring about destructive decisions. The taxing occurred in the creation of money; and money was created (increases in the money supply
were brought about) in bank lending.

When a bank lends, it lends what John Thrifty has deposited with it. (I
owe both the name and the little parable to James P. Warburg, the banker
and adviser to Roosevelt, with whom Pound corresponded.[3]) It does not
ask John Thrifty; the fiction, as far as he is concerned, is that the money
is there in his account, waiting to be given to him the instant he presents
himself at the counter. There is no harm to him, because he knows that
in fact his money is lent out, and that unless it were, he could receive no
interest. But, for the purposes of the bank, the money he has deposited
with it suddenly has two functions. It figures as John Thrifty's spendable
money, ready for him to use, for example, to pay another man who has
an account at the same bank; and it figures as money out on loan to
someone else. The bank has thus doubled it, for the duration of the loan.
Since the bank never ceases to loan, a large body of money is thus created
by it, on which it receives interest which will eventually amount to further
capital.

Suppose now that the government wants to spend more money than
it possesses. It may borrow for the short term by issuing Treasury bills.
Thus each week the United Kingdom government offers at auction a certain number of these bills. Overseas central banks, overseas commercial
banks, and big commercial and industrial firms bid for these bills; the rest
are taken up by the twelve London discount houses, acting as a syndicate.
Thus these institutions loan to the government the money it wants, in

return for bits of paper that entitle them to get the same money back in a few months, plus interest, all to be paid by the taxpayer.

Surely this "new money" is merely old money, already possessed by these institutions, and now transferred to the government?

The banks, at least, did not possess it; it was John Thrifty's money, whose phantom double was still held by them in his account. Every time the banks extend a loan, it is on the strength of the money (it is the money) that John has deposited with them. In present British banking practice, only 8 percent of his money need be kept in the bank ready for repayment to him should he ask for it. The other 92 percent is doubled by being fictionally present, and factually out on loan, earning interest for the bank's shareholders.

The same operation takes place when government bonds are sold to the banks. These mature after a long period or never, so that for a long period the taxpayer is paying interest to the banks for money that they have created.

The banks' debts, to put it another way, are used as money; and they are the only institutions that can do this. Governments cannot increase the money supply except by asking the banks to create it.[4] "Whether it be not a mighty privilege for a private person to be able to create a hundred pounds with a dash of his pen?"—Bishop Berkeley, in the 1730s, quoted by Christopher Hollis.[5]

It is not unnatural, unjust, that money should be created from nothing. It leads to the creation of real (nonmonetary) wealth. But there is no clear reason why private interests should profit from this process, rather than the public. It is said that banks, not governments, must create money, because banks are restrained: they at least create "on the basis of" real money, whereas governments would certainly print money unlimitedly. But if governments are so untrustworthy, why do these trustworthy banks lend to them? The reason why banks lend to governments is that governments have absolute power to tax, to find the future money to repay the loans. The same power could be the basis of government creations of credit, and therefore of money.

And what is the trustworthiness of banks, when any bank balance sheet shows that if the John Thrifties withdrew their deposits more rapidly than usual only some 8 percent of their money would be available and the banks must collapse? " 'You exaggerate,' says the objector. 'The financial system does not collapse, because the Government steps in with special measures to prevent the final calamity.' 'Exactly,' " answers Bishop Berkeley in effect, " 'and do you not see what that proves? It proves that the bank is lending money to the community not, as is pretended, on the credit of the bank but rather on the credit of the community itself.' "[6]

As C. H. Douglas wrote, "The modern State is an unlimited liability corporation, of which the citizens are the workers and guarantors, and the financial system, the beneficiary."[7]

So far the citizen is merely paying a tax to private interests on new money supply. But governments do not normally pay off their borrowings except by further borrowing; hence the national debt. ("The earth belongs to the living," said Thomas Jefferson as quoted by Pound (*P*, 256), but the living inherit this burden.) The interest payments are a massive continuous transfer of wealth from the taxpayer to banks and bondholders.

Once monetary wealth is accumulated, it can be "played" against real wealth. It could not be played unless it had a value—unless, that is, someone wanted it badly; and it is wanted by you and me, as a means of exchange. The game consists of betraying this need, of making money unstable as a means of exchange, by affecting its value as against real (nonmonetary) wealth. The holder contrives to find the moment when it will profit him to sell his accumulated pounds sterling for gold, or aluminum futures, or real estate, or Deutschmarks; and his selling affects the value of the pound. Or, says Pound, if he is a big enough fish, he may be able to influence, for his own purposes, national decisions that affect the currency. Canto XXXIII describes such a case. The Federal Reserve System is one of the two central monetary control institutions of the United States, but it judiciously interweaves public with private interests. The Federal Reserve Banks' loans to the (private) member banks affect general interest rates and money supply, and hence inflation and deflation. In May 1920, according to a Senate speech by Senator Brookhart, there was a secret meeting of the Federal Reserve Board, the Class A directors of the Federal Reserve Banks (who are also private bankers), and the advisory council. It was decided to restrict loans to the member banks.[8] The Governor of the Board, says Canto XXXIII, even

> put into the mouths of the directors of the Federal Reserve banks the words that they should say . . . "You have got more than your share, we want you to reduce, we can not let you have any more."

He also

said to them: wd. suggest, gentlemen, you be careful not to give out anything about any discussion of discount rates disturbs everybody immediate rush never discuss in the newspapers . . .

What, for the unsuspecting man in the street, is an imminent change in the value of his means of exchange, is a chance of profit for those who know:

> . . . & Company's banker was in that meeting, and next day he was out after a loan of 60 millions, and got it. Swiftamoursinclair but the country at large did not know it. The meeting decided we were over inflated.
> [XXXIII, p. 164]

Pound became more obsessively concerned with these value manipulations as the war threatened, and then destroyed, what he saw as Mussolini's attempt to create the ideal society. "The elements remain the same: debts, altering the value of monetary units, and the attempts, and triumphs of usury, due to monopolies, or to a 'Corner' " (*P*, 170). The sleight of hand, the falsification whereby the unit of exchange was invisibly transmuted, was the particular aspect of monetary economics that became the substance of the historical part of the Cantos after the Second World War.

Pound was probably not overworried by parasitism in itself, or what Lenin, according to Pound, called "a class, or rather a stratum, of *rentiers*, i.e. persons who live by 'clipping coupons,' who take absolutely no part in any enterprise" (*P*, 299). But he was worried by the effects of such groups as a force.

> 'and having got 'em (advantages, privilege)
>   there is nothing, italics *nothing*, they will not do
> to retain 'em'
>   yrs truly   Kungfutseu
> [LXXVII, p. 464]

If a reformist government appears in some banana republic, there are ways in which it can be unsettled very quickly. And Italy in the 1930s, as Pound saw her, was trying to emerge from the position of a banana republic. Mussolini asserted his country's independence from the international financial web, and the result, Pound believed, was the League of Nations Sanctions of 1933, an attempt at economic strangulation, on the excuse that Italy was building an empire in Africa. Pound compared this to British attempts to strangle the American colonies ("le sanzioni inglesi") before 1776 (*OS*, 1360).

There was also the question of stifled human creativity, debased products, and the consequent debasement of body, mind, and environment. The money market requires rapid and continuous profit; a bank manager does not favor a low-interest project over a high-interest project merely because the former produces more wealth for the community in the long run. If you want a loan, open a newsagent's (cigarettes, Coca-Cola, and the *Sunday Express*). Produce cars that require leaded petrol. The child's vital strength is sapped before he can defend himself.

> *With Usura* [. . .]

> no picture is made to endure nor to live with
> but it is made to sell and sell quickly
> with usura, sin against nature,
> is thy bread ever more of stale rags[. . .]

> Usura slayeth the child in the womb
> It stayeth the young man's courting
> It hath brought palsey to bed, lyeth
> between the young bride and her bridegroom
> CONTRA NATURAM
>   [XLV, pp. 229–30]

And so, as Marx records in Canto XXXIII,

> report of '42 was merely chucked into the archives and
> remained there while these boys were ruined and became
> fathers of this generation . . .
>   [XXXIII, p. 162]

The proposals scattered in Pound's writing might, then, be summarized as follows. Governments should themselves create new money when they need it (Jefferson had proposed this in slightly different terms: *P*, 296). New issue should be limited to the amount of real wealth that the government expects to be created nationally during the period of the loan. Governments should index the values of important necessities and, by regulating money supply, hold the value of the currency steady against them (creating a "commodity dollar"). (The United States Constitution, Pound held, required the government to control the purchasing power of the currency.) Private interests should be allowed to lend only that money they possessed; and interest rates should be strictly controlled.

These are more or less practical and rational ideas. But two aspects of his language baffled and alienated Pound's contemporaries. One was his insistent repetition of simple and obscure conundrums: "Money is not a commodity," "Money does not create wealth." The other was the Freudian concreteness of his images, strangely mixed up with a theological tone. His insistence on these simple distinctions was loaded with a certain anger because his contemporaries—Christians in particular—had abdicated the duty of relating mental clarity to moral implications. A share, he insisted, is not a bond. With shares, the lender participates in the risk of the enterprise: if it fails, his money is gone; if it does badly, there is no dividend. With bonds, whatever happens to the enterprise the lender has legal right to capital and interest. That in particular is the bearing of the word "Usury," as Pound defined it (XLV, p. 230), and part of the reason why the word became like a malediction to him. The Church had once cared about these crimes, and now understood no such distinctions (cf. LII, p. 258).

Design, whether of earthenware bowls or carbon fibers, works with three things: present human wit and labor; a heritage of knowledge; and the integrity (coherence) of nature's structures. Finance denies the awe or reverence which is due to the latter two, and transfers that due to the former into money. It thus invests money with powers we associate with the result of all human creativity, hence with a mystique, seen in its language ("creative finance," "Watch your money grow!" "Does your money work as hard as you?"). The people who handle it become high priests, which is their function in present society. It is so because the public is willing to "buy" their metaphors. In a man like Pound, to whom the natural *is* God, both his perception of this behavior and his emotional response to it will necessarily express themselves in language which is at once concerned with nature (including the sexual and scatological) and theological:

Mill defined capital 'as the accumulated stock of human labour'.
    And Marx, or his Italian translator (U.T.-E.T. edition): 'commodities, in so far as they are values, are *materialised* labour,'

so denying both God and nature.

With the falsification of the word everything else is betrayed.
Commodities (considered as values, surplus values, food, clothes, or
whatever) are manufactured raw materials.

Only spoken poetry and unwritten music are composed without any
material basis, nor do they become 'materialised'.

The usurers, in their obscene and pitch-dark century, created this
satanic transubstantiation, their Black Mass of money, and in so doing
deceived Brooks Adams himself, who was fighting for the peasant and
humanity against the monopolists.

'...money alone is capable of being transmuted immediately into
any form of activity.'—This is the idiom of the black myth!

One sees well enough what he was trying to say, as one understands
what Mill and Marx were trying to say. But the betrayal of the word
begins with the use of words that do not fit the truth, that do not say
what the author wants them to say.

Money does not contain energy. The half-lira piece cannot *create* the
platform ticket, the cigarettes, or piece of chocolate that issues from the
slot-machine.

But it is by this piece of legerdemain that humanity has been thoroughly trussed up, and it has not yet got free. (*P*, 307–8)

An interviewer asked Allen Ginsberg about Pound's "obsession" with
money. Ginsberg held that it was a service to humanity: Pound had de-
mystified the banks. Like John Adams more than a hundred years before
him:

> Every bank of discount is downright corruption
> taxing the public for private individuals' gain.
>   and if I say this in my will
> the American people wd/pronounce I died crazy.
>   [LXXI, p. 416]

Fact and Hysteria

But this is the same Pound who strongly supported Mussolini's regime
even when it became Hitler's ally (immediately before the Second World
War). The *Pisan Cantos,* written immediately after the war, do not recant,
though this fact was somewhat obscured at the time of publication by

certain obscurities of reference and by publishers' deletions. During the war years, though not before, Pound seems to have come to admire Hitler, and Cantos written much later seem to turn him into a kind of misguided saint (XC, p. 606; CIV, p. 741). And Pound is held to have been anti-Semitic.

People in Italy during the war did not know what was happening to the Jews in Germany; Pound cannot be held responsible in that sense for the death camps. From the earliest days of his concern with usury, Pound had used "Jews" as a shorthand term for usurers—a symptom of a prejudice then widespread among the Anglo-Saxon middle classes; but whenever his attention was brought to the question of race he would carefully distinguish between Jewish financiers and those blamed by association. But it seems to me clear enough that by the time of his wartime broadcasts for the Mussolini regime he conceived of evil Jewish racial qualities, among which the presence of the good was generally secondary. He had in fact swallowed the whole nineteenth-century Jewish Conspiracy theory, with its imagery and antecedents stretching back to the popular persecutions of the Middle Ages.[9] His language on the subject of money was medieval, a sort of chant of lexical nastiness, filled with the suggestion of exotic and ancient tongues, much as Poe filled his artificial excitements with the Inquisition and dark jargon. The Hebrew word *neschek* ("usury") recurs. This piece was written "Circa 1941":

> The Evil is Usury, *neschek*
> the serpent
> *neschek* whose name is known, the defiler,
> beyond race and against race
> the defiler
> Τόχος   hic mali medium est   [Poison   here is the centre of evil]
> Here is the core of evil, the burning hell without let-up,
> The canker corrupting all things, Fafnir the worm,
> Syphilis of the State, of all kingdoms,
> Wart of the common-weal,
> Wenn-maker, corrupter of all things.
> Darkness the defiler

This serpentine darkness makes "wens" in much the same manner as, among Hardy's peasants, the presence of lovers stops the butter from turning. The conspiracy, once discerned, transforms the meaning of all things, which is a defining characteristic of paranoia.

Sero, sero! [Late, late!] learned that Spain is mercury;
that Finland is nickel. Late learning!
S[assoon] doing evil in place of the R[othschild]
                    [Addendum for C, pp. 798–9]

The antecedents for this state, in Pound's own work, seem to lie in his handling of a sense of social responsibility in which he identified with John Adams, and in the documentary/historical method through which he expressed this. Adams, and American material in general, drew from Pound an excessive desire for order, which led to a need for dogmatic and clear-cut statement. "The evidence," preferably on producible documents, had to be marshaled to support this. Perception of tones, contemplation and the unspoken kinds of knowledge, Dionysian impulse, went out of the window. (Ovid more or less disappears from the Cantos between XXVII [1928] and XCVIII [1958].) But documents offer no security; the "facts" on them are merely pawns or switching diodes among which a thousand possible patterns may spring up at the observer's suggestion, patterns which branch endlessly off the page into the fact-hoards of other documents. The conspiracy theory, replete with footnotes proving the case conclusively, seems to be a phenomenon of our time. Meanwhile the restless researcher is back at his desk in the British Museum, digging out the proofs to clinch his footnotes. So Pound's mind seemed to explode into a mad fragmentation of documents during and after the war.

The earlier Cantos are full of turbulence, of "Mediterranean gods; startling, sudden [. . .] Gods tricky as nature" (*L*, 273), of Ovid. The sea is one of the governing metaphors of the first three; sudden change is celebrated. Pentheus is the fool: the man who would try to hold Dionysus and ecstasy in bonds. And even in the first American material, concerning Thomas Jefferson (Cantos XXXI–XXXIII), Pound tries to show the value of instinct as a political quality. (There is a connection between Jefferson and Mussolini the Dionysian.) But Jefferson is rather intractable material for this. There is no "Eleusis" in him: no song, sensual knowledge, religion-and-rite-as-mystery. Canto XXXIV deals with John Quincy Adams, son of Jefferson's friend John, and he is made Eleusinian by texture:

> Oils, beasts, grasses, petrifactions, birds, incrustations,
> Dr Mitchell's conversation was various. . . .

That opens the Canto, and it closes with ecstatic popular celebration:

> The firemen's torchlight procession,
> Firemen's torchlight procession,
> Science as a principle of political action
>
> Firemen's torchlight procession!

But a check of the sources makes this presentation seem a little factitious.[10] And in between this opening and this close all shows a mind of eighteenth-century American (still Puritan and classical) limitations. (John Quincy died in 1848.)

And the Jefferson group is the last Cantos section in which Pound holds up instinct as a political ideal. In his prose he is soon forcefully rejecting Jefferson in favor of John Adams, who with his descendants is "our norm of spirit" (LXXXIV, p. 540). Now Adams, as Pound presents him, is the principle of stability, of immovable conscience—indeed, of the Puritan "plymouth-rock conscience" that Pound ironically prided himself in, in a letter to Harriet Monroe in 1912 (*L*, 12). One of Adams's chief political functions in the Cantos is to warn against the hidden, insidious usurpations of money power that work through, and manipulate, democracy—by, for example, corrupting terminology.

The China Cantos, published simultaneously with the John Adams Cantos in 1940, pull history toward the two poles of softness, obfuscation, intrigue (associated with women and Buddhists), and social order, on which the verbal tone insists more and more excessively and irritably. This anger returns in full force in the *Rock-Drill* (1955) and *Thrones* (1959) sections, which betray a hysterical fear of all that is unknown and amorphous. In the Chinese parts of *Thrones*, the ideal is discipline and again discipline, inner and outer. Meanwhile the emotional coherence of this poem's sensibility has collapsed: it moves endlessly between the two poles of Erebus and the Empyrean, grasping at fragments of cleanness and light, while the black void gapes.

Now this move toward a hysteric sense of order goes together with a move toward documentation felt as documentation (assemblage of hard written matter), rather than, for example, as voices. Already in the Jefferson Cantos (the first documentary section after the Malatesta), there is much less voice differentiation. Only the two men Jefferson and Adams "speak" (to each other, in their letters), for the most part; and they are much less oral men. The prewar culmination of the documentary method is seen in the Adams Cantos, where Pound strives to bring to life a uniform surface, which is the voice of John Adams himself, as registered in his *Works* (almost the sole source). Like a recording engineer reprocessing an early disk, Pound can do no more than heighten certain contrasts of tone. But by this time Pound is in any case not so much concerned with the emotional depth communicated in such ways. He is now much less interested in the qualitative Fact of an era; much more interested in the atomic, material facts, and formulae, and distinct rational decisions. And that is part of the problem I am approaching.

But there is a contradictory tendency. Adams is the legal researcher, hunting for the truth in the hidden texts (thus the archetypal Protestant act: translating the Bible). But the ancient terms from the ancient legal authorities, alien and exotic in distance and tongue, come to seem in themselves the fount of the mystic law. Pound heightens this effect, seeming to prefer Adams snippets that have bits of Latin in them to those without. These phrases, chanted, are emblems of the Mystic Books:

> Whereof memory of man runneth not to the contrary
> Dome Book, Ina, Offa and Aethelbert, folcright
> for a thousand years
>
> [LXVII, p. 387]

The *Pisan Cantos* in many ways set themselves apart from this progression. But thereafter Pound develops a way of coming at documents so that they render up this dislocated mystic authority instantly (and without the intervention of memory, which in the *Pisan Cantos* has a quite different effect). Plunging into a sea of arcane documentation, omitting (as so often) the syntactic connections that give the phrase its meaning in context, he places on his page a detail that has become not historically "luminous" (a term from his *New Age* articles of 1911: *P*, 21–2), but numinous: "2 doigts to a boodle, one bawbee: one sixty doigts" (XCVII, p. 671). Chinese characters in particular have this role. They are both world-shattering and perfectly private, because they are clues to hidden patterns of force that only this researcher can understand: 'Wang's middle name not in Mathews 燊' [XCVI, p. 653].

The typical source for one of these Clues is an academic footnote. And the form of many of these late Cantos is an arrangement of footnotes, to which footnotes will be found in such parallel publications as *Versi Prosaici*, and in Pound's enormous outpouring of fragmentary correspondence, communications to scattered journals, and written marginal annotations in printed volumes in this period.

It is possible that both prose (documentation) and history were a mistake for Pound. Ford may have put his finger on the problem when he accused Pound of hating literary decoration in prose, and loving the "STRONG STORY," both because he disliked prose itself and because of a Puritan bent. And "you *might* harden into the Puritanism of the Plymouth Rock variety—which would be a disaster" (*PF*, 45). It is possible that Pound was fundamentally unsuited to prose reality, and that what he called (*P*, 167) the forty-year effort of "schooling" himself to deal with the grim, the hard, with human fallibility and error—in a word, the "Dark Forest"—was unnatural for a writer who was essentially Ovidian; and that a hysterical exaggeration of a New England heritage was the result.

Still it seems to me that until the war years Pound's sense of history was not yet irrational. To give an analogy: any Latin American with a sense of social justice might be justified in seeing, in one sense, a conspiracy between the American corporations, the State Department, the International Monetary Fund, the large banks, and the wealthier groups in his own country. That is, effectively, collusion exists. But it is merely instinctive, shifting and temporary, and the various conspiracies, transient and amorphous, are a product and not a cause. I think Pound was at such a mental position in about 1939, as far as usury was concerned. As far as the Jews were concerned, he thought that too many Jews were prominent in usury, but demanded (reasonably enough if that were true) that Jews seek out their economic criminals and disown them, and dissociate themselves from usury by attacking the many very visible non-Jewish financiers (*P*, 299–300; *PF*, 165).

With the steady tightening of Pound's mental processes, and with the coming of the war, both positions were fatally modified. Instinctive collusion in financial and governmental circles became, in Pound's mind, grand conspiracy; the presence of Jewish figures in high finance became, to Pound, Jewish control of high finance.

By about 1939 he was tending in the direction of a general theoretical anti-Hebraism on the level of cultural roots (cf. e.g., *L*, 331–2). But what he thought of as Hebraic on this level was what he also identified with Protestantism (in particular Calvinism): materialist and Manichean attitudes, destructive of the sense of immanent godhead in the world and in rite. And finally there is Pound's dislike of the "Middle-European," the cosmopolitan, the culturally fluid. Here the approved image is of a small-town republican stability, such as we find it in John Adams or in Dante (note the ideal of Cincinnatus in both):

> Sempre la confusion delle persone
> principio fu del mal della cittade,
> come del corpo il cibo che s' appone.

> Ever was mingling of persons
> the source of the city's woes,
> as piled-on food is of the body's.
>
> [*Paradiso*, 16.67–9]

But it is most likely that Pound would have latched on to quite other archetypes for these tendencies than the Jews, had not both history and his own development created in him the kind of dualism that needs a strong single focus for its animus, and provided that focus in inherited images of the Jewish race.

The Jews were a traditional scapegoat, ready for Pound to latch on to. One factor in this was a vicious circle of primitive fear and convenient hypocrisy. Thus the fact that particular Jewish families have been prominent for some centuries as moneylenders seems partly traceable to the fact that Christendom forbade Jews most occupations except the occupation of money lending—which was forbidden to Christians as being sinful. This itself was partly a manifestation of those dark medieval feelings about Jewry that stemmed merely from their position as an unabsorbed cultural Other. But in turn it gave Jewish moneylenders a vulnerability that kings were not slow to exploit, and intensified suspicion and hatred of Jews. These welled over into pogroms in times of social unrest. Prejudices still hardly developed from these ancient origins were common currency in the American Populism of Pound's youth, as among middle-class intellectuals in the Edwardian London to which he migrated in 1908.

Jung has described how fears of conspiracy are fostered by an abnormally heightened, simplified sense of good/evil dualism, which in turn tends to appear in times of social disturbance. And if we seek to explain why Pound shifted, from about 1939 onward, toward witch-hunting it seems to me necessary to remember his position of isolation in a country at war. War hysteria is powerful and takes many forms, and at any point during the present century one can find actions by otherwise reasonable men and women that have no other explanation.

Some find such moral attitudes irrelevant to the value of verse, even when they are present in the verse. But the profundity or otherwise of the moral understanding in a poem is a considerable factor in the interest (or otherwise) of the poem. I should like to persuade the reader that the breakdown in Pound's moral values in a certain area at a certain time does not necessarily affect those elsewhere.

Notes

1. This paragraph is based on Wallace Martin, *"The New Age" under Orage* (Manchester/New York: Manchester University Press/Barnes & Noble, 1967).

2. *Economic Democracy* (published as a book in 1920) was serialized in *New Age* from June 1919. See reviews by Pound in *P*, 207–12.

3. James P. Warburg, *The Money Muddle* (New York: Knopf, 1934).

4. For Treasury bills, cf. A.C.L. Day, *The Economics of Money* (London: Oxford University Press, 1968), pp. 77ff., and Herbert V. Prochnow (ed.), *The Federal Reserve System* (New York: Harper & Row, 1960), p. 59; for rediscounting as cover for note issue, cf. Warburg, *Money Muddle*, pp. 35–6, and Prochnow, *Federal Reserve System*, p. 97.

5. Christopher Hollis, *The Two Nations* (London: Routledge, 1935), p. 60.

6. Ibid., p. 59.

7. C. H. Douglas, *The Monopoly of Credit* (London: Chapman & Hall, 1931), p. 14.

8. See William Chace, "The Canto as Cento: A Reading of Canto XXXIII," *Paideuma*, vol. 1, no. 1 (Spring-Summer 1972), pp. 89–100.

9. *EPS*, p. 60; cf. pp. 62, 97–8, 110, 114, 177–9 and passim; *P*, p. 340. On the "Protocols of the Elders of Zion," cf. *EPS*, p. 115.

10. In the source, Adams is complaining about these processions, and saying that one should follow the political principle of acting as patron to scientific studies. See *The Diary of John Quincy Adams 1794–1845*, ed. Allan Nevins (New York: Charles Scribner's Sons, 1951), p. 559.

Bibliography

Passages in the Cantos are referred to by Canto number (in roman numerals) and the number of the page in *The Cantos of Ezra Pound* (New York: New Directions, 1972). However, in some cases the text of *The Cantos of Ezra Pound* (London: Faber, 1964) is preferred.

Abbreviations

EPS: Ezra Pound, *'Ezra Pound Speaking': Radio Speeches of World War II*, ed. Leonard W. Doob. Westport, Conn.: Greenwood Press, 1978.

Int: D. G. Bridson, "An Interview with Ezra Pound." Chapter 13 in this book.

L: Ezra Pound, *The Selected Letters.*

OS: Ezra Pound, *Opere scelte*, ed. Mary de Rachewiltz. Milan: Arnoldo Mondadori, 1970.

P: Ezra Pound, *Selected Prose.*

PF: Ezra Pound and Ford Madox Ford, *Pound/Ford: The Story of a Literary Friendship*, ed. Brita Lindberg-Seyersted. London: Faber, 1982.

"Safe with My Lynxes"

Pound's Figure in the Carpet?

MASSIMO BACIGALUPO

◆ ◆ ◆

IN THE EARLY CANTOS Pound was in the process of defining some of the main features of the Secret History of his poem. Canto VII closes announcing the Time of the Assassins (to use Rimbaud's phrase): while deferring to Henry James, "eternal watcher of things," somewhat awkwardly conflated with the sinister duke Alessandro de' Medici, Pound sympathizes largely with Alessandro's murderer Lorenzino, who is none but the poet and stands for vitality and action, which are to Pound valuable for their own sake. Lorenzino is "more full of flames and voices." That Pound was the source of a lot of sound and fury between 1908 and 1960 is unquestionable.

In early 1920, however, while giving the final touches to Cantos V–VII and drafting Part II of *Hugh Selwyn Mauberley*, Pound was undergoing a crisis, documented by these poems and by a letter T. S. Eliot wrote John Quinn on 25 January:

> The fact is that there is now no organ of any importance in which he can express himself, and he is becoming forgotten. It is not enough for him to publish a volume of verse once a year—or no matter how often—for it will simply not be reviewed and will be killed by silence.

. . . As I consider that Pound and Lewis are the only writers in London whose work is worth pushing, this worries me. I know that Pound's lack of tact has done him great harm. But I am worried as to what is to become of him. (358)

A reviewer of *Quia Pauper Amavi* (which includes such notable work as "Langue d'Oc," "Moeurs Contemporaines," the sustained "Three Cantos" of 1917, and *Homage to Sextus Propertius*) had announced a fortnight earlier in *The Observer*: "In himself Mr. Pound is not, never has been, and, almost I might hazard, never will be a poet" (Stock, 287). It was not long before Pound parodied this in *Mauberley*: "The case presents no adjunct / To the Muses' diadem." It may have been at this time that the present Cantos XIV–XV, Pound's excremental hell for the English, were drafted.

Through the good offices of Quinn, Pound was appointed correspondent for the *Dial*, and this (Eliot wrote Quinn on 10 May) "had a great effect in raising his spirits" (382). The *Dial* was to publish between 1920 and 1923 the early versions of Cantos IV–VIII, and the twelve "Paris Letters," which deserve to be reprinted. Disenchanted with England and doubtful about the value of his work, Pound returned to Venice and Sirmione, where he wrote (as a serial for the *New Age*) the estranged account of his childhood, *Indiscretions*. In spring 1921, after a brief return to London and a stay on the French Riviera, he moved to Paris, where at first he occupied himself with music, sculpture, and with the translation of Rémy de Gourmont's *Physique de l'amour, Essai sur l'instinct sexuel*. In a "Postscript" to the latter he followed up some remarks he had made in "Psychology and Troubadours,"[1] by outlining the theory of sexuality which we find in *The Cantos*, particularly in the 1920s. The "Postscript" is dated 21 June 1921, close upon Midsummer Day—probably no coincidence, for at this time Pound's mind was markedly veering toward the occult. Some months later he announced that on 30 October 1921, his thirty-sixth birthday, and the date of the completion of *Ulysses*, a new pagan era had commenced, and to this he alludes explicitly in his 1922 articles on Joyce: "L'année du centenaire de Flaubert, première d'une ère nouvelle."[2] This is not only a metaphor, but a reference to Pound's private astrology.

These speculations were encouraged when, on 2 January 1922, Eliot arrived in Paris from Lausanne with the draft of *The Waste Land*, on which Pound went to work in a quasi-editorial capacity, and with much excitement. When Eliot returned to London on 12 January 1923 he brought with him Pound's corrections, and when he sent back a revised version later that month Pound responded on "24 Saturnus" (i.e., 24 January according to the *Little Review* Calendar) with his famous letter of "complimenti."³

This was accompanied by a personal breakthrough, which, after a two-year stalemate, resulted in the composition of an "Eighth Canto," soon to be relocated, in a slightly revised form, as Canto II: manifesto of the new "era" and celebration of its god, Dionysus. By rehearsing (a) the grudging admiration of Troy's elders for the beauty of Helen, (b) the marine intercourse of Neptune and Tyro (a further borrowing from *Odyssey* 11, where Tyro's story is told), and (c) Dionysus' epiphany to the pirates who attempt to sell him into slavery, Pound tells us in three ways that the godhead cannot be fettered by convention and that it triumphs over all obstacles, and goes on to announce the establishment of his own libertarian reign:

> And Lyæus: "From now, Accœtes, my altars,
> Fearing no bondage,
>> fearing no cat of the wood,
> Safe with my lynxes,
>> feeding grapes to my leopards,
> Olibanum is my incense,
>> the vines grow in my homage."
>
> [II.8–9]

Thus in *The Cantos* Pound seeks to reverse the march of events decried in *Mauberley* ("Christ follows Dionysus"): the god of leopards regains the throne usurped by Christ. (This canto has also been read as a covert attack upon Prohibition.) Pound's program is reminiscent of Nietzsche's revaluation in the classical tradition of the Dionysian element as against the Apollonian. But Pound only paints a picture, or presents a variation on mythical themes, thus to some extent concealing his fervor. As with Homer, Andreas Divus, and "The Seafarer" in Canto I, we are chiefly aware of a process of layering: the principal source is Ovid, yet Ovid is also but one link in a textual chain reaching back to the Homeric "Hymn to Dionysus" (a logical follow-up to the quotations from the "Hymn to Aphrodite" in Canto I) and forward to Ovid's Tudor translator Arthur Golding, whose *Metamorphoses* (1567), "the most beautiful book in the language" (*ABC of Reading*, 127), Pound had particularly in mind—for what is he after but the utmost beauty? In fact Canto II is a great advance on Cantos IV–VII, bringing into the poem a new clarity, which one is tempted to call French. Yet we must correct the statement about beauty, since E.P., unlike his alias

Mauberley, is after something more, nothing less than the new (pan-aesthetic) Era, and this was to make *The Cantos* both formidable and tragic.

So it happened that the discouragement of 1919–1920 gave way to enthusiasm and to a sense of omnipotence. Pound conceived his own image *sub specie aeternitatis,* saw himself as a reincarnation of Dionysus (30 October according to the Pound Calendar is the "Feast of Zagreus"), and appropriated the god's feline totems: leopards, lynxes, and cats. This theophany is anticipated by a group of "Nine Poems" published November 1918 in *The Little Review*, which includes "Glamour and Indigo" (after Arnaut Daniel), the mystical and erotic "Phanopoeia" ("You are englobed in my sapphire. Io! Io!"), and "Cantus Planus," which in 1926 Pound was to use, disregarding chronological sequence, as an envoi to *Personae*, his *Collected Poems*:

> The black panther lies under his rose tree
> And the fawns come to sniff at his sides:
>
> Evoe, Evoe, Evoe Baccho, O
> ZAGREUS, *Zagreus,* Zagreus,
>
> The black panther lies under his rose tree.
> ‖ Hesper adest. Hesper ‖ adest.
>   Hesper ‖ adest. ‖

By way of Catullus' address to the evening star, Zagreus (one of the names for Dionysus in the Eleusis mysteries) is identified with Hymenaeus, the god of the wedding night. At the close of the first plentiful "day" of Pound's poetry, the word is resolved in music, as it were anticipating the nuptials to follow (and the anapestic meter of *The Cantos*: "And the fawns / come to sniff / at his sides").

In Canto V (where the Catullus poem is quoted again) there is a further reference both Dionysian and autobiographic: "Fracastor had Zeus for midwife, / Lightning served as his tweezers."[4] In a letter of 1916 Pound rehearsed his early life as follows:

Biographical or otherwise: Born in Hailey, Idaho. First connection with vorticist movement during the blizzard of '87 when I came East, having decided that the position of Hailey was not sufficiently central for my activities—came East behind the first rotary snow plough, the inventor of which vortex saved me from death by croup feeding me with lumps of sugar saturated with kerosene. (Parallels in the life of Fracastorius.) (72)

On the evidence of Canto V, it appears that Pound sees a connection between his rescue from death during the blizzard through kerosene and Fracastor's delivery through the lightning of "midwife" Zeus. But these are motifs of the myth of Dionysus, whose mother Semele was "shot to atoms" (Canto XCII) by the lightning of Zeus, who saved the infant by sewing him within his thigh—hence Dionysus' epithet "binatus" (*digonos* in Greek, see Canto LXXIV).

The theme is clarified by the final arrangement of Cantos I and II: on the one hand Ulysses, the poet as man; on the other Dionysus, the poet as god. The two are again contrasted in the first lines of the second sequence of Cantos, which links up with the elliptic finale of Canto I and goes on to the "divine or permanent world" (*Letters*, 210):

> So that the vines burst from my fingers
> And the bees weighted with pollen
> Move heavily in the vine-shoots:
>   chirr—chirr—chir-rikk—a purring sound,
> And the birds sleepily in the branches.
>   ZAGREUS! IO ZAGREUS!
>
>   [XVII.76]

The Greek cry "*io*" (previously appearing in "Phanopoeia") is also Italian for "I." "God am I for the time" was Pound-Propertius' comment on his nights with Cynthia. The exclamation signals the Panic moment in which man is at one with the cosmos; it is the cry of orgasm:

> By prong have I entered these hills:
> That the grass grow from my body,
> That I hear the roots speaking together,
> The air is new on my leaf,
> The forked boughs shake with the wind.
>   [XLVII.238]

Here the speaker is both a tree (as in "The Tree," the introductory poem in *Personae*) and the very earth out of which the grass grows. With Walt Whitman he could say, "If you want me again look for me under your boot-soles"—though Pound's tone is typically more orotund and biblical.

It is worth noting that in Canto XVII birds and bees produce, in their drunken stupor, the "purring sound" of the god's favorite animals. And in the middle Cantos:

Desolate is the roof where the cat sat,
Desolate is the iron rail that he walked
And the corner post whence he greeted the sunrise.
In hill path: "thkk, thgk"
        of the loom
"Thgk, thkk" and the sharp sound of a song
      under olives
When I lay in the ingle of Circe
I heard a song of that kind.
      Fat panther lay by me
                [XXXIX.193]

These are all variations of a single scene constructed "ideogramically" by the addition of new brushstrokes every time it recurs. The cat's journey leads from urban squalor to the pleasance in the hills above Rapallo, Pound's *locus amoenus*, where he can still hear Circe's looms and her singing. Since Pound associated Circe with Olga Rudge, the mother of his daughter, and with her house on the hills "under olives," and since she did not sing but performed on her fiddle the *Chanson des oiseaux* by Clément Jannequin as revised by Francesco da Milano and Gerhart Münch, he added this last new stroke in March 1941:

    We have heard the birds praising Jannequin
      and the black cat's tail is exalted.
        (*Letters*, 348; *Cantos*, 820)

And in the second Pisan Canto he simply reproduced Münch's score in Olga's handwriting as an homage to his companion and a material token—as it were, a photograph—of his pan-aesthetic, naturalistic, and erotic dream.[5]

Before leaving this figure in the carpet of *The Cantos*, let us watch Ezra Pound bearing up in all humility to his divine calling for the benefit of a bemused W. B. Yeats:

Sometimes about ten o'clock at night I accompany him to a street where there are hotels upon one side, upon the other palm trees and the sea, and there taking out of his pocket bones and pieces of meat he begins to call the cats. He knows all their histories—the brindled cat looked like a skeleton until he began to feed it; that fat grey cat is an hotel proprietor's favourite, it never begs from the guests' tables and it turns

cats that do not belong to the hotel out of the garden; this black cat
and that grey cat over there fought on the roof of a four-storied house
some weeks ago, fell off, a whirling ball of claws and fur, and now avoid
each other.[6]

At Rapallo, where he made his home in 1924, Pound imagined he was safe
with his lynxes. Yet his Dionysian fate was not to be accomplished until
September 1943, when he fled northward from Rome before the advancing
Allied army, a rucksack (*zaino*) on his back, the ruins of his dream about
him:

> the man out of Naxos past Fara Sabina
> "if you will stay for the night"
> "it is true there is only one room for the lot of us"
> "money is nothing"
> "no, there is nothing to pay for that bread"
>   "nor for the minestra"
> "Nothing left here but women"
>   "Have lugged it this far, will keep it" (il zaino)
>   No, they will do nothing to you.
> "Who *says* he is an American"
>   a still form on the branda, Bologna
> "Gruss Gott," "Der Herr!" "Tatile ist gekommen!"
>   Slow lift of long banners
>   Roma profugens Sabinorum in terras
>   [LXXVIII.498]

This is the "Provincia Deserta" of Pound's last and most dramatic walking
tour, as it flashes in the mind of the D.T.C. prisoner, who also is (or was)
"the man out of Naxos."[7] As in the older poem, a deep sympathy, nearly
an oceanic feeling, links him to the simple people that help him. At Pisa
he was finally to be reunited with his feline love: "O lynx, my love, my
lovely lynx" (Canto LXXIX).

After the breakthrough of the Dionysian Canto II, Pound made quick
progress on his poem. During July 1922, he drafted five cantos on different
topics, the first of which, concerned with the Renaissance world of Sigismondo Malatesta, was to occupy the poet (who inspected the sites of the
condottiere's feats and searched Italian libraries for documents) until April
1923, expanding in the process into the present four Malatesta cantos,
perhaps Pound's most complex persona, and the model of the subsequent

historical-poetical ventures of *The Cantos*. It was fitting that Eliot's *Criterion*, which opened its inaugural issue with *The Waste Land*, should close its first volume by devoting twenty-one pages of issue 4 to the Malatesta sequence, which is a very Poundian and epic response to the Twilight of the West depicted in Eliot's despondent poem.

Notes

1. An important essay of 1912, reprinted in the later editions of *The Spirit of Romance*.

2. Pound, "James Joyce et Pécuchet," rpt. Read, 201. See also "Ulysses," *Literary Essays*, 408. The calendar of Pound's new era "p.s.U." (i.e., "post scriptum *Ulysses*"), printed anonymously in the *Little Review* 8.2 (Spring 1922), 2 and 40, and noted in Read, 192, is partly a joke, partly a scheme of the mythical universe of *The Cantos*. It is ironic that Pound's post-*Ulysses* Era actually antedated by several months Mussolini's Fascist Era (the numbering of which Pound later adopted).

3. This letter is misdated 24 December 1921 in Pound's *Letters*, 169, and in Eliot's *Letters*, xxvi.

4. This is Pound's expansion in the Faber *Cantos* of 1954. The New Directions text preserves the reading of the first printing (*Dial*, 1921): "Fracastor (lightning was midwife)."

5. For Pound's excitement about and reflections on the Jannequin-Da Milano-Münch process of transmission, see *Guide to Kulchur*, 151–152.

6. W. B. Yeats, *A Packet for Ezra Pound*, rpt. in *A Vision*, 5–6. By a curious coincidence of literary history, this very garden in front of the seaside hotels was the home of another famous cat, the protagonist of Hemingway's concise "Cat in the Rain."

7. In the *Metamorphoses* and in Canto II, Bacchus is taken aboard the pirate ship and asks to be taken to Naxos: "Illa mihi domus est, vobis erit hospita tellus" (3.637). See also *Oro e lavoro* (1944): "On the 10th of September last, I walked down the Via Salaria and into the Republic of Utopia, a quiet country eighty years east of Fara Sabina" (*Selected Prose*, 336). In the last lines of the quoted passage, Pound reaches his destination and is greeted by the Tirol family with whom his daughter Mary was living. See de Rachewiltz, *Discretions*, 184–190. "Provincia Deserta" (1915), one of Pound's most characteristic and accomplished poems, remembers elegiacally his 1912 walking tour in Southern France.

Works Cited

de Rachewiltz, Mary. *Discretions*. Boston: Little, Brown, 1971.

Eliot, T. S. *The Letters of T. S. Eliot: Volume 1: 1898–1922*. Ed. Valerie Eliot. London: Faber, 1988.

Pound, Ezra. *ABC of Reading*. New York: New Directions, 1960.

————. *The Cantos*. 13th printing. New York: New Directions, 1995.

————. *Guide to Kulchur*. Norfolk, Conn.: New Directions, 1952.

————. *The Letters of Ezra Pound 1907–1941*. Ed. D. D. Paige. New York: Harcourt, Brace, 1950.

————. *Literary Essays of Ezra Pound*. Ed. T. S. Eliot. London: Faber, 1954.

————. *Selected Prose*. Ed. William Cookson. London: Faber, 1973.

Read, Forrest, ed. *Pound/Joyce: The Letters of Ezra Pound to James Joyce*. New York: New Directions, 1970.

Stock, Noel. *The Life of Ezra Pound*. London: Penguin, 1974.

Yeats, W. B. *A Vision*. London: Macmillan, 1962.

Extracts from *Ezra Pound and the Erotic Medium*

KEVIN ODERMAN

❖   ❖   ❖

Introductory Note by Peter Makin

[Oderman argues that pound had a curious idea about the relation between sex and godly visions that is a key to interpreting numerous passages in *The Cantos*. Yet at every stage of its development, Pound expressed this idea obliquely and in code. In his early essay "Psychology and Troubadours" (1912), Pound's claim is that the medieval troubadours had a heightened sensitivity to the gods' presence for a very concrete reason: they did not move easily from sexual desire to fulfillment. Their customs imposed "delay," and the psychic effect of this was a focusing, an intensity of vision. So the troubadour's lady became for him an alchemist's stone. It's clear that this idea related to Pound's own experience: in his own early poems, at times the gods seem to be manifesting themselves to a seer who is involved in a sexual encounter of some kind. Much later Pound would argue in a famous passage that the writers and painters of the earlier Italian Renaissance had no interest in the human body for itself but only as the outer manifestation of the moving intelligence within and, likewise, had no interest in a world of mechanical matter but only in a godly "universe of fluid force" that the truly seeing eye could perceive intersecting with that. It was this mystical "universe of fluid force," of "magnetisms that

take form," that was revealed to the lover whose sexuality was thus channeled in the proper way. In the 1920s, Pound read further in the biology
of sex and developed these ideas in rather extraordinary ways. He persuaded
himself that, since the human brain "exteriorizes" form by imagining (let
us say) a poem or a sculpture or a building and then creating it, and since
the human sperm "exteriorizes" form in the sense that the resultant human being is first mapped out in it, there was an intimate physical relation
between sperm and brain, and—again—the man whose sexual activity
involved "delay" might develop into a genius just because of the "relative
. . . retention" of sperm. This latter idea does not directly affect *The Cantos*
much. But, as Oderman shows, if we are familiar with Pound's general
ideas about forms of sexuality as a door to vision, and learn how to read
his codes, it becomes possible to read many *Cantos* passages that are otherwise vapid, fragmentary, or obscure.]

. . . IN 1933 POUND WROTE TO VIOLA BAXTER JORDAN that years of his
life and work had been devoted to the investigation of "uplift," of specific
kinds of sexuality, and that his interest in Provence reflected this general
interest, because it was there that the subject had been properly understood.[1] This suggests that . . . Pound's own writings ought to bear witness
to his thought. And they do, but the mode of statement, as we will see,
is extremely elliptical. It also suggests a beginning, another beginning,
Pound's most outspoken treatise on the subject of Provence: "Psychology
and Troubadours." By 1916 Pound's thinking about the "psychic function"
of sexuality had taken on sharp outlines; if it had ever been, it was no
longer emotion alone. Pound became more than "le Byron de nos jours,"
as H.D. at one point called him;[2] for Pound sexuality stood at the threshold
of the *mysterium*, though he saw clearly enough that for many it was a
source only of dissipation. Those are the ones who stopped with Circe.

Servants of Amor: The Early Poetry

> *You may take this if you like* cum grano.
> —Pound, "Psychology and Troubadours"

In a footnote to "Psychology and Troubadours,"[3] commenting on a "recent
lecture by Mr. Mead,"[4] Pound makes the curious assertion that "there
would seem to be in the legend of Simon Magus and Helen of Tyre a

clearer prototype of 'chivalric love' than in anything hereinafter discussed"
(*SR*, 91). Unfortunately, Pound seems never to have written down just
what that "prototype" was; or perhaps, in deference to the reticence about
bald statement he found in the "trobar clus" (troubadour closed composition), he simply chose to remain silent on the point. Initially, it seemed
to be just another enigmatic footnote, but then I remembered having seen
Simon Magus and Helen of Tyre mentioned before, in Charles Williams's
short history of the church, *The Descent of the Dove*.[5] There, in a discussion
of the early church, Williams mentions a spiritual "method" aimed at
calling forth an experience of the Spirit. It was

> dangerous but dangerous with a kind of heavenly daring. There grew
> up, it seems, in that young and ardent body an effort towards a partic-
> ular spiritual experiment of, say, the polarization of the senses. Our
> knowledge of it is very small, and is indeed confined to a famous passage
> of St. Paul, to a letter of St. Cyprian's, and to one or two disapproving
> Canons of various Councils. The method was probably not confined to
> the Church; it is likely to have existed in other Mysteries. The great
> necromancer Simon Magus carried with him on his wanderings a com-
> panion who may have been for that purpose, and there were attributed
> to her high titles.[6]

Including, it seems, Helen of Tyre. There is something very Poundian about
Williams's going on so about this as yet unspecified method of the "polarization of the senses," for which purpose Simon Magus perhaps carried
about Helen of Tyre. We learn shortly that the method, as practiced within
the church, did not involved a breach of Christian morality: "This is clear
from that passage in St. Paul [still unspecified!] which shows that in some
instances the experiment broke down owing to the sexual element between
the man and the woman becoming too pronounced."[7] And finally, somewhat later, we find out what he is talking about: "The women—*subintroductae* as they were called—apparently slept with their companions without
intercourse."[8]

    I then remembered another enigmatic statement in "Psychology and
Troubadours": "I have no particular conclusion to impose upon the reader;
for a due consideration of Provençal poetry in 'trobar clus,' I can only
suggest the evidence and lines of inquiry. The Pauline position on wedlock
is of importance—I do not mean its general and inimical disapproval, but
its more specific utterances" (*SR*, 95). The passage which both Williams

and Pound seem intent to gesture at but not cite, is to be found in Paul's so-called advice to virgins (1 Corinthians 7.25–38, especially 36–38). It is not particularly suggestive; the King James version reads:

> But if any man think that he behaveth himself uncomely toward his virgin, if she pass the flower of her age, and need so require, let him do what he will, he sinneth not: let them marry.
>
> Nevertheless he that standeth stedfast in his heart, having no necessity, but hath power over his own will, and hath so decreed in his heart that he will keep his virgin, doeth well.
>
> So then he that giveth *her* in marriage doeth well; but he that giveth *her* not in marriage doeth better.

If the evidence here seems almost nonexistent to the lay reader, Williams's and Pound's position is not beyond the bounds of the scholarly interpretation of the passage. While I don't want to enter the debate here, it is perhaps appropriate to note that *Peake's* Bible commentary lists as one of three possible glosses: "The custom of *virgines subintroductae* may have arisen early and this would explain the reference to virgins here . . . Before monasteries and nunneries were built, the custom was common; bishops fulminated and councils legislated against it as it was open to scandal."[9] The question is not whether it ever existed, but if it existed so early within the church. Pound, apparently, thought it did.

ONE RETURNS TO "PSYCHOLOGY AND TROUBADOURS," after this short excursion, with a clearer sense of the locus in which Pound's comments there are to be understood. Baldly, sexual dalliance, of one sort or another, has been for certain individuals the source of contact with, for want of a better term, a visionary reality. While the details of this experiment remain, perhaps properly, veiled, it should be obvious that modern romantic effusions about the simple act are not indicated. Pound himself lampooned such drivel in his "Fratres Minores," noting that "the twitching of three abdominal nerves / Is incapable of producing a lasting Nirvana."[10] What we have instead is a sublimation, in the erotic encounter, of the lover's heightened sensitivity, Williams's "polarization of the senses."

Whether or not the "best modern scholarship" is willing to see a resurgence of this experiment in Provence is beyond the scope of our enquiry; what is pertinent is that Pound thought he did. Once we have circumscribed this locus, "Psychology and Troubadours" admits of only one reading: the essay is laced with cryptic references to the role of sexuality in the psychology of the troubadours; indeed, it would seem to be at the very basis of the psychology of the "servants of Amor." The temptation is to summarize the whole lot, but perhaps a couple of illustrations will suffice. Consider the following, peculiarly Poundian, "scientific" figure.[11]

> Sex is, that is to say, of a double function and purpose, reproductive and educational; or, as we see in the realm of fluid force, one sort of vibration produces at different intensities, heat and light. No scientist would be so stupid as to affirm that heat produced light, and it is into a similar sort of false ratiocination that those writers fall who find the source of illumination, or of religious experience, centered solely in the philo-progenitive instinct. [*SR*, 94]

About three pages later Pound returns to the same figure:

> The electric current gives light where it meets resistance. I suggest that the living conditions of Provence gave the necessary restraint, produced the tension sufficient for the results, a tension unattainable under, let us say, the living conditions of imperial Rome.
> So far as "morals" go, or at least a moral code in the modern sense, which might interfere in art, Arnaut can no more be accused of having one than can Ovid. Yet the attitude of the Latin *doctor amoris* and that of the *gran maestro de amor* are notably different, as for instance on such a matter as delay. Ovid takes no account of the psychic function. [*SR*, 97]

It is worth noting that Pound has circumscribed his subject in a rather careful manner: sexual experience is not the source of illumination but one source, nor is this just any sexual encounter, but one characterized by restraint, delay, and tension. And these, I think we must infer, are necessary rather than sufficient conditions for the success of the experiment. Furthermore, running throughout the essay is an emphasis on the character of the lover, who must have "a particular constitution of nerves and intellect."

At one point, Pound states, "The problem, in so far as it concerns Provence, is simply this: Did this 'chivalric love,' this exotic, take on mediumistic properties?" (*SR*, 94). It is, I think, basically a rhetorical question, except, perhaps, as it applies particularly to Provence; he had already stated, in a footnote on Cavalcanti, "For effect upon the air, upon the soul, etc., the 'lady in Tuscan poetry' has assumed all the properties of the Alchemist's stone" (*SR*, 90). What is particularly suggestive is that after a series of similar questions, he simply states, "For our basis in nature we rest on the indisputable and very scientific fact [Pound!] that there are in the 'normal course of things' certain times, a certain sort of moment more than another, when a man feels his immortality upon him" (*SR*, 94). It's the Poundian call to the experiential ground—we are to expect such experiences because they occur in "the natural course of events" (*SR*, 97). Furthermore, after a thumbnail sketch of those drawn to ecstatic cults, Pound announces, "One must consider that the types which joined these cults survived, in Provence, and survive, today—priests, maenads and the rest—though there is in our society no provision for them" (*SR*, 95). That such types survived in Provence, for the purposes of "Psychology and Troubadours," is relevant; that they survive today, is, in the immediate context, a superfluous and therefore significant observation. Perhaps Pound was merely extending the logic of his argument to its natural conclusion, but in light of his own early poetry, it seems more likely that he was looking toward his own life and work.[12]

Almost twenty years later, in "Terra Italica," we find Pound still writing around the question of the educative aspect of sexuality for men of a certain temperament, culminating perhaps in the single, trenchant phrase "For certain people the *pecten cteis* is the gate of wisdom" (cognates, the one Latin, the other Greek, each a euphemism for the genitalia). . . . [13]

A GREAT DEAL HAS BEEN MADE of Pound's use of flowers as a kind of "erotic floral symbolism," for instance, and most famously, in "Coitus":

> The gilded phaloi of the crocuses
>   are thrusting at the spring air.
> Here is there naught of dead gods
> But a procession of festival,
> A procession, O Giulio Romano,
> Fit for your spirit to dwell in.
>
>   [*P*, 110]

How those thrusting crocuses suggest those gilded "phaloi," very satisfying for the Freudian sensibility! (And Pound's sexuality has attracted a good deal of attention from Lacanian critics.)[14] But, for a Freudian, those next lines must be a little surprising, not to say incomprehensible. However, if one assumes the psychology of "Psychology and Troubadours" rather than the psychology of Freud, the transition is clear. The sexual encounter occasions vision, and here the vision is of a procession of the gods. Pound, of course, isn't explicit; he introduces the gods by the backhanded "naught of dead gods," leaving it to us to draw our conclusions. Presumably Giulio Romano serves as a shorthand notation for the style of the vision, and Ruthven's gloss on the passage is perhaps remotely appropriate to the case: "he [Giulio] painted mythological scenes as though they were something he had experienced and not merely read about: in his art the pagan gods live on" (a sentiment which is certainly consistent with Pound's thinking if we delete "as though").[15] In any case, in this poem, as in "The Flame," Pound plainly suggests that the locus of the vision is a sexual encounter. He is not always so straightforward.

Sometimes, indeed, Pound simply suppresses the situation altogether, and gives us a kind of cryptogram of the visionary moment. All we are really left to base our guesses on is the language, and the sphinxlike surface of the poem. "Heather," I think, falls into this class.

> The black panther treads at my side,
> And above my fingers
> There float the petal-like flames.
>
> The milk-white girls
> Unbend from the holly-trees,
> And their snow-white leopard
> Watches to follow our trace.
>
> [*P*, 109]

Consider the dreamlike or visionary atmosphere of the poem, the use of words like "*petal*," "*flame*," and "*trace*,"[16] and the opposition of the black panther and the snow-white leopard, recalling Pound's comment that "at any rate, when we do get into contemplation of the flowing [Pound's universe of fluid force] we find sex, or some correspondance [*sic*] to it, 'positive and negative,' 'North and South,' 'sun and moon, or whatever terms of whatever cult or science you prefer to substitute" (*SR*, 93). That the panther and the leopard are to correspond to the polarities of a man and a woman in a sexual encounter must, of course, barring some external evidence, remain speculative. But that Pound was capable of transforming an experience to this degree to get it into a poem is demonstrable: one need only compare "Shalott" and the prose note following it in the *San Trovaso Notebook*, where the poem is said to have been inspired by the "essences of beauty" seen in the colors of the dawn's "reflexion" (*CEP*, 322).

In the poem, however, the Lord of Shalott, prince of dreams, speaks and mentions neither the dawn nor its colors. One would not want to push the point too hard; "Heather" is cryptic in the extreme.

About midway between poems which clearly embody a sexual encounter and an attendant visionary moment, such as "The Flame," and suggestive utterances like "Heather," there are poems like "Canzone: Of Angels," which exhibit the same configuration of a visionary reality, a lady, and a man feeling his immortality upon him—but with the sexual locus seemingly suppressed. "Canzone: Of Angels" begins familiarly enough:

> He that is Lord of all the realms of light
> Hath unto me from His magnificence
> Granted such vision as hath wrought my joy.
> Moving my spirit past the last defence
> That shieldeth mortal things from mightier sight,
> Where freedom of the soul knows no alloy,
> I saw what forms the lordly powers employ.
>
> [*CEP*, 139]

There follows an extended description of the "similitude" of the three splendors employed by the lordly powers which the speaker has seen in vision. What comes after is one of the most interesting passages in all of the early poems:

> The diver at Sorrento from beneath
> The vitreous indigo, who swiftly riseth,
> By will and not by action as it seemeth,
> Moves not more smoothly, and no thought surmiseth
> How she takes motion from the lustrous sheath
> Which, as the trace behind the swimmer, gleameth
> Yet presseth back the aether where it streameth.
> To her whom it adorns this sheath imparteth
> The living motion from the light surrounding;
> And thus my nobler parts, to grief's confounding,
> Impart into my heart a peace which starteth
> From one round whom a graciousness is cast
> Which clingeth in the air where she hath past.
>
> [*CEP*, 140]

The language, of course, is hopelessly archaic, which probably accounts for the omission of the poem from *Personae*; but the figure is wonderful, and

I think it is one of Pound's first successful attempts to embody the "radiant world," or as he variously calls it, the "universe of fluid force." The attempt for Pound is in the way of a recovery, because, as he says, "We appear to have lost the radiant world where one thought cuts through another with clean edge, a world of moving energies *'mezzo oscuro rade,' 'risplende in sè perpetuale effecto,'* magnetisms that take form, that are seen, or that border the visible."[17] The recovery, however, is always possible in a world which has a "permanent basis in humanity." The radiant world is there and available to perception; "We are not shut from all the thousand heavens."

We should remember that Pound's ultimate interest is not in the lady herself but in the visionary reality she makes available. To put it crudely, she functions as a "mantram" or analogue of the alchemist's stone; she is a means to an end. Pound's early poetry does not suggest that he thought the sexual encounter was the sole means of approach. For instance, it is not by chance that Pound mentions as an example of "magnetisms that take form" in the radiant world "the form that seems a form seen in the mirror" (*LE*, 154). As early as *A Lume Spento* he had reported, in "On His Own Face in a Glass," that he saw not one face but a "myriad," a "ribald company," a "saintly host" (*CEP*, 34). We miss the point entirely if we read this as some kind of metaphor for a multifaceted personality; here too Pound speaks directly from experience. He sees many faces in the mirror; they are forms seen in the radiant world. What we have is another method of recovering the radiant world, which we "appear" to have lost, another "experiment." Pound's commentary on Cavalcanti is again instructive; he finds in Guido "*natural demonstration* and the proof by experience or (?) experiment" (*LE,* 158).

In "Canzone: Of Angels," the quality of the movement of the diver at Sorrento figures the visionary movement of the beloved. The pattern of the movement is the same, and the diver in the vitreous indigo embodies that movement within the sensible world (of "normal" experience). While the beloved's movement in the realm of fluid force is something which is difficult for the uninitiated to imagine, we can feel our way toward that perception by "meditating" (Pound out of Richard of St. Victor) on the pattern which is manifest in the diver's rise. The lover sees the beloved move within a "lustrous sheath" which imparts motion from the surrounding light (the radiant world).[18]

The obvious question is how does the lover's perception of the beloved within the radiant world relate to the vision of the three splendors which has preceded it? By now it should be clear that the vision itself has sprung from the encounter of the lover with the beloved, touched on in the lines "And thus my nobler parts, to grief's confounding, / Impart into my heart

a peace which starteth / From one round whom a graciousness is cast."
She is the source, or the "mantram," of his vision. . . .

Divagation: Physiology

> The study of physiognomy shd. be encouraged.
> —Pound, *Guide to Kulchur*

I turn now to a "divagation" from the more manifestly literary dimensions
of Pound's visionary eroticism to what can only be termed its physiological
dimension. However, such a direction only appears to be away from the
literature, because Pound divulges in his writings on physiology a good
deal about his thinking that bears forcefully, if obliquely, on the visionary
side of his poetry. There is something more here than a bizarre aside,
however bizarre an aside it may be. The primary texts for this diversion
are Pound's "Translator's Postscript" to Remy de Gourmont's *The Natural
Philosophy of Love*, certainly one of the most scandalous items in the entire
Pound bibliography, and his little-known review of Louis Berman's *The
Glands Regulating Personality*, "The New Therapy."[19]

ON THE FACE OF IT, few of Pound's dicta seem less promising as material
for exegesis than his assertion in the "Translator's Postscript" that "it is
more than likely that the brain itself, is, in origin and development, only
a sort of great clot of genital fluid held in suspense or reserve" (*NPL*, 169).
Stunned laughter is the obvious response. Indeed, the tonalities of "great
clot" and the postscript as a whole suggest that Pound enjoyed composing
it, but we should not let the tone of the postscript or its disclaimers ("I
appear to have thrown down bits of my note somewhat at random" [*NPL*,
178]) interfere with our seeing that it is a careful piece of writing and
deserves a careful, exegetical reading.[20]
   . . . Pound's postscript diverges from the *Physique* in significant ways. . . .
For instance, while Gourmont by and large restricts the mode of his analysis to description of external behaviors and inferences drawn from them,
Pound "introspects it" when he can, and speculates on the significance of
these subjective data in terms of physiology (or a simulacrum thereof); it
is only to this extent that he is "extremely material and physical and
animal" in his analysis. Furthermore, it is a small but daring step from the
development of cerebral capacity in a species to the development of cerebral capacity in an individual—a step Pound takes, and self-consciously.

Pound espouses the Lamarckian view that changes in the species occur as changes in an individual, which are then "passed on." On the basis of an introspection, Pound argues that such mutations happen suddenly,

> with a conviction for which anyone is at liberty to call me a lunatic, and for which I offer no better ground than simple introspection. I believe, and on no better ground than that of a sudden emotion, that the change of the species is not a slow matter, ... I believe that the species changes as suddenly as a man makes a song or a poem, or as suddenly as he *starts* making them. [*NPL*, 174]

The iterated *credo* is telling. Despite the qualifications this is no modest statement, because to know by introspection an advance in the species one must be the individual to make it.

WITH THE SITE OF POUND'S ENQUIRY determined, the postscript seems less difficult, and we are better prepared to deal with the notorious statement quoted at the beginning of the chapter, "it is more than likely that the brain itself, is, in origin and development, only a sort of great clot of genital fluid held in suspense or reserve." The meaning of this passage hinges on Pound's characterization of the genital fluid: "the power of the spermatozoid is precisely the power of exteriorizing a form" (*NPL*, 169). Readers of Pound's *The Cantos* should be on familiar ground here, for this is the power of the acorn to exteriorize the form of the oak: "oak leaf never plane leaf" (87/573). The relationship of this power, of the seed to cast a form, to the functioning of the brain is, presumably, an example of what Pound calls in the postscript "as yet uncorrelated phenomena" (*NPL*, 169). The link, for Pound, is that the brain functions in a like manner; it has an "enormous content" as "a maker and presenter of images" (*NPL*, 169). That the functions are analogous is clear, and it is in the realm of analogies that Gourmont can speak, and Pound quotes him, of "fecundating a generation of bodies as genius fecundates a generation of minds" (*NPL*, 173). But Pound is saying more than that; he is asserting a physiological relation between the exteriorizing functions of the spermatozoid and the brain. At this the intuitive mind balks, and demands a little coaching.[21]

Pound makes a poor coach, offering instead a few red herrings by way of explanation for what he thinks is the physiological basis of the functional parallelism of the brain and sperm. At one point he cites "the lack of any other known substance [besides sperm] in nature capable of growing into brain" (*NPL*, 169) as evidence for the relation, but the obvious objection "or into an arm" suggests that this is an indirection. The real link is more introspective than this, and is introduced clandestinely. It will be remembered that Gourmont's correlation of intelligence to "profonde" copulation was a matter of genital design, of the depth of penetration. Though Pound takes this correlation as his starting point, he never returns to it in its Gourmontian form; instead, he silently amends it to a correlation between intelligence and a specific kind of copulation, characterized in such terms as "suspense," "reserve," and "retention," a characterization that leads him to note that "A flood is as bad as a famine" (*NPL*, 170–71). Nothing here about design, because this is not Gourmont. Pound's version:

> Species would have developed in accordance with, or their development would have been affected by the relative discharge and retention of the [spermatic] fluid; this proportion being both a matter of quantity and of quality, some animals profiting hardly at all by the alluvial Nile-flood; the baboon retaining nothing; men apparently stupefying themselves in some cases by excess, and in other cases discharging apparently only a surplus at high pressure; the imbecile, or the genius, the "strong-minded." [*NPL*, 169]

The effect of "relative discharge and retention" remains constant; in species, those retaining nothing suffer an atrophy in their development, and vice versa; in man, it is a question of individuals: excess discharge possibly leading to imbecility, retention leading to strength of mind, even to genius (remembering the qualitative dimension that crosscuts the simply quantitative question). There is here, of course, a significant echo of Pound's assertions in "Psychology and Troubadours," where he insisted on the importance of "delay" in the sexual encounter, if it is to serve a "mediumistic" function in the psychic life of the lover (*SR*, 97). This suggests that the compact experience remains the same, but depending on the character of the work, Pound emphasizes one or another aspect of it. From every perspective, though, indulging in simple copulation is lampooned as an inferior approach to sexuality; here it is stupefaction by excess. . . .

The Cantos: First Assay

> What remains, and remains undeniable to and by the most hardened objectivist, is that a great num-

ber of men have had certain kinds of emotion and,
magari, of ecstasy. They have left indelible records
of ideas born of, or conjoined with, this ecstasy.
—Pound, *Guide to Kulchur*

Simple magnitude, not to mention complexity, makes any "first assay" of
The Cantos a perilous encounter. To circumscribe the subject, I will focus
on a single canto—25. The choice is not entirely arbitrary; 25 is not an
extraordinarily difficult canto among those in which Pound's visionary
eroticism plays a large part. . . . But more important, the analysis of a connected passage in the context of a single canto has the positive virtue of
revealing Pound's poetic strategies and providing a sense of the relation of
mediumistic sexuality, as a subject, to some of *The Cantos*'s more celebrated
themes. . . .

> And Sulpicia
> green shoot now, and the wood
> white under new cortex
> "as the sculptor sees the form in the air
> before he sets hand to mallet,
> "and as he sees the in, and the through,
> the four sides
> "not the one face to the painter
> As ivory uncorrupted:
> "Pone metum Cerinthe"
> Lay there, the long soft grass,
> and the flute lay there by her thigh,
> Sulpicia, the fauns, twig-strong,
> gathered about her;
> The fluid, over the grass
> Zephyrus, passing through her,
> "deus nec laedit amantes."
> Hic mihi dies sanctus. . . .
>
> [25/117–18]

Sulpicia in the grass dominates this passage, is present throughout it, provides the persona of the beloved, over which Pound layers, ply over ply,
elements of his visionary eroticism. In the first section Pound invokes the
"metamorphic moment" by recurring to the motif of man-as-tree—a signature of metamorphosis from "Hilda's Book" onward. In the *Personae* of

1926 it is most visible in "The Tree," written for Hilda Doolittle when they were both teenagers, but it is also apparent in "A Girl." These two poems deserve to be juxtaposed in this context, and I'll quote them in their entirety. In reading them, we should keep in mind the erotic context suggested by "A Girl," Pound's assertion in "Psychology and Troubadours" that "myths are only intelligible in a vivid and glittering sense *to those people to whom they occur*" (*SR*, 92, my emphasis), and that in his "Arnold Dolmetsch" Pound described the origin of myth experientially, as a man walking "sheer into 'nonsense' " (*LE*, 431), giving, suggestively, as an example a man who created a myth to make palatable his experience of having "turned into a tree" (*LE*, 431). Here is "The Tree":

> I stood still and was a tree amid the wood
> Knowing the truth of things unseen before,
> Of Daphne and the laurel bow
> And that god-feasting couple olde
> That grew elm-oak amid the wold.
> 'Twas not until the gods had been
> Kindly entreated and been brought within
> Unto the hearth of their heart's home
> That they might do this wonder-thing.
> Nathless I have been a tree amid the wood
> And many new things understood
> That were rank folly to my head before.
>
> [*CEP*, 35]

"A Girl":

> The tree has entered my hands,
> The sap has ascended my arms,
> The tree has grown in my breast—
> Downward,
> The branches grow out of me, like arms.
>
> Tree you are,
> Moss you are,
> You are violets with wind above them.
> A child—*so* high—you are,
> And all this is folly to the world.
>
> [*CEP*, 186]

In reading these poems we must not deny the "nonsensical" element—
a man becoming a tree—by taking cover under the word "metaphor."
Pound insists on nonsense with the word "folly" in the last line of each
poem. Of course, the objective observer would not see the lover transformed into a tree, but Pound is proceeding by feeling, and he feels that
"things do not remain always the same. They become other things by swift
and unanalysable process" (*LE*, 431). The erotic encounter (implicit in "The
Tree," explicit in "A Girl") occasions the metamorphic moment. That this
is true in the passage I have quoted from Canto 25 is an evidential judgment, but the evidence is there, although incomplete. As Hugh Kenner
has shown us, the Sapphic fragment had structural implications for Pound,
and in his own poetry Pound began to proceed by fragmentation.[22] "The
Tree" and "A Girl" are part of the ideogram, even though they are not
part of *The Cantos*, and they are evidentially important for our understanding of the Poundian ellipsis in Canto 25; but there are passages in *The Cantos*
which bear on this one as well.[23] The most important is in Canto 20, where
we read:

> The boughs are not more fresh
> where the almond shoots
> take their March green.
>   [20/89]

For those who haven't perused Pound's notes for Canto 20 this must seem
even more elliptical, but this ellipsis is demonstrably explicable, and will
help us to bridge the gap in 25. A page later in the published version of
20 we read:

> from her breast to thighs.

In the notes these passages are continuous; the comparative "more" is
answered by its "than":

> The bough is not more fresh
>   where the almond shoots
> take their March green, than she
> square from the breasts to thighs.[24]

Thus, the notes to 20 reveal Pound's suppression of the erotic context in
favor of the fragment. The evidence suggests a similar procedure in the

> green shoot now, and the wood
> white under new cortex

of Canto 25.[25]

If the statement in the "tree motif" which introduces our passage in 25 is, by Pound's definition, mythic, what follows is not. The mode of statement changes, but the subject—Pound's erotic, "unofficial mysticism"—remains the same. That Pound should take up the subject in a different manner immediately following the introduction of the tree motif provides further oblique support for my interpretation of that motif's significance in Canto 25 by the implied cohesion of the text. What Pound does is poach a little from his own prose (*Gaudier-Brzeska*) in describing the ground of the "real" sculptor's work—"the form in the air." In this case, the passage from 25 elaborates what is only a dim hint in the prose: "The real sculptor 'sees' or is aware of, not only all the sides of his work, but of the 'through,' that is the diameters that can be passed through it from any angle."[26] Clearly the discussion of Gaudier-Brzeska is couched in technical language, but it is no coincidence, I think, that Pound passes directly from this to Gaudier's "Hieratic Head of Ezra Pound"—which I have already suggested is implicated in Pound's erotic preoccupations. Besides the resonance with his own prose, "as the sculptor sees the form in the air / before he sets hand to mallet" recalls what by Pound's time had almost become a topos, the sculptor seeing his sculpture *in the stone* before he began work. The variation is an interesting one and consistent with Pound's views of the raw materials of art. For Pound, the artist brings his idea, or form, to the material; he does not take his inspiration from it (despite vorticist strictures against models). Beyond that, the "form" which the sculptor sees in the air is described in a way which suggests the subtle bodies Pound's notes lead us to expect in the canto. It's transparent, but visible. It's seen, not imagined. To understand the presence of this "form" in this context, we must recognize that the force of the passage (and the one which immediately follows) is the force of simile: "as the sculptor," "As ivory uncorrupted." The form seen by the sculptor is *like* the form seen by the lover, and it is not like "the one face" seen by the painter, which here conveys simple reception ("Rubens' meat" in the terminology of Pound's "Cavalcanti"). Pound introduces the simile in this context to locate the kind of perception, in visual terms, experienced by the lover. It is a perception of, seemingly, a transparent subtle body. Of course, we can infer the erotic dimension of this passage—that a lover is implicated at all—

only by our knowledge of Pound's other works: early poems, prose, and notes. On its own, the difficulty of the passage would be insuperable.

The referent of "As ivory uncorrupted," which follows immediately after the simile of the sculptor's form in the passage under discussion, is problematical. The syntax is too broken to provide many sure clues. The phrase may refer back to the form seen by the lover, but as a visual description it seems unlikely because of the opacity of ivory (though old ivory does have a sheen and sometimes seems to cast light, which would conform to Mead's descriptions of the *augoeides*). But the colon which follows the phrase seems to indicate that the referent is forward, in the passage which follows, with its return to Sulpicia in the grass:

> As ivory uncorrupted:
> > "Pone metum Cerinthe"
> Lay there, the long soft grass,
> > and the flute lay there by her thigh,
> Sulpicia. . . .

It is Pound who puts Sulpicia in the grass. In volume 3 of the works of Tibullus, where Sulpicia's poems are bound up and where Tibullus addresses poems to her, we do not find her in the grass, with or without a flute. Pound has reworked his material radically, keeping only the love between Sulpicia and Cerinthus (implicit) and the phrase "pone metum Cerinthe, deus nec laedit amantes" (Put fear aside, Cerinthus. God harms not lovers),[27] and even that phrase is cut into pieces, varied, and shorn of its original context (Sulpicia on her sickbed, comforting Cerinthus). If Pound revised his source so heavily, he must have done it toward some end, and it is that end which we need to discover if we are to comprehend the introductory "As ivory uncorrupted."

By laying Sulpicia in "the long soft grass" Pound effects a localization of the lovers, a localization which is mildly suggestive, undulant, even erotic. The addition of a flute here is suggestive as well. She does not play it; perhaps she has lain it aside, favoring, for the moment, love to song. But beyond the literal level, the flute probably has a phallic significance, not so much as a symbol as a description born from habits of indirection. It's almost a discretion. But in an indiscreet letter to Viola Baxter Jordan, Pound likens the appearance of the phallus to a flute—dissociating "phallus" (erect) from "penis" (flaccid).[28] If we can admit that the flute here is probably (and we can't expect a greater certainty) an oblique description of a phallus,[29] then Pound's distinction between phallus and penis would also be relevant, suggesting not only that she has her lover with her there in the grass but that he is in a state of readiness.

We are, perhaps, getting closer to understanding to what "As ivory uncorrupted" refers. The colon which follows it suggested that the referent was subsequent; there, we found what appears to be a cryptic reference to a phallus. That the "ivory uncorrupted" refers to the phallus is, I think, highly likely. The following passages from other cantos, which are clearly related to 25, provide further evidence for the attribution. From 21:

> Phoibos, turris eburnea,
> > ivory against cobalt,
> And the boughs cut on the air,
> The leaves cut on the air
> The hounds on the green slope by the hill,
> > water still black in the shadow.
> In the crisp air,
> > the discontinuous gods. . . .
> > > [21/99]

And from 29:

> > Let us consider the osmosis of persons
> nondum orto jubare;
> The tower, ivory, the clear sky
> Ivory rigid in sunlight
> And the pale clear of the heaven
> Phoibos of narrow thighs,
> The cut cool of the air,
> Blossom cut on the wind. . . .
> . . . .
> The white hounds on the slope. . . .
> > [29/145]

These ivory towers are obviously phallic in intent: "rigid in sunlight." The two passages also exhibit other facets of the ideogram of visionary eroticism. The "mythic" tree motif is suggested by the boughs, leaves, and blossoms, here "on the air" or "on the wind." The apparitional appearance of the gods is suggested by "In the crisp air, / the discontinuous gods" (*spezzato*). And the hounds on the green slope recall a passage in Canto 17:

> And the goddess of the fair knees
> Moving there, with the oak-woods behind her,
> The green slope, with the white hounds
> > leaping about her. . . .
> > > [17/76]

All of which recall the silver hounds of "The Return," who accompany the returning gods:

> Gods of the wingèd shoe!
> With them the silver hounds,
> > sniffing the trace of air!
> > > [*CEP*, 198]

(Gods who, we will later find, "have not returned. 'They have never left us' " [113/787].) And all of these poems, with the exception of "The Return," are dawn songs, and from *A Lume Spento* on Pound wrote an inordinate number of *albas*, aubades, dawn songs. This poetry is thick with associations, but always the thread, never the whole web. It's a poetry that invites turgid critical prose.

If we grant, then, that the ivory of "As ivory uncorrupted" refers to the flute which in turn is phallic, and the whole is descriptive of an erotic encounter, there remains the question of why this ivory should be "uncorrupted." I think it can be understood, in a general way, as an instance of an implicit distinction between two kinds of sexuality in *The Cantos*: clean, hygienic sexuality and unclean, even diseased sexuality (a distinction which crosscuts any question of vision).[30] The "uncorrupted" is an avowal of cleanliness, perhaps even of ritual cleanliness, and is set against the corrupt or polluted sexuality of the defamers—the homosexuality of the Honest Sailor (12/56–57), the "condom full of black-beetles" of the Hell Cantos (14/63), and the "whores for Eleusis" (45/230), to mention only three examples of "corrupted" eroticism.

The passage from Canto 25 under discussion continues:

> Sulpicia, the fauns, twig-strong,
> > gathered about her;
> The fluid, over the grass

Zephyrus, passing through her,
              "deus nec laedit amantes."
Hic mihi dies sanctus. . . .

[25/118]

The first two lines here return to the mythic mode, the "twig-strong" of
the fauns echoing the tree motif, the fauns themselves "mythic" for a state
of being. Again, Pound is his own best commentator. In "Religio," Pound
wrote:

> What is a god?
> A god is an eternal state of mind.
> What is a faun?
> A faun is an elemental creature.
> What is a nymph?
> A nymph is an elemental creature.
>
> [*SP*, 47]

What Pound means here by "elemental creature," a phrase he would have
later avoided, is to be understood in light of the "Note Precedent to 'La
Fraisne' " of *A Lume Spento* where Pound quotes one "Janus of Basel":

> "When the soul is exhausted of fire, then doth the spirit return unto
> its primal nature and there is upon it a peace great and of the woodland
>
> *"magna pax et silvestris."*
>
> Then becometh it kin to the faun and the dryad, a woodland-dweller
> amid the rocks and streams
> *"consociis faunis dryadisque inter saxa sylvarum."*
>
> [*CEP*, 8]

And later in the "Note" in his own voice:

> I because in such a mood, feeling myself divided between myself corporal
> and a self aetherial "a dweller by streams and in woodland," eternal
> because simple in elements
> *"Aeternus quia simplex naturae"*
>
> [*CEP*, 8]

The last quotation helps to explain the others, in that not only does it betray the customary descent to experience, which seems to stand behind all of Pound's writings on extraordinary events, but it also identifies the experience as a "mood," and for Pound myths were explications of "moods." This particular mood, whose statement involves the evocation of fauns, is described in two ways, which Pound probably understood as two elements or stages of a single mood. Perhaps "When the soul is exhausted of fire" is the immediate condition for Pound's "feeling myself divided between myself corporal and a self aetherial." But most pertinent for our study, this last state sounds a great deal like the dissociation of the subtle from the gross body we observed in Pound's notes for Canto 25, when the subtle body moved without a corresponding movement in the corporeal body. The fauns, then, may be a mythic statement of what the notes describe literally.[31]

From the mythic statement implicit in his treatment of the fauns, Pound moves back to description in the line that follows, describing "the fluid" as it passes over the grass. The definite article "the" draws our attention to the word "fluid."[32] Here the word surely indicates what Pound called in "Psychology and Troubadours" "the universe of fluid force" (*SR*, 92), which the analysis of that essay suggested was experienced by the lover in moments of visionary perception in the erotic encounter. It touches, as well, on another motif which Pound returns to again and again, which we can here christen "Sub Mare," after the poem of that name, which opens as "The Tree" and "A Girl" close, with a self-conscious recourse to the nonsensical:

> It is, and is not, I am sane enough,
> Since you have come this place has hovered round me,
> This fabrication built of autumn roses,
> Then there's a goldish colour, different.
>
> And one gropes in these things as delicate
> Algae reach up and out, beneath
> Pale slow green surgings of the underwave,
> 'Mid these things older than the names they have,
> These things that are familiars of the god.
>
> [*CEP*, 194]

In our passage, the "Sub Mare" motif is indicated by the fluid's flowing *over* the grass, the very grass Sulpicia is reclining on.

THE NEXT LINE IN OUR passage also appears to be nonsensical: "Zeph-yrus, passing through her." This may be yet another return to the mythic mode, indeed, the appearance of "Zephyrus" suggests that it is; but Zeph-yrus here may simply indicate the wind. In light of the evidence adduced to show that Pound was probably writing about the clairvoyant seeing of a subtle body around the gross body of the beloved (Sulpicia), it is possible that this apparently nonsensical passage simply refers to the wind passing through Sulpicia's subtle body, the *augoeides,* rather than through her cor-poreal body. This reading makes sense of what is otherwise nonsensical, though the skeptical may—understandably—have recourse to some phrase like "rank folly."

There remain, for explication in our passage, only the two Latin phrases. "Deus nec laedit amantes" completes the "Pone metum Cerinthe," as men-tioned earlier. I said there that Pound had taken the phrase out of its original context, and it may be that by embedding it in this new context of a visionary erotic encounter, he has refocused its significance; perhaps rather than soothing the fear of the lover at the potential loss of the beloved to death (as in Sulpicia's poem), the phrase is meant as a reassur-ance for the lover who has "walked sheer into 'nonsense' " (*LE*, 431).

The "Hic mihi dies sanctus" which closes our passage is a particularly interesting one, in that the "mihi" seems to have an autobiographical force, as an authorial intrusion, a temporary setting aside of the mediating per-sonae of Sulpicia and her Cerinthus. Furthermore, the "sanctus," the ho-liness of the day, confirms the implicit spirituality with which Pound in-vests the passage throughout. For Pound, Sulpicia and Cerinthus have performed a rite there in the grass. The "sanctus" prescribes the tone of the passage as a whole.

A rereading of the passage, once the spade work has been done on the phrases which constitute it, reveals that it is not as fragmentary as it originally seemed. It is *superficially* fragmented; Pound moves, on the surface of the poem, from one mode of statement to another and back again, suggesting by the merest phrase those other of his poems and prose pieces which we need to recall to make the passage comprehensible (and some works the general reader cannot know, such as his notes). The passage is very elliptical, even excessively elliptical, but beneath the fragmentation there is one experience, approached in many ways. The implied poetics revealed by this passage is not the poetics of Pound the popularizer. There are two *Cantos,* an exoteric *Cantos* and an esoteric *Cantos,* and this passage is from the latter book.[33] . . .

Notes

1. Ezra Pound to Viola Baxter Jordan, 14 September 1933, Beinecke Library, Yale University, New Haven, Connecticut.

2. H.D., *End to Torment, A Memoir of Ezra Pound*, ed. Norman Holmes Pearson and Michael King (New York: New Directions, 1979), p. 43.

3. Pound wrote to Dorothy Shakespear, on 13 July 1912, about "Psychology and Troubadours" that "the thing is bad but has paragraphs. It is utterly—as a whole—incomprehensible—but that was necessary. One can not write & convey information at the same time." Ezra Pound and Dorothy Shakespear, *Their Letters 1909–1914*, ed. Omar Pound and A. Walton Litz (New York: New Directions, 1984), p. 131. Difficult, if not incomprehensible, Pound's early correspondence with Dorothy might have provided a good deal more evidence for this study than it does if Dorothy hadn't practiced self-censorship, as the editors note: "We believe that between 25 and 30 of the earliest letters are missing, probably burned. Dorothy would have certainly destroyed the most personal ones. This would be quite in keeping with her practice in later life of cutting small sections from letters and destroying the rest" (p. 369). I noted lacunae at several points in the correspondence when it seemed that the subject of visionary eroticism might well have come up. For instance, on 12 September 1911 Dorothy writes, cryptically, "Yes. How are intimacy & mystery combined? Therein lies the whole root of the matter" (p. 57). What teases is that this is in response to a letter which, though it touches on the mystical, does not discuss the relation between "intimacy & mystery," but which does end with the editorial information *"rest of letter missing."* Still, the correspondence is valuable, not only for particular information, but for the general portrait it provides of the young Pound. Of greatest relevance for this study, the letters document the very large place of the occult in Pound's interests at that time. With respect to poetic composition, for instance, Pound wrote to Dorothy on 28 October 1911, "As for the rest I wonder if we can not look at the beginning of things as a sort of divine phantasmagoria or vision or what you will and the 'vagueness' etc as a sort of smoke—an incident in the much more difficult process of drawing down the light, of embodying it, of building it into the stiffer materia of actualities. The whole thing a process of art, of the more difficult art in which we are half media & half creators." *Their Letters*, p. 76.

4. G. R. S. Mead, editor of the theosophical journal *The Quest*, where Pound's "Psychology and Troubadours" first appeared.

5. Charles Williams, *The Descent of the Dove* (Grand Rapids, Mich.: William B. Eerdmans, 1972).

6. Ibid., p. 11.

7. Ibid., p. 12.

8. Ibid., p. 13.

9. Matthew Black, ed., *Peake's Commentary on the Bible* (London: Thomas Nelson and Sons, 1962), p. 958.

10. Ezra Pound, *Personae* (New York: New Directions, 1971), p. 148.

11. See Ian F. A. Bell, *Critic as Scientist: The Modernist Poetics of Ezra Pound* (London and New York: Methuen & Co., 1981), for a fascinating account of Pound's scientific metaphors. Bell demonstrates how current Pound's language was by unearthing not only many of Pound's direct sources, but by demonstrating as well the degree to which such language was "in the air." Bell argues that Pound's use of the language of science to describe extraordinary experience was a function of the author's relations with his audience—that Pound was simply searching for an acceptable idiom. According to Bell, "The problem, again, was that of the trans- lation required by modernity: of finding an available lexicon for experience that was seemingly arcane and certainly private and communicatively unintelligible; of sustaining a public, and publishable, status for the myths of psychic or mystic phenomena" (p. 138). I find this argument convincing but incomplete. Pound, following the lead of the "trobar clus," hoped to be writing essays and poems that were available on two levels, one for the crowd, one for the elect. So there is always an element of obfuscation in his treatment of "mystic phenomena." Thus, Bell's insistence on Pound's desire to "seek a public voice" (p: 140) for such phe- nomena, his "*struggle* to maintain for the modern world the value of mystical perception" (p. 141), oversimplifies Pound's intent by collapsing Pound's two au- diences into "the modern world." Walter Baumann is surely right in arguing for the "magical" in Pound's late as well as early work: "behind the formidable 'sci- entific' vocabulary the same magic continued." W. Baumann, "Ezra Pound and Magic: Old World Tricks in a New World Poem," *Paideuma* 10 (Fall 1981): 202–24. Much of Pound's science is veneer-thin.

12. Pound's willingness to see a "permanent basis in humanity" may have been encouraged by Allen Upward. In *The Divine Mystery* Upward had said "I have to ask the reader to keep in mind that the earlier and later cults and beliefs that we have been considering flourished—as they still flourish—side by side, in the same geographical area, in the same city, and often in the same mind." A. Upward, *The Divine Mystery* (1915; rpt., Santa Barbara, Calif.: Ross-Erickson, 1976), p. 147. States of mind which once found a social expression persist without one, are recoverable.

13. Ezra Pound, "Terra Italica," in *Selected Prose*, ed. William Cookson (New York: New Directions, 1973), p. 56. For more on the *pecten cteis* see Peter Hamilton Laurie, "The Poet and the Mysteries," Ph.D. diss., Brown University, 1976, p. 5.

14. There have been three recent Lacanian readings of Pound's sexuality: Alan Durant, *Ezra Pound, Identity in Crisis* (Brighton: Harvester Press, 1981); Paul Smith,

Pound Revised (London: Croom Helm, 1983); Robert Casillo, "Anti-Semitism, Castration, and Usury in Ezra Pound," *Criticism* 25 (Summer 1983): 239–65. Although these three studies have their virtues, they do not address the occult dimension of Pound's sexuality. In a real way, then, their studies are strictly irrelevant in the context of my investigation. But, because they base their interpretations of Pound on many of the same passages that I deal with here, a few remarks about their work are in order. All three studies are highly critical of Pound and his work. Pound invites the ad hominem like no other poet in our tradition, and Durant, Smith, and Casillo exploit the opportunities. They mean to explain Pound's more conspicuous failings, his fascism, anti-Semitism, and sexual chauvinism, in terms of the Lacanian version of the castration complex. While the translation into Lacanian terminology does provide a coherent frame in which to view Pound's "phallocentrism," it obscures Pound's own understanding of sexuality. When Pound's views diverge from the Lacanian model, they are left out (intentionally or not). So, the "erotic medium" escapes notice in oversimplifications like this: "The propriety of the sexual act, then, depends upon its function. If it is part of the process of natural productiveness then sexuality is celebrated; if not, then it is despised and condemned as perverted." Smith, *Pound Revised*, p. 55.

These studies are radically reductive. I am not sure whether the fault lies in the Lacanian perspective, or in the heavy-handed way in which Lacan is applied, but the result is the same. Readers who want to understand Pound are less likely to find passages like the following helpful than an impediment: "Rebuttal of genital privation by replacement of the penile appendage in women can enable the fetishist to renounce the fact of anatomical difference, and so partially forestall the field of the symbolic by superimposing this continued defensive captation of the ego upon a previous visual suppression." Durant, *Ezra Pound*, pp. 129–30. James Hillman (among others) has convincingly argued that psychoanalytic readings are themselves fictions, sometimes useful fictions, but not "facts." See J. Hillman, *Healing Fictions* (Barrytown, N.Y.: Station Hill, 1983), pp. 1–49. While Lacan, I suspect, generally observes the distinction, Durant, Smith, and Casillo do not.

It is symptomatic of these studies that Durant ends his investigation with "by no means an easy question": "If the *Cantos* cannot in any way be read as Pound intended, since the emergence of desire everywhere undermines the repression which sponsors conscious, didactic meanings, the question arises if there are any conditions at all in which the poem can be read with pleasure" (pp. 186–87). What is particularly telling is that Durant tries to answer this question *theoretically*, but that his reading of the poem leads him to such a question itself calls into question its usefulness.

I believe that critics interested in a psychological explanation of Pound's sexuality would do better to start with James Hillman, "Toward the Archetypal Model of the Masturbation Inhibition," *Loose Ends* (Zurich: Spring Publications, 1975), pp. 105–25.

15. K. K. Ruthven, *A Guide to Ezra Pound's Personae* (1926) (Berkeley and Los Angeles: University of California Press, 1969), p. 52. For a note on Pound's use of sources in "Coitus," see Peter Davidson, "Giulio Romano at the Spring Marriage," *Paideuma* 11 (Winter 1982): 503–10. Davidson appends photographs of Romano's sixteenth-century frescoes from the Sala di Psiche of the Palazzo del Te in Mantua, photographs which amply document Romano's style.

16. "Trace" occurs frequently, as in "Canzone: Of Angels," and "Canzon."

17. Pound, in the passage preceding this one, places "our" loss between Cavalcanti and Petrarch. Ezra Pound, "Cavalcanti," in *Literary Essays of Ezra Pound*, ed. T. S. Eliot (New York: New Directions, 1968), p. 154.

18. Pound describes this "passage" of the beloved in several early poems; it is, I think, the subject of the first stanza of "Canzon" and of "Gentildonna." It's interesting that Pound seems to favor kinetic over static representations of the beloved seen in the radiant world, though static images do occur, as in "Canzon: Of Incense," where the lady simply wears a "cloak of graciousness" that "gloweth" about her. This is consistent with Pound's characterization of the same reality as the "universe of fluid force," with the emphasis on fluidity.

19. Ezra Pound, "Translator's Postscript," in Remy de Gourmont, *The Natural Philosophy of Love*, trans. Ezra Pound (New York: Rarity Press, 1931), and Ezra Pound, "The New Therapy," *New Age* 31 (16 March 1922): 259–60.

20. For a Lacanian reading of the "Postscript," see Durant, *Ezra Pound*, pp. 104–7.

21. Not all commentators think that Pound is being more than metaphorical in the postscript; Riddell, for instance, argues that "Pound's metaphors, which may appear more like a mystical physiology than a scientific text, cannot be taken literally, but can be read back into his theory of language and into his Imagist doctrine." Joseph N. Riddell, "Pound and the Decentered Image," *Georgia Review* 29 (Fall 1975): 573. While the latter is plausible, I must insist that the postscript is just what Riddell fears it is, "mystical physiology."

22. Hugh Kenner, *The Pound Era* (Berkeley: University of California Press), pp. 54–75.

23. Such as "her crotch like a young sapling" in 39/194, but that is, perhaps, simply simile.

24. Pound, holograph drafts for Canto 20, Beinecke Library.

25. In light of the preceding "physiological divagation" it is possible that "cortex" here refers not only to the tree but to the "evolutionary" effect of the experience on the lover's brain.

26. Ezra Pound, *Gaudier-Brzeska* (New York: New Directions, 1970), p. 145.

27. Tib.. 3.10.15. (Loeb translation).

28. Ezra Pound to Viola Baxter Jordan, 14 September 1933, Beinecke Library. He attributes the comparison to the "dark lady." Pound insisted on the dissociation in a letter of 17 April 1924 to William Bird as well, collected by D. D. Paige in *The Letters of Ezra Pound: 1907–1941* (New York: Harcourt, Brace and World, 1950), but the relevant sections were expurgated, presumably as offensive.

29. It is significant, surely, that Pound has "the flute" rather than "her flute."

30. As early as "Psychology and Troubadours" Pound had insisted on the possibility of a clean, but not visionary, sexuality: "In Catullus' superb epithalamium 'Collis O Heliconii,' we find the affair is strictly on one plane; the bride is what she is in Morocco today, and the function is 'normal,' and eugenic" (*SR*, 96). Of course, that he says "strictly on one plane" suggests that it could be on more than one.

31. As an index of the continuing density of our passage, it is worth noting that the phrase "gathered about her," used to describe the fauns, echoes the description of the hounds in Canto 17, cited earlier: "Leaping about her." Seemingly every phrase echoes another, or several others.

32. Durant, who also argues that the flute is phallic, seems to think "the fluid" here is "emission spilt on the grass." *Ezra Pound*, p. 182. Poets sing of many things, but not this.

33. Of course, even when Pound *intends* to be didactic he is often dauntingly difficult, as readers and critics alike attest. For an account of the nature of the difficulty Pound presents the reader, see James J. Wilhelm, *Il Miglior Fabbro: The Cult of the Difficult in Daniel, Dante, and Pound* (Orono, Maine: National Poetry Foundation, 1982). However, Wilhelm does not emphasize sufficiently, in his discussion of Pound, what he calls the "hermetic" element, the willful "opaqueness" of one who "does not want to promulgate [his] ideas to the vulgar crowd" (p. 3). This is always an *additional* difficulty when Pound addresses the erotic medium.

Bibliography

Cantos references are to *The Cantos of Ezra Pound*. London: Faber, 1975.

Abbreviations

CEP: Ezra Pound, *Collected Early Poems.*
LE: Ezra Pound, *Literary Essays.*
NPL: Remy de Gourmont, *The Natural Philosophy of Love*, tr. Ezra Pound. New York: Rarity Press, 1931.
P: Ezra Pound, *Personae: The Collected Shorter Poems.* New York: New Directions, 1971.
SR: Ezra Pound, *The Spirit of Romance.*

A Metaphysics of the State

PETER NICHOLLS

◆   ◆   ◆

I Ethics and Obligation

In view of Pound's increasingly instrumental claims for language, it is not surprising to find that [in the late 1930s] he began to reappraise the loosely dialectical structure of Cantos XXXI–LI. If the poem was to provide an effective guide to action, a whole series of questions about ethical "rightness" and obligation would have to be confronted more directly. The problem was clear from the first half of Canto XXXIX. There Pound had celebrated the practical intelligence, the "mythopoeic" habit of mind, but he had tended to use the Homeric world as a means of bracketing or suspending questions which we should normally ask about actions which are praised for their quality of directedness and motivation. It was in order to define these qualities more precisely that Pound, in 1937, began an intensive study of the texts of Confucius and Mencius.

He had long been interested in China, and indeed Noel Stock suggests that he had been reading Confucius as early as 1907.[1] We know from his correspondence that Pound was again exploring Confucius's writings (probably the *Ta Hio*) in 1914,[2] and there are sporadic references to Confucian ethics in his articles from then on. His enthusiasm intensified during 1922 and 1923, the period in which he drafted the Confucian Canto XIII. Here

Pound celebrated Confucianism as a doctrine of responsibility and order, contrasting it with the "other-worldliness" of Christianity:

> And Kung gave the words 'order'
> and 'brotherly deference'
> And said nothing of the 'life after death'.

Pound's interest in Confucius continued to grow. In 1928 he published a translation of the *Ta Hio*; by 1934, he was speaking "as a Confucian," and a year later he wrote of "the scalding need for Confucian teaching."[3]

With the exception of Canto XIII, Pound's interest in the Chinese philosopher had so far made little direct impact on the poem. When he returned to the Confucian texts in 1937, however, the aim of his researches was in part to discover a coherent and systematic ethical base for *The Cantos*. It was at this point that Pound's deep attraction to classical mythology came into conflict with his new commitment to Confucian ideals. The collision of interests became a major theme of *Guide to Kulchur*:

> The Homeric world, very human. The *Odyssey* high water mark for the adventure story, as for example Odysseus on the spar after shipwreck. Sam Smiles never got any further in preaching self-reliance. A world of irresponsible gods, a very high society without recognizable morals, the individual responsible to himself.[4]

Pound's feelings about the *Odyssey* are certainly more mixed than they had been in Canto XXXIX, and there is here a definite uneasiness about speaking of a "high society" which lacked "recognizable morals." It is the emphasis on social "irresponsibility" which explains Pound's growing hostility to Greek culture and his preference for the Roman:

> Plato's *Republic* notwithstanding, the greek philosophers did not feel communal responsibilities. . . . The sense of coordination, of the individual in a milieu is not in them. . . .
> Rome was the responsible ruler. The concentration or emphasis on eternity is not social. The sense of responsibility, the need for coordination of individuals expressed in Kung's teaching differs radically both from early Christian absolutism and from the maritime adventure morals of Odysseus or the loose talk of argumentative greeks.[5]

In *Guide to Kulchur*, much is made of the capacity of Platonism to subvert the social order, yet, briskly dismissive as Pound's argument is, one cannot help feeling that he is wrestling with his own strong attraction to that sensuous neo-Platonism which had played such an important part in the earlier Cantos. What Pound is seeking is a way of integrating the visionary impulse into the social instincts which underlie "responsibility"; he thus draws a fundamental distinction between "the ecstatic-beneficent-and-benevolent, contemplation of the divine love, the divine splendour with goodwill toward others" and "the bestial, namely the fanatical, the man on fire with God and anxious to stick his snotty nose into other men's business."[6] The distinction suggests an important transition from the visionary affection and eroticism of the earlier Cantos to an idea of "benevolence" as that socially motivated feeling which so far has emerged explicitly only in the historical sections of the poem.

   This development, aided by his study of the Confucian texts, was closely related to Pound's search for a position from which to oppose the liberal dichotomy of state and individual. . . .

II Pound's China

By 1938, Pound had decided upon two main sources for the next sequence of Cantos: de Mailla's *Histoire générale de la Chine* and *The Life and Works of John Adams.*[7] Once he had made his way through these multivolume works, he composed the sequence with unusual speed. Cantos LIII and LIV were in typescript by February 1939, and only two days later he reported to Ronald Duncan that he was busy with Canto LVI.[8] At the beginning of March he was working on Canto LXVII, and on 6 March he informed Henry Swabey that he was "retyping Cantos 52/71."[9]

   The speed with which this sequence took shape was partly due to Pound's extensive reliance on two main sources. Yet one suspects too that, as the political situation in Europe grew more uncertain, he was hastening to produce a body of materials which might provide guidance in the crisis to come. In fact there are signs that Pound conceived these Cantos as an act of direct political intervention, that they were designed to provide precedents for the fascist regime, and perhaps even sanctions for Mussolini's seizure of power. " 'History,' " Pound wrote in Canto LIV (p. 280), " 'is a school book for princes' " and the various references to contemporary Italy were surely intended to create an implicit meshing of the modern culture with that of Confucian China. Canto LII makes this alignment explicit ("Thus we lived on through sanctions"—p. 257), and there are subsequent references to "the first Quindecennio" (LIV, p. 282), to "a charter of labour" (LIV, p. 287), the "confino" (LV, p. 297), installation of granaries (LV, p. 298), the agricultural policy of "Ammassi" (LXI, p. 335), and to Italian submarine maneuvers in honor of Hitler's visit in 1938 (LIV, pp. 279–80). At one point Pound seems to address Mussolini directly: "TSONG of TANG put up granaries / somewhat like those you want to establish" (LV, p. 298). These sporadic references might not seem particularly important given the room they occupy in Cantos LII–LXXI, but the whole sequence is concerned with the idea of "revolution" and, as the "Make it New" ideograms in Canto LIII suggest, the central notions of "renewal" and legitimacy were, for Pound, implicitly linked to the *rivoluzione continua* of Italian fascism.

The purpose of these new Cantos was to explore what he referred to in *Guide to Kulchur* as "the ideas of authority, of participation, of duty."[10] In view of what has already been said of his developing idea of the state, it was perhaps not surprising that Pound should have been drawn to the Confucian history of de Mailla. The early Chinese histories differed from the epic narratives of the West in several important respects. In the first place, they were generally lacking in heroic and tragic elements, and they exemplified none of that moral neutrality so characteristic of the Western epic.[11] They had, too, a directly practical function and were aimed not at a small group of scholars but at a bureaucratic elite whose ability to learn from the past was a mark of their aptitude for coping with current affairs of state.[12] The actions of individuals only occupied a place in such records insofar as they related to the functioning of a clearly defined social group. Confucian historians were primarily concerned with type and reoccurrence, but—this was important for Pound—their lack of attention to the individual did not lead to any "intellectualistic" overview. One scholar observes of these chronicles that they are characterized by

> on the one hand, the lack of personal features—the individual is absorbed into and disappears behind the group, of which he is but a specimen; and on the other, the absence of any abstraction which would allow a synthesis—concrete detail predominates and despite its repetitive character stands in the way of generalisations.[13]

Here, then, was a form of history which might provide an alternative to the heroic "irresponsibility" of the Homeric *paideuma*, and one which promoted an idea of continuity and renewal without sacrificing specificity of detail.

The attention to a continuous body of ethical values also helps to explain the lack of interest shown by many Chinese historians in the military deeds and stratagems which make up such a vital component of the historical *materia* of the West. When, for example, Chu Hsi came to edit the *Comprehensive Mirror* (the principal source for de Mailla's *Histoire*) he rigorously excised the accounts of military campaigns which figured in the original records.[14] This was but one example of the general tendency to see the story of internal conflicts and barbarian invasions as subordinate to the main theme of China's enduring institutions.[15]

Pound was attracted to this type of history partly because its rhythms were so alien to the Western intelligence, and partly because it supplied a model of recurring patterns of order and stability across massive tracts of time. As a result, the Chinese Cantos exhibit a more deliberately abstractive handling of the past, reading history with an eye to its hidden "typological" configurations. This has an immediate impact on the language of the poem. A clipped shorthand substitutes naming for evocation, producing a narrative more concerned with forerunners and "reincarnations" than with the immediate (and momentary) object of its attention:

> KONG sank in abuleia. TANG rising.
> And the first TANG was KAO TSEU, the starter.   *a.d. 618*
> And that year died Li-Chi that had come to his rescue
> with a troop of 10,000. The war drums beat at her funeral
> And her husband drove back the tartars, Tou-kou-hoen.
> [LIV, p. 285]

Pound refuses to linger on these events, partly because the motif of decline and fall suggests a historical principle, but also because the pace of the narration and the vicissitudes it records are designed as a contrast to the recurring emphasis on endurance and stability (a few lines later we have, "Built thus for two hundred years TANG"). That we discover only a line later that Li-Chi was a woman (daughter of the Emperor Kao Tseu) is typical of the way in which throughout the sequence Pound obstructs our interest in the individual. Compare these lines from earlier in the same Canto: "OUEN kept up mulberry trees / and failed with his family" (LIV, p. 285). It is this kind of writing which has often been considered loose and slovenly.[16] The degree of deliberateness behind Pound's second phrase, however, should make us pause, for the almost brutal lack of consequence registered in that line (and in many others) does seem to represent a deliberate rhetorical strategy. Pound wants the reader to gain from this idiom a sense of confrontation with an alien culture, a culture for which such "failure" is less an example of personal moral weakness than of a loss of connection with values which are deeply embedded within a complex and continuous structure of social practices. There is no prying into domestic intimacies here; Pound's deliberate lack of specificity is meant to point up Ouen's "failure" as a deviation from a permanent moral principle, and his chosen idiom places it uncomprisingly within the public domain.

This section of the poem has no place for the dramatically rich "antinomianism" which gave color to the early Cantos. Instead, Pound's handling of his ancient subject matter and the elaborate decorums which it records yields a highly stylised idiom and format of presentation. The result is to create a past which is conditioned less by historical density than by an almost "spatial" feeling for events situated in time. The rapid variation of names, dynasties, and regimes actually tends to displace the strictly linear movement of Pound's source. Things recur and endure, and we have the sense of events coexisting in time rather than fulfilling some progressive evolutionary design. Pound's concern is with continuity and extent ("the Wall was from Yu-lin to Tsé-ho"—LIV, p. 285), and the effect is one of an almost timeless interpenetration of past and present as history yields its "permanent" moral insights ("Law of MOU is law of the just middle, the pivot"—LIII, p. 269). Within this hugely extended past, the individual no longer appears as the primary basis for historical development, and Pound attends instead to the continuities of language, law and custom which gave Chinese culture its appearance of enduring stability.

In line with this new perspective, there is an underlying sense of the land as a determining factor in China's past (as Karl Mannheim remarks in his discussion of conservative thought, land is often seen as "the real foundation on which the state rests and develops, and only land can really make history"[17]). Pound's concern with what Mannheim calls "time-transcending, spatially determined, material entities as the basis of history" arises out of a feeling for land as a factor more fundamental than class or money in determining the particular character of Chinese society. We can already detect his emotional attraction to the vast extendedness of the Chinese landscape in the poems of *Cathay*, but, where in the earlier volume this was tied to a sense of seasonal recurrence and enduring patterns of social manners, the immenseness of China's land mass sponsors in the Dynastic Cantos a reverence for the authority and institutions which have guaranteed its apparent political stability ("1600 leagues of canals 40 ft wide for the / honour of YANG TI of SOUI"—LIV, p. 285). While many of the poems of *Cathay* make that landscape a locus of separation and loss, in the Chinese Cantos the land is an image of totality, at once the source of productivity and "authentic" labor, and a basis which sustains the all-pervasive forms of law and custom. The lack of particularity in this section is directly related to Pound's sense of the land as a kind of abstract presence (it is, we might say, land rather than landscape, lacking as it does his characteristic attention to specific natural objects).

The impact of a "spatial" view of history on the writing is easy to discern. There is a new transparency of diction, a clear, almost stately precision:

> Grain price was high when TAÏ entered
> > a small measure cost one bolt of silk, entire.
> If a prince piles up treasure
> > he shares only his surplus
> Lock not up the people's subsistence.
>
> > > [LIV, p. 286]

The idiom has, too, a homespun (and deliberately "unpoetic") concreteness ("Make census / Give rice to their families / Give them money for rites"— LVI, p. 308), and the prosody affirms a world of fundamental clarities by employing the end-stopped measure of the earlier visionary sequences:

> > RITE is:
> Nine days before the first moon of spring time,
> that he fast. And with gold cup of wheat-wine
> > that he go afield to spring ploughing
> > that he plough one and three quarters furrows
> > > and eat beef when this rite is finished. . . .
> > > > [LIII, p. 271]

Loss of order is registered by an undermining of this language; the writing becomes slatternly, the firmer measure verging momentarily on dissolution:

> MOU-TSONG drove out the taozers
> > but refused to wear mourning for HIEN his father.
> The hen sang in MOU's time, racin', jazz dancin'
> and play-actors, Tartars still raidin'
> MOU's first son was strangled by eunuchs. . . .
> > > [LV, p. 291]

From the dialectic of tones across the sequence we can see that Pound is trying to work toward a language of moral injunction. The difficulty is that of articulating the "permanent" truths without lapsing into what is, for him, the highly inappropriate but all too accessible rhetoric of biblical didacticism. Pound finds this hard to avoid ("Was observer of seasons, saying: / Take not men from the plough"—LIV, p. 285), but the purging out of archaism and the refusal now to use the privileged singing voice as the vehicle of "higher" insights are signs of his attempt to construct a newly transparent moral discourse, "luminous" in its simplicity and directness, and penetrating back beyond the perverse "selfishness" of Christianity to a common language closely in touch with man's essential nature. Yet previous interventions by "ego scriptor" have been awkward enough, and one detects a certain embarrassment, a worry about pompous attitudinizing, behind the new didactic tone. Hence Pound's self-conscious levity and the often clumsy use of colloquialism ("jobs for two millyum men"—LIV, p. 285), which are intended to counterbalance the more studiously honorific passages ("Died KAO TSEU . . . Died the Empress Tchang-sun CHI"—LIV, p. 286) and to enforce a toughly pragmatic idealism: "The 10th a charter of labour / and the last on keepin' up kulchur" (LIV, p. 287).

The new didactic tone is directly related to Pound's increasing commitment to an ideal of paternalistic authority. As the poet is drawn more to models of benign but absolute authority, so he is less willing to trust to the reader's ability to "infer" relations between the materials assembled in the poem. The didactic tone is maintained throughout, and with this goes a starker and more stylized version of Pound's concept of "strong" government than anything we have had so far. *The Cantos* now celebrates rulers such as Yong Tching, who "sought good of the people, active, absolute, loved" (LXI, p. 334), and Pound quotes from the *Mencius* to affirm that "A good governor is as wind over grass" (LII, p. 266).[18]

It is tempting to read such passages simply as covert endorsements for what Pound had already described as Mussolini's "gentle" authority,[19] but, although this hovers in the background, the Chinese Cantos are also engaged in an attempt to refer ethical questions to a "pre-political" level where the paradigm of justice is encoded in myth. Much depends here upon our acceptance or rejection of that principle of "benevolence" which, for Pound, locates the origin of law in nature and human nature. In these Cantos, vast spaces intervene between ruler and subject, giving the relationship an almost iconic quality. For the Western liberal—and this is the point Pound makes by implication—such distances are the sign of the individual's alienation from the state; for Pound himself, they function to disperse power and to render authority truly "indirect." The imperial fiat expresses not the will of one man, but sanctioned precepts which are governed by the interrelation of social and natural orders. Hence, I think, Pound's attention to ancient rites, superstitions, and ideas of "cosmic" justice which, if located in the Western tradition, would give rise only to Voltairean ridicule. The function of these ominous disturbances of the phenomenal order is to deflect instances of immoral behavior from being questions of consciousness and self-direction and to register them instead as violations of nature.

It is to the point to note here that Pound's 1937 study of Chinese texts also included a close reading of the *Mencius*, a work which provides a subtle extension of ideas in the Confucian canon. Mencius is best known for his theory of the goodness of human nature. Whereas, in Legge's words, "the utterances of Confucius on the subject of our nature were few and brief,"[20] Mencius took this as his major theme. Human nature, he said, is motivated by a benevolence which is rooted in the "heart" and which distinguishes man from beast. Pound's idea of the disposition to virtue ("the *directio voluntatis*") finds an echo here, since Mencius sees morality not as an arbitrary and artificial set of rules imposed on man from outside, but as a formal principle of human nature. Morality has a natural base in man's being ("Mencius said, 'All men have a mind which cannot bear to see the sufferings of others' "[21]), and Heaven, in contrast to its Christian counterpart, is not seen as a source of legislation removed from man: " 'Benevolence, righteousness, propriety, and knowledge are not infused into us from without. We are certainly furnished with them.' "[22] For Mencius, social obligations are defined through the exercise of this natural benevolence, and the complex hierarchy of feudal relationships is bound together by feelings of sociability which have their origin in familial affection. There is here a difference in emphasis between Mencius's and Confucius's thought: as D. C. Lau observes, "for Confucius benevolence was the totality of the moral qualities in man. For Mencius, benevolence was more specifically the virtue that characterizes the relationship between parent and child."[23]

It is Mencian "benevolence" which underlies Pound's idea of paternalistic authority in the Chinese Cantos. Political obligations are traced back to the organic unit of the family, and Pound's new attention to filial values comes to displace the erotic sexuality which had played such an important role in the earlier Cantos. In view of this, it is at first sight surprising to find that of the very few references made here to familiar texts, most are to Guido's Canzone. These reminders of visionary passion seem quite at odds with the ethos of Confucian China until we realize that Pound is seeking to free them of their libidinal associations and transform them into signs of the rectitude which governs the "social affections."[24] Guido's poem

is now engaged in a new context, developing those hints of authority and
"right reason" which we have already discerned in Canto XXXVI:

> De libro CHI-KING sic censeo
>   wrote the young MANCHU, CHUN TCHI,
> less a work of the mind than of affects
> brought forth from the inner nature
> here sung in these odes.
> Urbanity in externals, virtu in internals
>   some in a high style for the rites
> some in humble;
> for Emperors; for the people
> all things are here brought to precisions
> that we shd/ learn our integrity
> that we shd/ attain our integrity
> Ut animum nostrum purget, Confucius ait, dirigatque
> ad lumen rationis
>   perpetuale effecto/
> That this book keep us in due bounds of office
>   the norm
> fshow what we shd/ take into action;
>   what follow within and persistently
> CHI KING ostendit incitatque. Vir autem rectus
> et libidinis expers ita domine servat
> with faith, never tricky, obsequatur parentis
> nunquam deflectat
> all order comes into such norm
> igitur meis encomiis, therefor this preface. . . .
>   [LIX, p. 324]

The Latin is from Lacharme's translation of Chun Tchi's "preface" to the
Shih King, and Pound introduces the phrase from the Canzone ("perpetuale
effecto") to bring that earlier evocation of effective intelligence into line
with the Confucian principle of "reason." The "light" of the "possible
intellect" (its "tract or locus") is now the *lumen rationis,* the "norm" of good
government. "Right reason" thus denotes a natural law rooted in the
virtues of filiality and self-discipline whose pervasiveness and "perpetual
effect" constitute the immanent authority of the "ethical state." As we
have seen, Pound tends to read the Canzone as an expression of the control
and refinement of passion, and in that sense the "rectitude" of the Italian
poem, its precision of word and rhythm, is analogous to the Confucian

"norm." Once the two are brought together, the idea of "affection" can be made to encompass the whole hierarchy of feudal relationships ("domine servat," "obsequatur parentis").

This passage is pivotal in the development of *The Cantos*: "illumination" no longer entails fragmentary and discontinuous insights, but reveals instead a metaphysical principle of formal hierarchy. We have, in fact, the fulfillment of that "reversal" of the neo-Platonic theory of emanation described above. Hugh Kenner's insight, that Pound's Confucianism is indelibly colored by the very Taoism he so ardently rejects, is of central importance here, though the effect of his argument is to make the position of the Chinese Cantos a somewhat equivocal one. Before 1943, says Kenner, Pound's "need was for a moralist of statecraft, not a metaphysician," and he goes on to crystallize this distinction in the varying use of the word *tao*. Whereas in the *Analects* this signifies a "unitive, normative" ethics, in the *Chung Yung* it is "a principle [which] pervades not only human conduct but the universe. . . . Pound was to call it "the process"). Kenner argues that it was not until he had finished work on the Chinese Cantos that Pound "came to grips with the doctrine of the pivot."[25]

It is clear, however, from the essay on Mencius that Pound had been studying the *Chung Yung* in 1937. Furthermore, he had already used the word "process" to describe the "way" (*tao*), explaining that "at no point does the Confucio-Mencian ethic split away from organic nature. . . . The nature of things is good. The *way* is the process of nature, *one*, in the sense that the chemist and biologist so find it."[26] It is, I think, more accurate to describe this statement as "neo-Confucian" in its blending of elements; it is certainly not "Taoist" in Kenner's sense of "a tradition of thought that talks of harmony with the universe rather than of modes of government."[27] Pound castigates that form of "quietism" throughout the Chinese Cantos, but his own conception of "statecraft" could hardly be described as a secular one. In fact Canto LV has already provided this metaphysical definition of "rationality":

> Lux enim per se omnem in partem
> Reason from heaven, said Tcheou Tun-y
>   enlighteneth all things
> seipsum seipsum diffundit, risplende
>   Is the beginning of all things, et effectu. . . .
>   [LV, p. 298]

"Reason" is here conceived as pervasive order and "proportion" emblematized by light; it is quite clearly a cosmic principle. The Latin refers us to the diffusive *virtù* of light in Grosseteste's cosmology, and this is aligned with the Confucian concept of "reason" as underlying the ordered operation of all things. That Pound's Confucianism contained this metaphysics even before he began work on the *Chung Yung* is confirmed by his early translation of the *Ta Hio.* Where, in the 1928 version, we find "the luminous principle of reason which we receive from the sky," Pound's later translation situates that "light" in "the process of looking straight into one's own heart and acting on the results."[28]

It seems clear, then, that the references to light in the Chinese Cantos support a metaphysics of the state, a view of political relationships which Pound now describes variously as "totalitarian," "hierarchical," or "organic": "The corporate concept has implicit in itself the idea of organic composition. The liver is not the rival of the lungs; the small glands do not repeat the function of the heart but work as complements to it."[29] At moments like this, Pound is simply rephrasing the fundamental tenets of fascist ideology. Elsewhere, however, he tries to express the concept in less overtly political terms, making "totalitarian" synonymous with "totality" and referring to a "hierarchy of values."[30] It was partly because of Pound's way of searching history for models of a "metaphysical" order that he came to see the eighteenth century as a period of radical dislocation. The rationalism of the Encyclopaedists destroyed the *"sense of gradations*—thing[s] neither perfect nor utterly wrong, but arranged in a cosmos, an order, stratified, having relations one with another."[31] In his later version of this essay, Pound explains that "the degrees of light and motion, the whole metaphoric richness begin to perish. From a musical concept of man they dwindle downward to a mathematical concept."[32] These remarks contain many of the contradictions which were implicit in Pound's metaphysics of the state. How, for example, was this set of views to be maintained in the contemporary world? One solution was to accept the ideological claims of fascism, as Pound had done in his metaphor of the "body politic." Another was to work to recreate the lost "metaphoric richness," though this implied that the paradigm of the state could be constructed only in discourse and not in reality. A third possibility was to take as a model a historically remote society where the chain of authority was simply and clearly defined, and where "nature" was still conceived of as a simultaneously material and sacral entity.

Although Pound was, as we shall see, quite prepared to accept Mussolini's "ruralization" policies and his promotion of agrarian Catholicism as authentic signs of the reconstitution of such a model, he was perhaps wiser than he knew in directing his poem back toward ancient China. The "hierarchical" model depended upon a rudimentary division of labor and a low level of economic competition; Mencian "benevolence" could not survive as an ordering principle in the face of the "false" equality of the marketplace, and had Pound devoted these Cantos to modern Italy his controlling concepts would have stood starkly revealed as but an ideological "camouflage." Yet the attention to ancient China also had its disadvantages, since it now became clearer than ever that Pound's ideal state could have a material basis only in a precapitalist economy. "Mencius distinguishes a tax from a share, he is for an economy of abundance," said Pound, and he concluded that "Mercantilism is incompatible with Mencius."[33]

Although the Chinese Cantos make much of the "distributive policies" of enlightened rulers, the implied link with Pound's Douglasian theories is tenuous to say the least. In fact, he was drawn to the feudal society of early China partly because its economy seemed to operate less in terms of money than of "goods." The development of mercantilist interests could only weaken a social structure based on moral principles of "responsibility" and "obligation"; Pound had already spoken of "the damage done in England by commutation of duty of overlords to their people into mere money payments."[34]

This growing attraction to simpler, feudal societies was closely related to Pound's changing view of the artist's role. The new paternalistic tone of the Chinese Cantos was in part a product of his movement away from his early liberal notions of the avant-garde toward a conception of the artist as spokesman for the values of the just state. The artist's heightened perceptivity was no longer the mark of his marginal status, but rather a measure of that special freedom which brought with it clearly defined duties and responsibilities. The feudal model thus entailed a redefinition of the writer's role:

> Liberty is not defendable on a static theory. Certain measures of liberty are *de facto* possessed first by the "small number of people," secondly by the official aristocracy, who assume habitual exemptions and do not discuss anything, thirdly by bohemia and the intelligentsia who feel little or no responsibility but who discuss everything. Fourthly in a clumsier manner by those who have easy money.[35]

The "small number of people" refers, presumably, to the phrase Pound constantly quotes from Machiavelli ("Gli uomini vivono in pochi") and suggests the familiar ideal of a natural aristocracy. The right to freedom of this group is paramount; Pound implies that as producers of culture its members enjoy a privilege which is superior, but analogous, to that of the "official aristocracy," which possesses lands and titles but is intellectually inert. One might not expect Pound to be so deferential to this second "aristocracy," but there is a deliberately hierarchical ranking of the four groups, "habitual exemptions" standing in contrast to the "clumsiness" of "easy money." These remarks involve more than a conventional disdain for the *nouveau riche*, since. . . . Pound does seem to think of property as a sort of material equivalent to writing.

A particular sense of "property" is involved here, and in comparing the writer to the "official aristocrat" who is free *de facto* because of his hereditary possession of landed wealth, Pound is making a tacit connection between ownership and social obligation. This entails a basic division between "permanent" property and that which is consumed on acquisition, and Pound's attachment to feudal particularism depends in part upon the concept of property defined through ownership of land (it is implicit in his line of thought that land should represent a communal heritage rather than a personal inheritance). Not only does land embody a system of rights and entitlements, it is also, like writing, a source of value which cannot be exhausted through appropriation.[36] Taken together, these qualities make land a property which has none of the disadvantages of "artificial" wealth produced by industry and commerce. An idea of stewardship is involved, land becoming the ground of right and social responsibility in somewhat the same way as artistic production provides the implicitly claimed basis for Pound's natural aristocracy.

One consequence of this set of ideas is to make the role of the reader an increasingly passive one. A certain amount of confidence in the writer's authority is needed in the Chinese Cantos, particularly since Pound's doctrine of "nature" is taken to be self-evident and fundamental in the same way that land was the basis of the social structure he describes. We might say too that the "metaphoric richness" of his feudal China is arguably the only means by which Pound can now avoid ideological "closure." . . . Pound would find it harder to give credibility to his metaphysics of the state when he began to seek it in materials which were both less remote in time and less amenable to a predominantly literary construction. . . .

Notes

Cantos references are to *The Cantos of Ezra Pound.* London: Faber, 1975.

1. Stock, *Life,* p. 220. For Pound's 1937 researches, see "Mang Tsze (The Ethics of Mencius)" (July 1938), *SP,* p. 96.

2. Letter to Homer Pound ([?] 1914), YL no. 365, p. 1.

3. "Mr Eliot's Looseness," *New English Weekly,* v, no. 4 (10 May 1934) p. 96; "Towards Orthology," *New English Weekly,* vi, no. 26 (11 Apr 1935) p. 534.

4. *GK,* p. 38.

5. Ibid.

6. Ibid., p. 223.

7. J.A.M. de Moyriac de Mailla, *Histoire générale de la Chine, ou annales de cet empire: traduites du Tong-Kien-Kang-Mou,* 13 vols (Paris, 1777–85); *The Works of John Adams,* ed. C. F. Adams, 10 vols (Boston, Mass., 1850–6).

8. Letter to Olga Rudge (21 Feb 1939), YL no. 1747, p. 1; letter to Ronald Duncan (23 Feb 1939), YL no. 1748, p. 1.

9. Letter to Katue Kitasono (3 Mar 1939), YL no. 1750, p. 1; letter to Henry Swabey (6 Mar 1939), YL no. 1752, p. 1.

10. *GK,* p. 43.

11. See, for example, D. C. Twitchett, "Chinese Biographical Writing," in *Historians of China and Japan,* ed. W. E. Beasley and E. G. Pulleyblank (London, 1961) p. 110 (cited hereafter as *Historians*). On the absence of "moral neutrality," see J. R. Levenson and F. Schurmann, *China: An Interpretive History* (Berkeley, Calif., 1969) p. 53.

12. See E. Balazs, "L'Histoire comme guide de la pratique bureaucratique," *Historians,* p. 87; and J. Needham, *The Grand Titration* (London, 1969) p. 241.

13. Balazs, in *Historians,* p. 78.

14. See J. Gray, "Historical Writing in Twentieth Century China," ibid., p. 194.

15. See Balazs, ibid., p. 82; and J. Harrison, *The Chinese Empire* (New York, 1972) p. 8. This undermines somewhat the importance which G. Mancuso, *Pound e la Cina* (Milan, 1974) p. 38, attaches to Pound's failure to refer to peasant uprisings in China.

16. Davie, *Ezra Pound: Poet as Sculptor,* p. 161, dismisses the writing of these Cantos as "pathological and sterile," mainly on account of Pound's abusive treatment of Taoism.

17. Mannheim, in *Essays on Sociology and Social Psychology,* p. 112.

18. See *The Works of Mencius,* trs. J. Legge, in *The Chinese Classics,* 5 vols (repr. Hong Kong, 1960) ii, p. 238. Legge's translation is the one used by Pound (see *L,* p. 297).

19. *JM,* p. v.

20. *Mencius,* trs. Legge, p. 57.

21. Ibid., p. 201.

22. Ibid., pp. 402–3.

23. Introduction to *Mencius,* trs. D. C. Lau (Harmondsworth, 1970) p. 41.

24. See C. K. Yang, Introduction to M. Weber, *The Religion of China* (New York, 1951) p. xxx: "Orgiastic and ecstatic elements, which might disturb the harmony of the social order or generate deviational tendencies, were thoroughly expurgated from the classics by Confucius and were suppressed from popular religiosity by rulers."

25. Kenner, *The Pound Era,* pp. 446, 455.

26. "Mang Tsze," *SP,* p. 101.

27. Kenner, *The Pound Era,* p. 456.

28. *Ta Hio, The Great Learning* (1928; repr. London, 1936) p. 7; *Confucius,* p. 27.

29. "I violini di Marconi" (18 July 1936), *EPM,* p. 393.

30. "Mang Tsze," *SP,* p. 104.

31. "The Jefferson-Adams Correspondence," *North American Review,* ccxliv, no. 2, p. 317.

32. *Impact,* p. 178.

33. "Mang Tsze," *SP,* pp. 100, 105.

34. *GK,* p. 261.

35. "Freedom de facto" (c 1940–1), *SP,* p. 275.

36. Pound notes of Mencius's economics ("Mang Tsze," *SP,* p. 108) that "The 'use' is utterly undodgeable. It does not mean exhaust."

Abbreviations

Confucius: Ezra Pound, *Confucius.*

Davie, *Poet as Sculptor*: Davie, Donald, *Ezra Pound: Poet as Sculptor.* London: Routledge & Kegan Paul, 1965.

EPM: *Ezra Pound and Music,* ed. R. M. Schafer. London: Faber, 1978.

GK: Ezra Pound, *Guide to Kulchur.*

Impact: Ezra Pound, *Impact. Essays on Ignorance and the Decline of American Civilization,* ed. Noel Stock. Chicago: Henry Regnery, 1960.

JM: Ezra Pound, *Jefferson and/or Mussolini.* New York: Liveright, 1970.

L: Ezra Pound, *Selected Letters.*

Mannheim, *Essays on Sociology and Social Psychology*: K. Mannheim, *Essays on Sociology and Social Psychology,* ed. P. Kecskemeti. London, 1953.

SP: Ezra Pound, *Selected Prose.*

YL: Yale Collection of American Literature, Letters of Ezra Pound. Beinecke Rare Book and Manuscript Library, Yale University Library.

Inventing Confucius

HUGH KENNER

◆　◆　◆

"ESTHETIC FINISH" IS APT TO MEAN "covering one's tracks." Pound's habit of not covering them keeps his processes before our eyes, and his reverence for tradition. "Tradition" (*trans* + *dare*) means "handing on." The Japanese names in *Cathay* register such a process: China to Japan to South Kensington. Similarly Divus's name in Canto I registers the existence of a Renaissance Latin Homer, and French phrases in the Chinese History Cantos an Enlightenment intermediary. And in Canto XIII, the Canto about Kung, enough proper names retain French conventions of transliteration to make the immediate source unmistakable: *Les Quatre Livres de Philosophie Morale et Politique de la Chine,* traduits du Chinois par M. G. Pauthier. My copy is dated "Paris, 1841." Pound's, of whatever printing, came to him at the time of *Cathay*,[1] 1914, bringing him a Confucius one could imagine speaking French maxims. Canto XIII presents such a Confucius:

> "When the prince has gathered about him
> "All the savants and artists, his riches will be fully employed."

("Savants" acknowledges Pauthier's idiom; "artists" is a link with the Sigismundo of Canto VIII. The authority is Pauthier's *Tchoung-Young,* xx–12: "dès l'instant qu'il aura attiré près de lui tous les savans et les artistes, aussitôt ses richesses seront suffisament mises en usage.") That was his first Confucius, commonsensical, practical, drawn chiefly from the *Analects* ("Les Entretiens Philosophiques"). It was also, so far as we can tell, the first Confucius known to China.

The *Analects,* despite a proportion of doubtful materials[2] in the last five of its twenty sections, seems on the whole an authentic record of things Confucius said. *The Book of Mencius,* almost as old, seems a pretty reliable record of the thought of a disciple of the disciples of Confucius's grandson. Between them they portray such a sage as Pauthier's idiom could domesticate: "*Sse* dépasse le but; *Chang* ne l'atteint pas," with the question, "Alors *Sse* est-il supérieur à *Chang?*" and the answer, "Dépasser, c'est comme ne pas atteindre;" whence

> And he said
>> "Anyone can run to excesses,
> It is easy to shoot past the mark,
> It is hard to stand firm in the middle."

But here we encounter Chu Hsi once more;[3] for Chu Hsi, the great twelfth-century neo-Confucian, detached from the *Li Chi,* that long Han Dynasty compilation on ceremonial usages, two sections which, added to the *Analects* and the *Mencius,* have ever since constituted the Four Books of Confucian China. In so doing Chu Hsi invented the Kung we know. For when the *Ta Hio,* Great Learning ("Great Digest"), is added Confucius becomes systematic, and when the *Chung Yung* is added, the Doctrine of the Mean, what Pound was one day to call "The Unwobbling Pivot," he becomes metaphysical.

Pound paid attention to the *Ta Hio* early; not long after writing the Kung Canto he rendered it "into the American language" from Pauthier's French, for publication (1928) by the University of Washington Book Store, Seattle.[4] It was 15 years before the *Chung Yung* seized his attention; during those years his need was for a moralist of statecraft, not a metaphysician.

The *Ta Hio,* meanwhile, was something to believe in. It tells us that the men of old, wishing their kingdoms to benefit by the luminous principle of reason which we receive from the sky, perforce commenced by penetrating and sounding what Pauthier blandly calls "les principes des actions," and moved on through moral knowledge and self-improvement to the rectification of their families and their states; whence peace and "la bonne harmonie" in the world. Though scholars find rhetorical chains of this kind suspiciously post-Confucian, the *Ta Hio* is anyhow very old, and Pound was happy to accept Chu Hsi's judgment that the first seven paragraphs had been written by Kung himself, "on the bo leaves." It was a welcome and authoritative dissent from what he took to be the Christian practice of minding one's neighbor's business before one's own, and it suggested that world harmony would spring from an ethic a single sheet of paper could encompass. On January 28, 1934, he answered Eliot's standing question, "What does Mr. Pound believe?": "I believe the *Ta Hio*."[5]

Still, one would like to know what "les principes des actions" may be, from the investigation of which the wise man must start. Digesting, gisting, such actions as Sigismundo's? That may have been the way to start.

BY 1936 POUND was studying Chinese characters. In that year the "Ideogramic Series"[6] commenced appearing: first Fenollosa's seminal essay, separated for the first time from the out-of-print *Instigations;* then the Pauthier-Pound *Ta Hio,* reprinted; then, as so often, the publisher dissolved his business. The third volume was to have been Williams's *In the American Grain,* inspection of which will indicate what Pound meant by "ideogramic." From the "Notes by a Very Ignorant Man" which he added to the Fenollosa reprint we find that he was searching with sporadic success through the leisurely entries in Morrison's multivolume dictionary (1815–22), where he found for instance the character 新 the founder of the Shang dynasty (1766 B.C.) inscribed on his bath tub: Make It New. "Renouvelle-toi complètement chaque jour; fais-le de *nouveau,* encore de *nouveau,* et toujours de *nouveau.*"[7] In "the American language," 1928, this had yielded "Renovate, dod gast you, renovate," but Morrison's was ampler: "From *hatchet, to erect, and wood.* To cut down wood. Fresh, new; to renovate; to renew or improve the state of; to restore or to increase what is good, applied to persons increasing in virtue; and to the daily increase of plants." The axe is at the right of the character, a tree at the bottom left. The full maxim repeats the character twice, with the day sign (sun) twice between; in Canto 53 we find,

> Tching prayed on the mountain and
> > wrote MAKE IT NEW
> on his bath tub
> > Day by day make it new
> cut underbrush

新
日
日

pile the logs
keep it growing.

Dorothy copied the ideograms[8] with pen and brush, inadvertently picking up two punctuation marks from the *Ta Hio* text; which means that by his time they *had* a Chinese text.

As they had: the Four Books in one volume[9] on thin paper, with an English translation and most elaborate footnotes, anonymous; Commercial Press, Shanghai: a piracy of the great work of James Legge, his two volumes squeezed into one by omitting his Prolegomena and his Indices. The most unlucky omission for Pound's purposes was the comprehensive glossary, which annotates every one of the 2,500 characters and distinguishes usages for nearly every occurrence. The student needs a dictionary therefore, and when he used this book in the Pisan camp Pound had a pocket dictionary as well;[10] but on a six-week retreat[11] in the late summer of 1937 he had no dictionary small enough to pack, and simply stared at the ideograms and the crib. "When I disagreed with the crib or was puzzled by it I had only the look of the characters and the radicals to go on from." He went "three times through the whole text,"[12] and rose from it with "a better idea of the whole and the unity of the doctrine . . . the constants have been impressed on my eye."

"There are categories of ideogram not indicated as such in the dictionaries, but divided really by the feel of their forms, the twisted as evil, the stunted, the radiant.[13]

"The mountain itself has a 'nature' and that nature is to come forth in trees, though men cut and sheep nibble."

It was the old western dream, a universal language; but expressed in *natural* signs. Gaudier had read some of the radicals at sight. Gaudier's time had been short. Might a man nearing fifty, though lacking Gaudier's eye, not make shift to decipher as it were the signatures of things? For this was his belief, which he had from his bones and also from Fenollosa, who had it from Emerson who had it, maybe from Chu Hsi's organicism, that in nature are signatures, that they attest a coherence, that honest man far apart in space and time may therefore read them alike:

It is of the permanence of nature that honest men, even if endowed with no special brilliance, with no talents above those of straightness and honesty, come repeatedly to the same answers in ethics, without need of borrowing each other's ideas.

Shun and Wan had a thousand years between them and when their wills were compared they were as two halves of a tally stick.

From Kung to Mencius a century, and to St. Ambrose another six or so hundred years, and a thousand years to St. Antonino, and they are as parts of one pattern, as wood of a single tree.

The "Christian virtues" are there in the emperors who had responsibility in their hearts and willed the good of the people.[14]

And ideograms being pictures of elemental things, in the Chinese written language, however speech had been babelized, the signatures of things lay patent for sages to use. (Never mind that Kung had talked; the written record is what we have.)

Here, then, lay the validation of his syncretism: his faith that honest men—Fenollosa looking at brush strokes, Major Douglas inspecting the books of an aircraft factory, Gaudier eyeing the cone and the cylinder, Cavalcanti attentive to the movement of his heart and of the Italian language—should have perceived a single moral reality: brought to full articulation in the Four Books.

And it would soon be time to tie together *The Cantos.*

LOOKING, THEN, at Legge's Confucius, *Analects* v.vi: "The Master said, 'My doctrines make no way. I will get upon a raft, and float about on the sea. He that will accompany me will be Yû, I dare to say.'[15] Tsze-lû hearing this was glad, upon which the Master said, 'Yû is fonder of daring than I am. He does not exercise his judgment upon matters.' " A picturesque opening, Kung upon a raft; a most lame and impotent conclusion, with a fussy footnote moreover suggesting three alternate lamenesses. Pound looked at the sign for *raft,* 桴, with the "tree" radical at its left; and looked at the last sign of all, 材, "tree" radical again; and was illuminated: "For the LOGS are there in the ideogram very clearly" (did he see a tree and a part-tree?): hence "Yu likes danger better than I do. But he wouldn't bother about getting the logs." "Implying I think that logs are used to make rafts. Nevertheless the translator in question talks about 'exercise of judgment,' losing we believe the simple and Lincoln-like humour of the original."

It was a lucky hit; though Legge's glossary would have told him only that what the second character means here is uncertain, we find it in Mathews's dictionary, entry 6661, as "Materials, stuff." In one compound it actually means "Department of Supplies," and combined with the sign for "tree" it means "timber." What Confucius was saying we had best leave to the Confucians, but Pound undeniably picked up something germane.

He was not always that fortunate, but that was thereafter his method: follow the crib, and when it flags, haruspicate the characters. If it flags, something is there to which the crib-maker was inattentive; and since these are natural signs, whatever is there need not take learning to see.

And ideograms began to punctuate *The Cantos.* And by November 1941 he was "making a real translation"[16] of the *Ta Hio,* though into Italian because shut off from English readers; and as to "the luminous principle of reason which descends from the sky," he had at last in January 1940 gotten his hands on the text of Scotus Erigena, for whom "Omnia quae sunt, lumina sunt."[17]

IN THE 1920s, at work on Cavalcanti, he had read of Erigena in Gilson's *Philosophie au Moyen Age.* He was very nearly the bearer of a secret doctrine: repeatedly condemned,[18] especially in 1225 and in part for his popularity among the Albigensian connoisseurs of fructive light, yet never extinguished: for centuries, with his neo-Greek theology, a perpetual temptation to the sober Latins. His theopanies—all things low lamps shedding diffuse divinity—shine where the neo-Platonic immateriality is perfused by a text of St. James and a text of St. Paul: "Every good and every perfect gift comes down from the Father of Lights" (James I.17) and "Omne quod manifestatur, lumen est" (Ephes. V.13). And they rhyme with Bishop Grosseteste's deduction of the whole universe from light: "Lux enim per se in omnem partem se ipsam diffundit," and when it has reached the extreme of its rarefaction, and hence its minimum of luminosity, it is that of which things are made. And Love, said Cavalcanti, takes rise in Memory's locus—"In quella parte dove sta memoria"—and radiates like Light, "himself his own effect unendingly":[19]

> Risplende
>   in sè perpetuale effecto.

Brooding on these matters, Pound had written of "the radiant world"

> where one thought cuts through another with a clean edge, a world of moving energies *"mezzo oscuro rade," "risplende in sè perpetuale effecto,"* magnetisms that take form, that are seen, or that border the visible, the matter of Dante's *paradiso,* the glass under water, the form that seems a form seen in a mirror, these realities perceptible to the sense, interacting.[20]

—radiant gists, for a while in the thirteenth century held in many intellects: the self-interfering patterns from which and through which and into which all corporeality constantly flows. Now might ideograms not represent these?

He assembled a Confucian "Terminology":[21]

示 The light descending (from the sun, moon and stars). To be watched as component in ideograms indicating spirits, rites, ceremonies.

明 The sun and moon, the total light process, the radiation, reception and reflection of light; hence, the intelligence. Bright, brightness, shining. Refer to Scotus Erigena, Grosseteste, and the notes on light in my *Cavalcanti*.

誠 "Sincerity." The precise definition of the word, pictorially the sun's lance coming to rest on the precise spot verbally. The righthand half of this compound means: to perfect, bring to focus.

That the lance should be the sun's, that "perfect" should mean "bring to focus," these are luminous intrusions. 戈, Mathews 3358, is a spear; 成, Mathews 379, is "to perfect," by one speculation spear plus cutting edge (at the left) plus man (enclosed):[22] a man able to bear arms, therefore mature. But Pound saw in the convergent gestures to the right of the character rays entering a focus, and did not care that such an etymology was impossible, before there were lenses. Add 言, a word, and we have 誠, Mathews 381, a word perfected, hence sincere, true, honest: but in Pound's world of light-philosophers "the sun's lance coming to rest on the precise spot verbally."

Marvelous nonsense? The character occurs some thirty-five times in the *Ta Hio* and the *Chung Yung,* and twenty-odd of its usages in the latter resonate with mysterious intensity which incites Legge to talk of "mystical significance."

> Hence to entire sincerity there belongs ceaselessness.
> Not ceasing, it continues long. Continuing long, it evidences itself.
> Evidencing itself, it reaches far. Reaching far, it becomes large and substantial. Large and substantial, it becomes high and brilliant.

Whatever this "sincerity" may be (the version is Legge's) one cannot wonder that it put Pound in mind of light: "Risplende in sè perpetuale effecto." When he finally tackled the *Chung Yung* in 1945, calling it after the look of its title character, 中, *L'Asse che non Vacilla, The Unwobbling Pivot,* he made this "sincerity" the attaining of precision of speech with oneself, a "clarifying activity" which starts with discriminating thing from thing, category from category, impulse from impulse, and (like light) "neither stops nor stays." De Gourmont's watchword, "dissociation," is behind this, and Arnaut's consonantal disjunction of word from word, and Cavalcanti's lost world "where one thought cuts through another with a clean edge, a world of moving energies," and Agassiz's reading of natural signatures, distinguishing fish from fish. And as to what Pauthier had called "pénétrer et approfondir les principes des actions," it now means Agassiz's kind of activity: "sorting things into organic categories," in Pound's mature view the primary moral act. 月 is not 月, he told one enquiring student.[23] Agostino di Duccio is no other stonecutter. Money is not a commodity. A share is not a fixed charge. In the *Pisan Cantos* if not in Cavalcanti, "memora" (verb) is not "memoria" (noun).[24] Which leads us to the operative *virtù* whereby Dick is not John, Ezra not Kung: the characterizing patterned energy.

Thus justifying, in a poem including history, ten thousand distinct particularities, to be distinguished without end in the faith that they will unify, leaves on one tree, trees in one forest, forests in one world. Throughout his long labor on *The Cantos,* the side of his mind that kept diversifying the poem was balanced by a tacit side that should unify it in due time. Preparing, keeping active, refining what should one day be the unifying force, was a contrapuntal activity, surfacing from time to time in interests the diversity of which bewildered readers. About 1914 he was thinking of his long poem with De Gourmont's "dissociation des idées" and Fenollosa's clustered particulars in mind. In 1917 he was occupied with Arnaut. In the early 1920s the theme was music; in the late 1920s, Cavalcanti; in the early 1930s, credit, an invisible *virtù;* after the mid-1930s, the dozen or so ideograms by which, he was convinced, Confucian wisdom was shaped. Each led to the next, and all, he postulated, would one day enter his final orchestration. But by 1940 Europe had blown up.

A MYSTIQUE OF IDEOGRAMS that touch on light had brought him a long way from the commonsense Confucius whose dicta about "order" and "brotherly deference" are recorded in the *Analects.* Such a Confucius, uttering maxims of statecraft, underlies the *Comprehensive Mirror for Aid in Government* which was the ultimate source of the Chinese History Cantos, and the Confucians who arranged the materials from which de Mailla worked saw millennia of history as an oscillation between unifying Kung and disastrous *tao*, the carriers of disintegration always the mystics whom the Cantos teach us to call "taozers."

> Down, down! Han is down
> Sung is down
> Hochang, eunuchs, and taozers
> empresses' relatives, came then a founder
> saying nothing superfluous
> cleared out the taozers and grafters, gave grain
> opened the mountains
> (56/302:315)

Very good, taozers, irresponsible peddlers of the ineffable; their doctrine, as old as Kung's, was as readily perverted toward froth as Kung's toward formalism. There was a vulgarized taoism which instead of cultivating indifference to death offered instead to render death indifferent by brewing an elixir of immortality:[25]

> And there came a taozer babbling of the elixir
> that wd/ make men live without end
> and the taozer died very soon after that.
> (54/288:300)

This tended toward alchemy and the transmutation of metals and other opiates for the people:

> another lord seeking elixir
> seeking the transmutation of metals
> seeking a word to make change . . .
> HOAI of SUNG was nearly ruined by taozers
> HIEN of TANG died seeking elixir
> (57/313:327)

But the Kung we can set against taozers is not the Kung of the Pivot, the Chung Yung, 中. This difficulty was not perceived by Pound, who finished his work on these Cantos before he came to grips with the doctrine of the Pivot; and then he was in more trouble than he perhaps knew.

This Pivot is a transcendental norm, not the Aristotelian mean at which we arrive by knowing and avoiding extremes, but the "great root of the universe" to apprehend which is to incorporate a rectificative energy that will never betray one toward extremes. (Hence "the unwobbling pivot," because it is not defined by what it avoids, but stays in one place.) Chu Hsi had brought this concept into Confucian philosophy. And as St. Thomas's theology alters the gospels though their words are unchanged, so such a conception, once brought near the *Analects,* alters the *Analects;* in particular it alters the bearings of a word Confucius used many times, 道,[26] the way, the path, the course one's action takes. As he uses this word in the *Analects,* it already denotes not any way but *the* Way: ethics is unitive, normative; there is a principle all good conduct follows. In the *Chung Yung,* however, such a principle pervades not only human conduct but the universe. Nature proclaims it, the sun awakens seeds by its efficacy, it is implanted in every human heart. So implanted, it is our rational nature; to cherish it and develop our lives in its manner is The Way (Pound was to call it "the process"). Chu Hsi has a note on this, which Pound in 1945 translated, "The main thing is to illumine the root of the process, a fountain of clear water descending from heaven immutable. The components, the bones of things, the materials, are implicit and prepared in us, abundant and inseparable from us." This "fountain descending from heaven," on the first page of Pound's *Pivot,* like "the tensile light, the Immaculata" on the last page, was conceived by a mind impassioned by Guido's "Risplende in sè perpetuale effecto," by Erigena's "Omnia quae sunt, lumina sunt," by Arnaut's great figure of the raining light, "lo soleills plovil": a mind intent on the unification of *The Cantos,* and disposed to perceive their characteristic imagery in the ideograms. And the brilliance of his language averts the fact that this clarifying order, this realization of the inborn transcending nature, for which he found the word *process,* is called 道: *Tao.* Yes, *tao.* The *Chung Yung* is dense with Taoism.

The neo-Confucianism from which Pound trustingly received the Four Books was an aspect of Chu Hsi's syncretic mode of thought. That mode, nominally Confucian, had assimilated much coloration from fifteen centuries of Taoism: from a tradition of thought that talks of harmony with the universe rather than of modes of government; that indeed tends toward anarchy in distrusting modes of government; that is quietist, not active, intuitive not intellective; that produces as model not the ruler but the hermit. So intrinsic are such impulses to the long story of China that we cannot sort out with any plausibility a Confucian orthodoxy which is radically something other. *Tao,* The Way, Confucius used the term repeatedly; we find it some eighty times in the *Analects* themselves. Chinese landscape painting, inviting the viewer to enter and lose himself, is Taoist,[27] so much so that Fenollosa's two-volume *Epochs* has never a good word to say for Confucianism. The Seven Lakes Canto, based on poems which accompany pictures, is Taoist in feeling. The Pound of "The Flame" who imagined his soul rolling back and growing translucent, consubstantiate with the blue of the Garda Lake—

> Call not that mirror me, for I have slipped
> Your grasp, I have eluded

—like the earlier Pound of "Hilda's Book" who imagined himself becoming a tree, and the later Pound of Canto XLVII who heard the "roots speaking together" and the sixty-year-old Pound who wrote in Pisa that "the sage delighteth in water"[28] (and might as well have written it in China), was Taoist in his deepest impulses, and it is not surprising that he could respond to places—for instance to Montségur of which he knew so little and guessed so well—with a geomancer's perception of hill and shade.

Yet hardly had the Seven Lakes Canto been printed when he was steeped in chronicles that inveighed against Taozers.

But do we not know—though Pound likely did not know—that the same Chu Hsi who blended *Tao* with Confucius also stood behind those anti-taoist chronicles? We do; Chu Hsi did; but the Comprehensive Mirror, highly tendentious, uses history, we also remember, to afford paradigms.[29] One of its recurrent paradigms is the folly of trusting anything practical to the likes of, say Henry Thoreau, whose archetypal political action was not to seek office but to get himself symbolically jailed. (Or shall we say, to Ezra Pound, another symbolic prisoner?) A Confucian official might taoize on holiday, painting landscapes;[30] a taoist might not govern; and if this is contrary to the doctrine of the *Chung Yung* in which the luminous clarifying principle will ameliorate the earth, well, it is contrary.

A man can grow committed to incompatible things. Pound's interest in the Fascism he idealized is continuous with his interest in the *Chung Yung*: in the belief that a ruler of sufficient sensibility, sufficiently steady will, could catalyze a whole people's *senso morale*. On the other hand taoist sanctions had been claimed for mere laziness:

> and the country was run by Yang Siun
> while the emperor amused himself in his park
>   had a light car made, harnessed to sheep
> The sheep chose which picnic he went to,
>   ended his days as a gourmet. Said Tchang, tartar:

> Are not all of his protégés flatterers?
> How can his country keep peace?
> And the Prince Imperial went into the cabaret business
> and read Lao Tse.
>
> (54/282:294)

De Mailla's readers would have recognized that: it is like the court of Marie Antoinette.

Somewhere to the right of such slither, Pound was convinced, but not as far to the right as Robespierre, was a domain where statesman of unitive sensibility brought order without tyranny. He fastened on John Adams, ten Cantos of finely culled citations that are bracing but aesthetically dispersive. Now the poem had to converge. He turned to the *Chung Yung.* But the Chinese History Cantos, which never allow one to suppose that Kung may rigidify as much as Tao may slither, had a one-sidedness difficult to integrate, and it is not surprising that the terminology he settled on in his 1945 version of the *Pivot* tends to interfere with the reader's ever discovering that the word rendered "process" there and in the *Pisan Cantos* is *tao*.[31]

These matters are not after all irreconcilable, but events were now driving Pound too fast for an overall view. He was hanging on by sheer faith and sheer willpower.

A LAST IDEOGRAM: *hsien:* 顯: Mathews 2692, to manifest, to display, to be illustrious. On the right, the 181st radical, *the head.* Top left, the *sun,* and below it what was once a picture of silk bobbins and now means *silkworms.* We find it in the Book of Odes, #267, quoted toward the end of the twenty-sixth chapter of the *Pivot,* the chapter with which Pound's version closes. Sun held his eye, and silk. Legge is flat: "How illustrious was it, the singleness of the virtue of King Wan!" Legge goes on to add that singleness likewise is unceasing. Once more, an impotent close. But the sun, the silk. And Pound rendered,

> As silky light, King Wen's virtue
> Coming down in the sunlight,
>   what purity!

To which he appended, for the last words of his *Pivot,*

The *unmixed* functions [in time and in space] without bourne.
                This unmixed is the tensile light, the
                        Immaculata. There is no end
                                to its action.

Sun and silk: the tensile light. Thus in the *Pisan Cantos,*

            Light tensile immaculata
                        the sun's cord unspotted
                "sunt lumina" said the Oirishman to King Carolus,
                                "OMNIA,
            all things that are are lights"

And above, on the same page,

        plowed in the sacred field and unwound the silk worms early
                                        in tensile 顯
            in the light of light is the *virtù*
                    "sunt lumina" said Erigena Scotus
                        as of Shun on Mt Taishan
            and in the hall of the forebears
                                as from the beginning of wonders
            the paraclete that was present in Yao, the precision
            in Shun the compassionate
            in Yu the guider of waters

                                            (74/429:455)[32]

The unspotted sun's cord, the tensile light, Erigena: derived from a character in which no one had ever had the eye to discern such wonders
before. That was his forte, the magnificent misreading. In the *Pisan Cantos*
splendor on splendor of diction is elicited in this way from characters used
as *mantrams,* to invent a Confucius far from the urbane sage of the *Analects,*
a light-philosopher and perhaps as much an invention as Chu Hsi's in the
twelfth century. As in his cloud chamber a physicist sees an electron's
trace, so Ezra Pound looking at ideograms in the 1940s was inspecting tracks
left, he was thoroughly convinced, by the patterned energies at the roots
of phenomena. I raise my eyes from this page and see a jet contrail, very
high, luminous pink in the dawn sky. Those who are skilled in fire may
read it. It proclaims Newton's third law, action and reaction, and Boyle's
law that unites the heat and the volume of gases, and Dalton's discovery

that cooling condenses water, and Snell's law of refraction whereby drop-lets grow luminous when sunlight enters them: self-interfering patterns, written in a lengthening trace in front of which, invisible, a hundred people are being carried through the high air.

Notes

1. "Dedication" to the Calcutta edition of his version (Gallup A58b). *Gaudier-Brzeska* (written 1915) has an epigraph from Pauthier.

2. H. G. Creel, *Confucius: The Man and the Myth*, 1949 (reprint entitled *Confucius and the Chinese Way*), 291–3. *Analects* XIII.iii, on purifying terminology, long a key passage for Pound, appears to be inauthentic (Creel 221, and 321 note 13).

3. L & S, 58; Creel, 243–4.

4. Gallup, 42.

5. *LE,* 86; for the date, *Make It New,* 3.

6. Gallup, 159.

7. Pauthier, *La Grande Étude,* II.x.

8. Her account, 1965.

9. *Letters,* #331. Pound's working copy being (1969) inaccessible, Mr. Omar S. Pound showed me a duplicate.

10. Unidentified, but existence vouched for.

11. "Mencius," 604/119.

12. "Mencius," 609/124.

13. "Mencius," 620/136.

14. "Mencius," 615/130.

15. "Mencius," 605/120.

16. Gallup, 167.

17. *Letters,* #336, 337.

18. During the Albigensian débâcle, Canto XXXVI tells us, "They dug for, and damned Scotus Eriugina." This is metaphorically correct. But when Pound wrote in Pisa (Canto 83) that they "dug up his bones in the time of de Montfort (Simone)" he was confusing him with his disciple Amaury de Bène, whose bones, three years dead, were exhumed and scattered in 1210. They have neighboring chapters in Fiorentino's *Storia della Filosofia,* much underlined by Pound. Confusing him with his disciple: first suggested, without benefit of the Fiorentino confirmation, by Achilles Fang, *Materials for the Study of Pound's Cantos,* unpub. Harvard dissertation, 1958.

19. This paragraph leans on an unpublished essay by Mr. Walter Michaels.

20. *LE,* 154.

21. Prefixed to his 1945 version of the *Great Digest.*

22. R. B. Blakney, *A Course in the Analysis of Chinese Characters,* 1926, 105.

23. *Letters,* #273.

24. EP to HK, letter, 1951, reproving an effort to regularize.

25. L & S, 127.

26. Creel, 122–3.

27. L & S, 112.

28. 83/529:564. See *Analects* VI.xxi.

29. L & S, 49.

30. L & S 110–18, a most clarifying discussion.

31. When Pound learned this himself it is difficult to say. The History Cantos picked up the word *tao* from a French prose with no ideograms; the Legge Confucius on the other hand offers ideograms and translation but no Chinese sounds. The apparent discrepancy between Kung's *tao* and de Mailla's could thus have escaped him for a long time. The dictionary when he turned up the character there would have offered the pronunciation *tao,* but that is not decisive even if he noticed it. Mathews's dictionary for example gives seventeen different characters with different meanings, all pronounced *tao,* and he may have supposed for a long time that Kung's *tao* and Lao Tse's were different words.

32. Early New Directions printings had the wrong ideogram here, and the Faber still has.

Bibliography

References to *The Cantos* are in the form "(74/447:475)." This means Canto 74, page 447 in *The Cantos,* New York: New Directions, 1970, and page 475 in *The Cantos,* London: Faber, 1964.

Abbreviations

Cathay: Ezra Pound, tr., *Cathay.* London: Elkin Mathews, 1915.

Gallup: Donald Gallup, *Ezra Pound: A Bibliography.*

Gaudier-Brzeska: Ezra Pound, *Gaudier-Brzeska: A Memoir.* Hessle: Marvell Press, 1960.

LE: Ezra Pound, *Literary Essays.*

L & S: J. R. Levenson and F. Schurmann, *China, an Interpretative History,* 1969.

Letters: Ezra Pound, *Selected Letters.*

Make It New: Ezra Pound, *Make It New.* London: Faber, 1934.

"Mencius": Ezra Pound's essay "Mang Tsze (The Ethics of Mencius)," *Criterion,* July 1938, 603–25, and *Impact,* 1960, 118–41. In dual page references, *Criterion* always precedes.

The Music of a Lost Dynasty

Pound in the Classroom

D. S. CARNE-ROSS

❖ ❖ ❖

M R. G., YOU BROUGHT UP AN IMPORTANT POINT last week which I rather brushed aside, in the bad way we people have. The cognoscenti may have settled it, to their own satisfaction; the general reader has not. You said: Is interpretation of *The Cantos* inevitably arbitrary—a matter of "making a lucky guess at what EP may have meant" by this or that cryptic allusion? Is the poem—this applies specially to the *Pisan Cantos*—irredeemably private, its logic at best the logic of personal association, so that reading Pound means stitching together a poem of one's own out of bits and pieces that catch one's fancy? I wanted to take Canto 81 this afternoon. The opening lines are as good a place as any to pursue Mr. G's question. The passage starts with some classical deities and is thus to some degree in the public domain, but then it seems to withdraw into Pound's own private experience. Why doesn't someone read a few lines and get them off the page? Anyone.

x   Zeus lies in Ceres' bosom
         Taishan is attended of loves
                   under Cythera, before sunrise

and he said: "Hay aquí mucho catolicismo—(sounded
                                    catoli*th*ismo)
        y muy poco reliHion"
and he said: "Yo creo que los reyes desaparecen"
(Kings will, I think, disappear)
That was Padre José Elizondo
                        in 1906 and in 1917
or about 1917
        and Dolores said: "Come pan, niño,"   eat bread, me lad—

Thank you, hold it there Mr. G, are you ready to shoot?

G Well, yes, I am. So this Elizondo said something that Pound thought important. But what he says here isn't important, that I can see. We just have to guess at what meaning the whole remembered conversation had for Pound. The single remark may be the hook that brings it all back to his mind. It doesn't bring it into mine.

D We had Elizondo before, though. That helps—

First perhaps we ought to look at the lines more formally, structurally. There are three sections or moments. The mythological prelude, in Pound's lyrical, cantabile style. One of the many Pisan dawn scenes. Then Padre Elizondo who in fact says two things, not obviously connected, in Spanish. This is in spoken, colloquial style and so is the third moment, also in Spanish, which consists of only one line.

G Who is Dolores?

A Spanish lady, I would think. What about the relation between these three moments? Since there's no punctuation at the end of the lines they just flow into each other. "Before sunrise / *and* he said. . . ." Why "and"?

D Doesn't Pound often use "and" to join passages that aren't obviously connected?

To . . .

D . . . make us look for the connection, I suppose. Because there really is a connection— and we've lost it?

I like that way of putting it. Pound distrusts hypotaxis which by subordinating one element to another disposes them in a hierarchial order which tends to weaken their natural force. Parataxis is more egalitarian. Though that isn't really the point. Pound's typical maneuver is to lay his elements side by side. So in the early poem that has become a demonstration piece he writes:

> The apparition of these faces in the crowd;
> Petals on a wet, black bough.

This isn't an elliptical simile. The petals and the faces don't stand in relation of analogy to each other. The two elements in their full strength, their full right, *confront* each other and do something to each other and together make a statement that couldn't be put in any other way.[1] It is a matter—though Pound may not have seen this at the time—of ceasing to treat things as mere objects to be pushed round by an all-important subject. It means giving *things* back their autonomy.

What are the first three lines of Canto 81 saying, do you think—whatever their bearing on the rest of the passage?

x *Zeus lies in Ceres' bosom. Sky and Earth—the sacred marriage, prefigured by the fertility rites in Cantos 39 and 47. Pound usually says Demeter, not Ceres, doesn't he? Taishan, the sacred Chinese mountain we've had a good many times. It's—*

MISS Q *(Who will say nothing more this afternoon) . . . an Italian mountain near Pisa transfigured by a piety Pound learned in China.*

x *All right. So Greece and China. Pound is always cutting between them.*

In a dark time we have to draw on all the world's resources. I am not myself convinced that we have the right to other people's resources; Pound thinks we do.—It's rather Greek China, isn't it, with those attending loves? Then back to Greece proper with Cythera which could be Aphrodite's island but here must mean the goddess herself. It's odd that Taishan is *under* Cythera. Aphrodite is not a sky goddess. The sacred mountain, anyway, ringed round by loves, and above them, Cythera or Aphrodite. And Zeus lies in Ceres's bosom. A kind of mythological flourish to get things going, perhaps. Or perhaps not quite that. And this leads somehow to Padre Elizondo. We've had him before, someone said.

x *(Riffling back) Yes, here he is, in Canto 77, "Padre José had understood something or other . . . learned what the Mass meant, / how one should perform it. . . ."*

Did we decide what Elizondo had understood?

H *I wrote down something you read from some critic. "Pound approves of church ritual"— Catholic ritual, I suppose that is—"in so far as it retains traces of the older pagan meaning."*

Then change of style, EP speaking: "The Church in sanity RETAINED symbols, look at Easter show in Siena Cathedral (Egypt etc.) Ceres, Bacchus."²

Does that help here?

H Pound probably means—

Is Pound speaking?

H All right, Pound makes this Elizondo say—

Sorry to be difficult but that still isn't right. We are to suppose that Padre Elizondo really did say this. He is a real man who on two occasions said something to Pound in his own Castilian Spanish. It is a cardinal principle of the poem that the materials it presents must be presented exactly as they are or were. A man's actual words, and as far as possible even the sound of his words, must be reported, the date, location, etc., must be given. As Pound sees it, this is part of the *evidence*. Elizondo is one of the poem's countless independent voices that bring their own independent witness, their tithe of understanding or knowledge or memory.

H Well anyway, this character says there's a lot of Catholicism—in Spain and I suppose Italy and places like that, but not much religion. "Religion" meaning the stuff in the first three lines, sacred marriages and what have you. That's what Pound calls religion. Why he thinks it is preserved in Catholicism I can't imagine. If that's what he does think.

X All Pound says or the critic says is that Catholic ritual retains traces of the older pagan meaning. No more than that. In Catholic countries there may not be much religion but there is still a bit and that bit preserves traces of the older religion. Is that it?

Don't ask me, ask the poem. Or rather, let it ask you. If our conversation this afternoon is to lead anywhere, it must be the poem that is guiding us.

G If this is so important to Pound, why doesn't he keep on with it? The stuff that follows about kings disappearing is a new tack altogether.

I wonder. Anyway, though Pound is didactic in a way no other important modern writer is, at his best he doesn't *tell* us what to believe. He presents the scattered elements of something, a belief or usage or whatever, and leaves it to us to put the elements together: with the force of a personal discovery. But I don't in fact think Elizondo's second remark is a new tack. I take it there is a distinction here: between the things we had better keep and those we can afford to let go. In a piece called *Patria Mia* written as early as 1912 Pound said: "One wants to find out what sort of things endure, and what sort of things are transient; what sort of things recur." The enduring / the recurrent / the transient: that triple distinction is in fact a governing principle of the poem. So here, the gods endure; the rites or mysteries recur; whereas kingship is a feature of the political and religious life of mankind that Pound as a republican American feels he can do without.

I see a sufficiently clear line that runs from the mythological prelude to Elizondo on religion, with a parenthetical distinction on the subject of kingship. What about the third moment, though—Dolores's "Come pan, niño"?

R *(Stiffly) I hope it isn't meant as some sort of analogue to Communion. At the Last Supper when Jesus broke bread he said, "Take, eat: this is my body." If this is what Pound has in mind, it's pretty blasphemous.*

I think you may well be right. Not about the blasphemy, though; Pound wouldn't see it like that.

Well, we have been through the passage, in a very provisional way. Why don't we play it over again and try to move round inside it more freely? Anyone.

X *Me again?*

You read very well before.

X   Zeus lies in Ceres' bosom
     Taishan is attended of loves
               under Cythera, before sunrise
     and he said: "Hay aquí mucho catolicismo—(sounded
                                        catoli*th*ismo)
          y muy poco reli*H*ion"
     and he said: "Yo creo que los reyes desaparecen"
     (Kings will, I think, disappear)
     That was Padre José Elizondo
               in 1906 and in 1917
     or about 1917
          and Dolores said: "Come pan, niño,"   eat bread, me lad—

Thank you. You read more as though it were a whole this time, not a series of new starts. But if it is a whole, as I suspect, a kind of unit within the poem's continuous movement, the thread that links the mythological prelude to Elizondo must somehow lead on to Dolores. Mr. R caught an allusion to the sacrament of Communion there. If that's right, we would expect that what Pound is after is the *trace* of the older pagan meaning preserved in the Christian sacrament, a trace of reliHion—as in the first three lines, presumably—preserved in catolithismo. So that Eat bread, me lad (let's suppose Dolores is speaking to her son), distantly repeating Take, eat: this is my body (Christ speaking to his flock), will somehow be related to Zeus lies in Ceres's bosom.

But are we justified in expecting this? Or are we doing what Mr. G objects to, putting our own arbitrary interpretation on fragments that in themselves are quite hermetic? I suppose we should ask: Has the poem done anything to suggest that we should attribute this sort of significance to bread?

Has it had anything to say about bread at all?

F *There is some stuff at the beginning of the previous canto where Pound used the same Spanish phrase, Come pan, niño.*

Good. I think the first page of Canto 80 may bear on our present passage.

F *And just before that he said, "an era of croissants / then an era of pains au lait." I took him to be referring to a particular period. Since Debussy came in just above, I suppose around 1900. Then there is a line that doesn't make any sense at all, "and the eucalyptus bobble is missing." Then, Come pan, niño.*

Hold the eucalyptus bobble for a moment. How does it go on?

F   that was an era also, and Spanish bread
                       was made out of grain in that era
                  senesco
                      sed amo

I grow old but I love. Then more about bread and grain, then the Latin phrase again. What the Latin has to do with bread. . . .

Hold the Latin for a moment too, along with the eucalyptus bobble. And you had better hold those croissants as well. We may need them. While we are at it, is there anything else in the poem about bread?

P *There was something earlier on about wild birds not eating white bread. In Canto 74, page 428 in our text.*

What was the context?

P It came just before a kind of religious ceremony, Catholic and Chinese mixed up. Oh yes, and he mentions Mount Taishan there too.

What do you suppose the birds had against white bread?

P Supermarket pap maybe, Italian style. Like in the Usura canto—

> with usura, sin against nature,
> is thy bread ever more of stale rags
> is thy bread dry as paper,
> with no mountain wheat, no strong flour

Very good. The perversion of bread there is part of a multiple perversion or sin against nature and the canto ends, you may remember, with what Pound sees as sexual perversion:

CONTRA NATURAM
They have brought whores for Eleusis

which he admits in a letter is "*very* elliptical." I don't want to lose the thread but perhaps we had better follow this up. As we are coming to see, *The Cantos* work in a cumulative way. You have somehow to read the single passage with the whole poem in mind. Whores for Eleusis, he says, "means that in place of the sacramental——in the Mysteries, you 'ave the 4 and six-penny 'ore . . . the degradation of the sacrament (which is the coition and *not* the going to the fatbuttocked priest or registry office) . . . ."[3] And so on in one of Pound's rather too rugged epistolary styles. In plainer words, uncorrupt sexual union is a sacrament akin to the sacrament of the sacred marriage that formed part of the mysteries at Eleusis. If this sounds a bit Henry Millerish, reread Canto 47. Pound's ideas about sex do not come up to Olympia Press standards.

I've not lost the thread, as you suppose. It is just that there are so many threads—one has to be very neat-fingered. I am still on Canto 81 and the phrase which I think may be the key phrase—Come pan, niño—which also turns up at the beginning of 80. We have discovered that there is a good deal about bread in *The Cantos*. Which may be proper enough, given the aims of the poem. It is a poem about building the city and it is a religious poem. (That's a very Poundian "and," I'm afraid.) It doesn't talk about "spiritual values," it teaches us the rudiments—about bread, for instance. It teaches us to honor all the ancient makings of man's hands that are filled with his sense of the holy. Religious people have always taken bread seriously. Christianity certainly did and so did the Greeks; you can call bread *Demetros karpos* in Greek, the fruit of Demeter. To find out what we have done to bread—read Giedion if you want the details[4]—and then to recover bread, the "sense" of bread, the taste of good bread: this, Pound would say, is a step toward building the city. Sorry about the lecture but *The Cantos* is this kind of poem.

By way of getting back to business, let's take a harder look at the first page of Canto 80 which as I said seems to bear on our passage from 81. There are several things there that we set aside just now. First, that eucalyptus bobble. This is I admit pretty cryptic but a poet has a right to a few such properties. The invaluable Mr. Kenner has preserved the story for us.[5] A eucalyptus tree grows on a hillside above Rapallo and coming down that way in 1945, flanked by two armed partisans, en route to America, and trial and perhaps death, Pound stooped to pick up a eucalyptus pip and took it with him, in memory of a sacred Italian landscape. In *memory*, that's the key notion, and in fact Pound himself tells us earlier, in Canto 74, page 435, all we need to know: "and eucalyptus that is for memory."

But what do you suppose the eucalyptus pip is doing *here*, between croissants and pains au lait and Come pan?

x *Since the eucalyptus pip is missing, it must mean . . . some failure of memory.*

And what has been forgotten?

x *Perhaps that bread—I don't know how to put this—was once a religious sort of thing. . . .*

We don't have the words for this now, I agree. That is why Pound has to be so indirect, why he can't simply *tell* us.

Then there is the Latin, Senesco sed amo, and at the start of the period another Latin phrase, "Amo ergo sum and in just that proportion." Love as the principle or condition of being—a kind of summation of the hymn to Aphrodite in the previous canto. Love and being; love and ageing—an oldish man conscious of time passed and still in love. *Love and time*, perhaps—love resisting the passage of time.

The third thing I asked you to hold was "an era of croissants." What about those croissants?

p *Crescent-shaped rolls, very nice with fresh butter and coffee for breakfast in Paris.*

Pound and his poem would certainly agree with you. Is there anything else, I wonder?

G *Need there be?*

No, but the poem is working at full pressure in these cantos and seemingly random particulars are coming together, building up. Remember the beautiful line at the end of 74, "So light is the urging, so ordered the dark petals of iron." Pound's favorite image of the rose pattern driven into the dead iron filings by the magnet. But now—so light is the urging—no longer *driven*: the filings, the discrete elements of experience—the dark petals—effortlessly take their place in the pattern. The pattern reaches out and claims them. Not that there aren't still plenty of obdurate particles that don't seem to fit in anywhere—though less than there used to be; we are learning to read the poem better these days. And no doubt there is a certain amount of unreclaimable slag. Pound was writing an entirely new kind of poem and had no way of knowing how much to put in.

But here the informing pattern is at work very strongly, hence I'm inclined to take a second look at those croissants. Croissant, from *croître*, *crescere*, is in French the crescent moon, the moon in her increase. There is a lot of lunar poetry in the Pisans. The moon—the moon goddess, Artemis—is one of the divine presences who come to the poet in his cage. There's the Franciscan "sorella la luna" at the start of 74; the moon as "la scalza" in 76, the bare-foot girl whose house has been broken (like Isotta's temple at Rimini and other sacred Italian buildings); the moon appears as the muse in the Poundian ideogram at the end of 77, dancing on a sixpence, bringing things into focus; the moon lights up the Pisan tower and baptistery at the start of Canto 79 which culminates in the hymn to Aphrodite. So as I said I'm inclined to think that Pound's sign-seeking, haruspicating eyes found Artemis and her crescent moon in those croissants.[6]

And if so, there is likely to be some relation here between Artemis and the other goddess who stands behind the Latin words just above, Amo ergo sum: Aphrodite, who was invoked so lyrically in the previous canto. Aphrodite and Artemis. . . .

G *This strikes me as totally arbitrary. Perhaps Pound does mean croissant to suggest Artemis and the moon. But how can we possibly be sure that this is a valid reading?*

If this were a short poem you would be perfectly right, we couldn't. But the passage does not exist in isolation; it asks to be read in the light of other, related, passages before and after—

G *Did you say* after*?*

Many long poems work this way—they have a spatial as well as a temporal aspect. Temporally, you move through them and A precedes B; spatially, you see the whole poem spread out before you, with A and B simultaneously present. When Milton has Adam and Eve pass "hand in hand" before God in the Garden, he wants us to think of the later scene where those hands will come apart and then, at the end of the poem, come together again.

In this same canto, page 500 in our text, the two goddesses are brought into a clear enough relation. There is a strange allegorical passage—it starts with the eucalyptus pip, I hadn't noticed—about the moon and suffering and different attitudes to suffering. Then at the bottom of the page Pound writes, "At Ephesus she had compassion on silversmiths." "She" is Diana of Ephesus, Artemis; that's in the public domain, or was. Silversmiths I suppose are makers, artists in general perhaps. Pound the artist is the center of consciousness in these cantos. And then, in opposition apparently to Artemis, Aphrodite: "Cythera egoista." The compassionate Artemis or moon goddess is somehow set against the merciless power of Aphrodite— *saeva*, he calls her elsewhere, harsh, savage. Then ten pages later the two goddesses are lyrically reconciled or united:

> (Cythera, in the moon's barge whither?
> how hast thou the crescent for car?

Daniel Pearlman, who discusses this whole canto very well in *The Barb of Time*, makes the neat suggestion that the open parenthesis (serves as a pictogram for the crescent, croissant moon.[7] Pound has always made full use of the typewriter's resources.

Does this seem to bear at all on the lines from 81 we started out with?

> (Silence neither unresponsive nor unproductive)

D *Perhaps it explains why Pound speaks of Taishan attended of loves under Cythera. Cythera, Aphrodite, is now in the moon's barge—she is the moon. The two goddesses are one. Doesn't the planet Venus at certain seasons appear in crescent form?*

The heavens were very much alive for Pound at Pisa. He hadn't much to look at.

Does this reconciliation or union of the two goddesses convey anything to us? I don't mean, Can we attach any possible significance to it? Of course we can. I mean, what sense does the poem as it is now developing lead us to expect? Does it, for instance, suggest the reconciliation of discordant forces or elements in the poem—and hence perhaps account for the new serenity that marks the writing of the later *Pisan Cantos*?

(Silence neither unproductive nor unresponsive)

The moon that grows and wanes speaks elegiacally to us of time's passing and the pain of that passing: the inconstant moon, emblem of time that steals from us what we love. "Man is in love and loves what vanishes," Yeats said. And Pound in an early canto (about a lover who tried artificially to arrest time's passing) said, "Time is the evil. Evil." The evil time is linear time that leaves the past behind in a limbo of dead things. But the poem has from the start been trying to establish another time, organic or seasonal time whose image is not a line but a circle or perhaps a spiral. (This is the argument of Pearlman's book and a very important one, though it may be that he makes it explain too much.) Linear time passes; seasonal time returns.

Time becomes an urgent problem for Pound at Pisa. He realizes suddenly that he himself is growing old and the friends of his youth are dying one by one. The Pisans are full of elegiac, heroic roll calls. Their death enforces the sense of irreparable loss under which these cantos are written, the destruction of so much of the Europe that Pound loves, the apparent failure of all he has struggled for. So against the ruinous action of linear time he sets the power of *memory*, memory that overcomes time by preserving what we love. And more than that. Memory shows that the past is not simply gone, passed. Pound somewhere speaks of the mind, memory, holding *resurgent* images. Can anyone remember where that comes?

D *At the start of Canto 76 we have*

> And the sun high over horizon hidden in cloud bank
> lit saffron the cloud ridge
> > dove sta memora

A morning scene, an hour or so after the dawn scene in 81. Saffron, Aphrodite's color, then a phrase from the Cavalcanti Canzone d'Amore which was incorporated into Canto 36, "where memory stands."

D *And this draws on a passage six pages earlier quoting another phrase from that poem—I have a mark in the margin—*

Your Ariadne's thread—

D . . . *where he wrote*

> and that certain images be formed in the mind
> to remain there
> *formato locho . . .*
> to remain there, resurgent ΕΙΚΟΝΕΣ

And then a bit later, in 76, there's the full statement:

> nothing matters but the quality
> of the affection—
> in the end—that has carved the trace in the mind
> dove sta memoria

Wherever the quality of the affection—Aphrodite—is strong enough to carve a trace in the mind, the past is preserved and its content, its images, rise up again and are renewed like the moon—Artemis—that renews herself each month. Or, since the crescent, croissant moon suggests growth, say that memories rise from the dark of the mind like flowers from the dark earth.

Memory, then, points to the existence of another kind of time that is not evil, seasonal time. For though it carries us to age and death, it holds everything and brings everything back in its perpetually self-renewing rhythm. But only when love is there. Hence, juxtaposing the two times, Pound writes:

> Time is not, Time is the evil, beloved
> Beloved the hours βροδοδάκτυλος

"Beloved," and *brododáktulos*, rose-fingered, Sappho's epithet for the moon. How gentle the words are. Aphrodite and Artemis: Love and Time . . .

Perhaps we are almost ready to start reading our passage from Canto 81. We have found how to move inside it fairly freely and let other passages from the poem flow into it. We have found words to say about it, to help us understand it . . . Or perhaps only to evade it?

> Zeus lies in Ceres' bosom

The sacred marriage of heaven and earth, someone said, prefigured by the fertility rites in Cantos 39 and 47. Fine, that's the kind of thing Poundian critics are expected to say. Yet what do we know of sacred marriages and fertility rites as we sit here this afternoon in a room in Boston and listen to the traffic go by? Are we simply deceiving ourselves with big words?

x *But you yourself said that the passage doesn't exist in isolation. The first line, for instance, has been . . . prepared for.*

That's true, yes. One of the special beauties of the *Pisan Cantos* is the way an incomplete phrase is planted so to say and emerges later on, still incomplete, and grows silently in the dark of the poem to emerge eventually in its perfect form.

A *You mean like "of sapphire, for this stone giveth sleep"* . . .

B *. . . which nine pages further on reappears as "for this stone giveth sleep"* . . .

C *. . . and then after twenty-four pages emerges fully grown in the couplet that closes a lyrical meditation:*

> Her bed-posts are of sapphire
> for this stone giveth sleep.

What is happening to us this afternoon? It is as though . . . the poem were taking over, and guiding us. As though we had learned to be silent and let the poem speak through us. . . .

G *Are we supposed to be able to remember single phrases for pages on end?*

Poets do expect this, yes. Not just Pound—Dante, for example. At the beginning of the *Purgatorio* he stands at the foot of the mountain and looks over the southern sea on which no man sailed and afterward returned. And Vergil girds him with the reed of humility, *com'altrui piacque*, as Cato had ordered. But the same phrase was used earlier on in a different context. We remember the great scene in the *Inferno* telling how Ulysses sailed on that sea and how his heroic, arrogant voyage ended in disaster when the waters closed over him, *com'altrui piacque*, as God willed. Dante counts on our recalling, juxtaposing, the two scenes. So does Pound, though his repeated phrases work differently. They grow in the dark while we aren't watching.

What about the first line of our passage, Zeus lies in Ceres's bosom? Mr. X, you said it had been "prepared for."

x Well, not exactly, but in Canto 77, page 470 in our text, there's the line

so kissed the earth after sleeping on concrete

and then something about Demeter which is Greek for Ceres. I don't know if that helps.

I think it does. When Pound first came to the detention camp, they put him in a cage with a concrete floor. After three weeks of this he broke down and was moved to a tent in the medical compound. And in gratitude he kissed the earth. This surely is a humanly understandable gesture, something that any of us might do if we were overwrought and in similar circumstances. It is not outside our experience, like the sacred marriage. Then Pound realizes the significance of what he has done and leaves a space to show that he is moving into a different kind of perception. He blocks it out with one of his verbal ideograms:

> bel seno   Δημήτηρ   copulatrix
> thy furrow

In Italian first, because the fair breast or bosom of earth he has kissed is Italian earth and must be addressed in her own tongue. Then he gives earth one of her sacred names, the name of the great earth goddess Demeter. And because sleeping on earth means sleeping *with* earth, if you have that way of looking at things, he adds "copulatrix." This is a mystery—"connubium terrae . . . mysterium," he writes later on—and the mysteries can't be uttered openly; they need their sacred languages which in the West are Greek and Latin.

What about "thy furrow"?

x There is a line not far from our passage in 81, near the end of 80:

Demeter has lain in my furrow

And just before that?

> with a smoky torch thru the unending
>   labyrinth of the souterrain
> or remembering Carleton let him celebrate Christ in the grain

The whole poem, as we've said so often, is governed by the seasonal rhythm of fall and rise, descent and ascent. The lines you have just read are obviously part of an ascent, a ritual that culminates in an ascent. The initiates must pass through a tortuous underground passage, a kind of testing, and at the end they emerge into the light and celebrate the god who has risen in the grain; Pound rather unexpectedly calls him Christ here. From the grain, bread, the fruit of Demeter: hence Dolores in the next passage can say to a child, Come pan, niño. And Pound adds here, "Demeter has lain in my furrow" because it is the sacred marriage with the earth goddess that makes this possible and grants men the continuing gift of bread.

F *But why* my *furrow? Surely the marriage is between Demeter and* Zeus—*Zeus lies in Ceres's bosom?*

In his usual way Pound gives us the elements separately: so that we may put the rite together for ourselves. Perhaps it would help, though, to have the whole scenario all in one piece. Where might we hope to find it?

(D nods a question toward a book in the middle of the table)

Yes, in the work we've drawn on so often, *The Golden Bough*. A note in my margin says that the passage we want is in chapter 12, near the start of the section called "The Marriage of the Gods." Can you find it for us?

D *This must be it. "In the great mysteries solemnised at Eleusis in the month of September the union of the sky-god Zeus with the corn-goddess Demeter appears to have been represented by the union of the hierophant with the priestess of Demeter"—*

Hence

Demeter has lain in my furrow

The poet is the hierophant who stands in for the god. As hierophant, he shows the sacred event to us, *to hieron.*

D *"The torches having been extinguished, the pair descended into a murky place"—*

Hence

with a smoky torch through the unending
labyrinth of the souterrain

Pound has changed the details a little.

D "... while the throng of worshipers awaited in anxious suspense the result of the mystic congress, on which they believed their own salvation to depend."

Mark the detached, scholarly tone of voice. Frazer couldn't have guessed that fifty years later this primitive ... belief would come to life again in a poem. Or perhaps with part of his mind he would have understood.

D "After a time the hierophant reappeared, and in a blaze of light silently exhibited to the assembly a reaped ear of corn, the fruit of the divine marriage."

Hence

let him celebrate Christ in the grain

Remember of course that corn is British English for wheat.

So this is what Pound is presenting in the lines from Canto 81 and in all the other passages that lead into and prepare for them. He starts, triumphantly,

Zeus lies in Ceres' bosom

with the divine union which the rite mimes. It is only *because* Zeus lies in Ceres's bosom, under Cythera or Aphrodite, who is now at one with the moon goddess, Artemis: love and time reconciled in the seasonal rhythm of nature, nature's divinity recovered and celebrated under the twin signs of love and returning time—it is only because of the sacred union of heaven and earth that Dolores can say, Come pan, niño. Only now do we understand what her words mean. We had ... forgotten that to eat bread is to take part in a great mystery. And yet it is the most homely, everyday thing there is.

P That's why he calls Demeter Ceres here. Ceres, cereal. . . .

G Wouldn't it have seemed more everyday to us if he had put it in English?

Pound puts it in English too. It has to go in Spanish, to his way of seeing, because it is only in Catholic cultures that traces of the old rites have been preserved and he has always been very much concerned with the process of preservation, of *transmission*. Hence Elizondo's two statements are necessary: Elizondo who had understood what lies behind the Christian sacraments and knew how to distinguish what endures and recurs from what passes away.

Zeus lies in Ceres's bosom: Come pan, niño: and the lines between and everything that leads into them from elsewhere: a single sentence enacting the recovered rite, the central mystery "venerable and articulate and complete."

So that's it then, it all coheres. Everything is perfectly clear. Or perhaps *not*, perhaps nothing is clear. Perhaps we haven't got it at all. I come back to the question I raised just now: What can the mysteries Pound tries to revive mean to us today? We make our classroom response; can we do anything more? So much of our work in class, with the older texts specially, and Pound's at his best is as ancient as any, is a matter of pretending to respond to things that are altogether outside our experience.

If it were easy to understand what these things mean, Pound would not have had to write *The Cantos*. A great deal stands in our way. "2 thousand years, desensitization" he called it at the end of Canto 92 (and just before spoke of "the degradation of sacraments"), two thousand years during which the mysteries meant almost nothing. The Catholic Church preserved a trace of them, he thought, but in today's world as a whole they are mere mumbo jumbo. We'd be embarrassed even to mention them outside class. So students of *The Cantos* have been forced to take Pound's gods and myths as simply part of the machinery of the poem, matters we "suspend disbelief" in while we get on with the business of reading—like the vegetation ceremonies that provide part of the machinery of *The Waste Land*.

For Pound they have always been very much more, though perhaps it is only with the *Pisan Cantos* that we see how *much* more. When these cantos came out in 1948, people who had been ignoring Pound's work for decades were reluctantly forced to admit that he did exist. They even found something there they could latch on to. It is mostly very obscure, they said, but at least he is writing *personal* poetry again—that being the only thing poets are now supposed to write. The Pisans are personal poetry and they aren't, but what is beyond question is that Pound's own tragedy put him at the center of the poem—the center of consciousness—as never before. Above all, it meant that his beliefs were *tested* as never before. In his book-lined study at Rapallo he had said: "I assert that the Gods exist." He had affirmed the life-giving powers of the mysteries, the saving rhythm of descent and ascent. In Canto 47 he had written:

> Falleth,
> Adonis falleth.
> Fruit cometh after.

Now it was Pound who had fallen: into a very convincing, quite unliterary hell. Would he rise again? Does fruit come after? Are the mysteries strong enough to lift up a man on whom the shadow of death has fallen? Do the gods exist, or are they simply part of a poet's fancy baggage?

The answer, we may say, is there in the 120 or so pages of the *Pisan Cantos:* in the sense that they record a great human victory. Pound does come through. We may put this down to his own personal toughness, an irreducible pigheaded heroism. God knows, I wouldn't want to underrate this. Pound is a great poet, I believe; he was also a very brave man. At the same time what these cantos show is that Pound won through because he felt he was sustained by the powers he had always believed in. He himself went down into the unending labyrinth of the souterrain, a dark night of the soul that left no room for "poetry," for make-belief. And he came up to look on the eternal elements and a nature once again brilliant with divinity. The army gave him a patch of ground to lie on and he found Demeter there and celebrated the marriage of Heaven and Earth. It must be the most astounding breach of military discipline since Coleridge joined the Fifteenth Dragoons.

And this is not all. The fact that when the test came, Pound's "pagan" beliefs did literally work points to something very important about those beliefs: they were always strangely, disconcertingly, literal. We may have stumbled on a feature of his work that has put so many people off.

Mr. R, you were offended earlier this afternoon when you found an analogy to the sacrament of Communion in Dolores's words about bread. From your point of view—I take it you're a Catholic—rightly so. For while Pound honors the Church for preserving traces of the mysteries, it is the mysteries themselves he believes in. The Church has lost their true meaning, their true form, and this is what he wants to recover. The trouble with Communion, he would say, is that the Church has left out the sacred marriage! He would say, I believe: When the founder of Christianity declared, "except a corn of wheat fall into the ground and die, it abideth alone; but if it die, it bringeth forth much fruit"—in saying this, Christ was reducing what had been a sacred truth—the truth of Eleusis—to a mere metaphor, a figure. Christian poets continued to use the myth of seasonal death and rebirth as a figure for man's spiritual rebirth. Both Dante and Milton so use the myth of Persephone. But it is *only* a figure, not the literal truth. Hence for the last two thousand years poetry has had to be "polysemous," as Servius said of Vergil and Dante said of himself and critics say admiringly of every important modern author except Pound.[8] Poetry has had to point away from the first, literal level to further levels of meaning, to "that which is signified by the letter," as Dante puts it; the thing, however concretely rendered, always "stands for" something else supposedly more important. But Pound is not polysemous; his first level doesn't point beyond itself. He is therefore not "complex" and in our critical language that means he is a simple-minded fellow, despite the surface complexity of his cultural allusions, though of course he writes very good verse. "*The Cantos* are never really difficult," Mr. Alvarez announces, confident that no one in his vicinage will correct him: Pound "says what he wants very skillfully, and he never has anything very difficult to say."[9]

Readers have in fact found *The Cantos* difficult but the difficulty which first confronts them—that surface complexity of cultural allusion—is not the real problem. The allusiveness of *The Waste Land* has not kept people away. I don't want to be facile and say that what is difficult about Pound's poetry is its "simplicity" but in a sense this is true. We feel that something is missing there; the whole reverberating dimension of inwardness is missing. There is no murmurous echo chamber where deeps supposedly answer to deeps. Not merely does the thing, in Pound's best verse, not point beyond itself: *it doesn't point to us.* The green tip that pushes through the earth in spring does not stand for or symbolize man's power of spiritual renewal. It is not polysemous. Pound's whole effort is *not* to be polysemous but to give back to the literal first level its full significance, its old significance, I would say. That green thrust is itself the divine event, the fruit of the marriage at Eleusis. Persephone is in that thrusting tip, and if man matters it is because he too has a share in that same power, he too is part of the seasonal, sacred life of nature. But only a part.

Meant as literally as Pound means it, this is very hard to take. Not only does it offend against the ways we have been taught to read literature; it is an offense against the great principle of inwardness or internalization that has put us at the center of things and laid waste the visible world.[10] It gives back to the visible world—a world "out there" that is not of our construction nor dependent on our collaboration—an importance it hasn't had for centuries. And in so doing it drastically reduces our importance.

Pound has been praised for the new "humility" he reveals in the *Pisan Cantos*—by critics not specially noted for that virtue. But his humility goes far beyond anything they have in mind. Take the passage in Canto 83 where he admiringly watches Brother Wasp building his mud house. To say that there is nothing remotely *de haut en bas* about his attitude doesn't sufficiently make the point. What is disconcerting is that Brother Wasp in no sense derives his significance from the inner world of the human observer and is quite as important as he is, rather more so indeed since he is closer to the divine sources, to what Pound calls the process. Listen to the way he celebrates the infant wasp's descent to the earth:

> The infant has descended,
>   from mud on the tent roof to Tellus,
> like to like colour he goes amid grass-blades,
>   greeting them that dwell under **XTHONOS XΘONOΣ**
> **OI XΘONIOI;**   to carry our news
>   εἰς χδονιους   to them that dwell under the earth,
> begotten of air, that shall sing in the bower
>   of Kore   Περσεφόνεια
> and have speech with Tiresias, Thebae

Donald Davie in an excellent passage speaks of Pound's "reverent vigilance before the natural world."[11] But there is more here even that that, a solemnity of accent that no other poet, perhaps, could have found for so "humble" an occasion. The little creature has been entrusted with the poem's central movement or theme, the Odyssean descent to the underworld to bring up new sources of strength.

Compare if you like Lawrence's poem "Snake." Lawrence is certainly respectful enough yet he is very self-conscious about it and has to assure us he "felt so honoured" that "one of the lords of life" had to come to drink at his water trough. The effect is to direct attention on Lawrence—and away from the snake. Whereas Pound can simply disappear. He doesn't tell us what he felt or try to persuade us of the wasp's importance. He lets the solemnity of his verse do that. Unlike Lawrence again, he can honor the nonhuman without feeling the need to rail at his "cursed human education." On the contrary, having celebrated the magnificence of Brother Wasp, he at once goes on to celebrate another magnificent act in the distinctively human field of high culture. "Uncle William"—Yeats—composing a poem as "perdurable," as free from the bonds of mortality, as the wasp's building activities. Brother Wasp and Uncle William confront each other, ideogrammatically, and together make a statement that could be put in no other way.

I read you a sentence from Alvarez just now, a typical enough piece of criticism, about Pound never having anything very difficult to say. Alvarez goes on to make his point by contrasting Pound and Eliot. "Ash Wednesday," he says, is obscure (unlike *The Cantos*, that is) "because it demands so much of the reader; preconceptions and obfuscations have to be stripped away in order to follow the delicate unfeigned shifts of feeling and argument." Sometimes it's a help when a critic manages to get things wholly back to front. You have all read "Ash Wednesday," I imagine. Apart from the difficulty for the non-Christian reader of having to take Christianity seriously, did the poem make demands on you greater than modern poetry normally does? Didn't you take those "delicate unfeigned shifts" of whatnot entirely in your stride? They are almost the minimal requirement of any good writing today. Eliot's poem is "difficult," I suppose, but it's the kind of difficulty we enjoy. It flatters our self-esteem; Pound's "simplicity" is chastening.

What our weekly conversations in this class have surely shown is that *The Cantos* demand enormously more of us, a departure from our normal ways of thinking about ourselves and the world more radical than most of us are prepared or even able to make. Century-old "preconceptions" and "obfuscations" have to be stripped away before one can even understand what Pound is saying. To read *The Cantos* means, in his own words, to recover "a lost kind of experience," a lost *unity* of experience within which the elements that have been separated come together again. So that to eat bread is once more to take part in a great mystery, the marriage of heaven and earth.

Years ago Pound himself once put it like this. Writing to a friend about the entrepreneurial activities that consumed so much of his time, he said: "I desire to go on with my long poem; and like the Duke of Chang, I desire to hear the music of a lost dynasty."[12]

Well . . . What I wanted to do this afternoon was read, and read, a single representative passage in such a way that what at first looks a muddle becomes entirely lucid—a lucidity not of our contriving or imposed on the text by arbitrary interpretation but there in the text, in the poem, waiting for us. Perhaps all I have succeeded in doing is to demonstrate that *The Cantos* are even more impenetrable than you were told when you signed up for this course. Or perhaps not. I can't tell from your patient, polite faces what you are really thinking. There's a way to find out, though. Why doesn't someone read the lines from Canto 81 just once more and then we'll call it a day?

G *I have a question. If Pound's poetry isn't polysemous, what justification is there for taking those croissants to signify Artemis and the moon?*

Mr. G, you are an invaluable man. You have just given us our first topic for next week. And now, who is going to read the lines?

x Me again?

Yes, you again. I want to hear if you are assisting at a sacred event.

x   Zeus lies in Ceres' bosom
                        Taishan is attended of loves
                                under Cythera, before sunrise
                        and he said. . . .

Notes

1. See Herbert N. Schneidau, *Ezra Pound: The Image and the Real* (1969) 62ff.
2. Boris de Rachewiltz, "Pagan and Magic Elements," in *New Approaches to Ezra Pound* (1969), ed. Eva Hesse, 194.
3. *The Letters of Ezra Pound, 1907–1941* (1950), ed. D. D. Paige, 303.
4. One industrious person actually does so after class and writes down some sentences from *Mechanization Takes Command* (1969) in the blank pages thoughtfully left by New Directions at the end of their edition of *The Cantos:* "The bread of full mechanization has the resiliency of a rubber sponge." (198) "The changed characteristics of bread always turned out to be in the interests of the producer. It was as if the consumer unconsciously adapted his taste to the type of bread suited to mass production and rapid turn-over." (201) "The question, 'how did mechanization alter bread?' cannot be put off and no doubt can remain about the answer. Mechanization has devalued the constant character of bread and turned it into an article of fashion for which newfound charms must ever be devised." (207) Pound would say: It is not "mechanization" that has taken command and devalued bread but *Usura.*
5. Hugh Kenner, *The Pound Era* (1971) 171–172.
6. Ibid. 450. Kenner thus describes Pound's approach to Chinese ideograms: "follow the crib, and when it flags, haruspicate the characters." (*Haruspex:* the priest who scrutinized the entrails of the sacrificial victims for signs.)
7. Daniel D. Pearlman, *The Barb of Time* (1969), 280, n. 49. See also the end of Canto 112:

8. *Polysemus,* πολύσημος, "having many significations." Charlton T. Lewis and Charles Short, *A Latin Dictionary* (1879), *s.v.* Dante said of his *Divine Comedy:* ". . . there is not just a single sense in this work: it might rather be called *polysemous,* that is, having several senses. For the first sense is that which is contained in the letter, while there is another which is contained in what is signified by the letter." "The Letter to Can Grande," in *Literary Criticism of Dante Alighieri* (1973), ed. Robert S. Haller, 99.

9. "Craft and Morals" in *Ezra Pound: Perspectives* (1965), ed. Noel Stock, 52–53.

10. Cf. C. S. Lewis: "that great movement of internalisation, and that consequent aggrandisement of man and desiccation of the outer universe, in which the psychological history of the West has so largely consisted." *The Discarded Image* (1964) 42.

11. *Ezra Pound: Poet as Sculptor* (1964) 175–177.

12. *Letters,* 128.

Res and *Verba* in *Rock-Drill* and After

DONALD DAVIE

❖   ❖   ❖

P OUND'S PREFERENCE FOR *RES* (things) over *verba* (words) is so
notorious, and has been reiterated so insistently by the master himself
(from the resounding Thomist declaration, "Nomina sunt consequentia
rerum," in the Gaudier memoir of 1917, through to his preferring on just
these grounds in *The Pisan Cantos* Ford's conversation to Yeats's) that, when
it comes to a choice or a showdown between a mimetic view of how
language relates to reality and a structuralist view, it seems clear that
Pound must stand with the conservative and nowadays somewhat embattled champions of *mimesis*. And yet, as people are beginning to notice,
Pound's own practice in *The Cantos* (throughout, but more markedly in the
later sequences, *Rock-Drill* and *Thrones*) lends itself more readily to explanation in structuralist than in mimetic terms—to the extent that there is
at least *prima facie* justification for Massimo Bacigalupo's charge that Pound
was culpably naive in not realizing how his own practice went beyond his
own mimetic theory. To be blunt about it, Pound's transition seem to be
frequently from *verbum* to *verbum* (by way of often translingual puns, fanciful
etymologies, echoings of sound) with no appeal over long stretches to the
res supposedly under discussion; Pound moves often from signifier to signifier, leaving the signified to take care of itself. The most obvious example,

first appearing very early in *The Cantos* and thereafter insistent enough to
be a sort of structural principle, is Pound's taking over from Aeschylus the
pun on the name of Helen (*helandros, helenaus, heleptolis*: man-destroyer, ship-
destroyer, city-destroyer) and extending it to apply to other Helens or
Eleanors, principally Eleanor of Aquitaine, but also Eleanor of Castile,
Eleanor of Provence, and others. This is obviously, and has duly been called,
"wordplay"; and I incline to think that the most pressing dilemma facing
Pound's admirers today is whether such "play" can be considered responsible (as most structuralist theories would agree that it can be), or else
must be declared irresponsible (as most mimetic theories have regularly
judged it).

If this seems to suggest that, whatever Pound's own asseverations to the
contrary, structuralist assumptions give us more access to *The Cantos* than
a mimetic approach, there are nevertheless difficulties in the way of the
structuralist. First of these is the assumption, made by most structuralists
though not all, that there is a radical breach between "the modern" and
all previous centuries of verse writing. Typical is John Steven Childs [*Paideuma*, 9–2, 289–307]: "it is not the interactions of characters which afford
meaning in Modernist literature; it is the mental character of the writer/
narrator himself which orders events and feelings" [p. 290]. Or again, "Modern poetry, eschewing directly social or didactic functions, is based on the
exploitation of non-referential discourse" [p. 293]. Both of these *dicta* plainly
go against the bent of Pound's temperament, so imbued with *pietas* toward
the recorded and inherited past, so ready to risk the didactic, and so
vowed—until the Pisan experience in some degree compelled otherwise—
to avoid the overtly and unashamedly "subjective." Moreover, in the one
case we have so far considered, Pound might vindicate his wordplay by
appeal to a precedent so far from modern as Aeschylus. Or else, if this
should seem only a debating point, consider another of Pound's ancient
masters, Ovid, who as Edgar M. Glenn points out [*Paideuma*, 10–3, 625–634]
indulged just the same wordplay in the *Metamorphoses* with the name of the
nymph Coronis, a pun on the names for raven (*corvus*) and for crow (*cornix*).
Structuralist criticism, it seems, must be ready to offer revisionist readings
of Ovid, no less than of a "modern" like Pound. And indeed it's entirely
possible that through the many centuries when Ovid has been admired, a
mimetic or prestructuralist understanding of language, and of how language traffics with reality, has failed to do justice to the power and vitality
of Ovid's mind; though poets like Dryden have delighted in Ovid's *logopoeia*
or word-play (his "turns"), one is familiar with apologetic scholarly com-

ments to the effect that this regrettable proclivity in Ovid is a price we must pay for his more solid virtues.

In any case *The Cantos* pose some real difficulties for that traditional criticism which I shall continue to call, somewhat loosely, "mimetic." A very bold and clear example is what Michael Alexander makes of some lines from Canto 95:

> I suppose St. Hilary looked at an oak-leaf.
> (vine-leaf? San Denys,
>   (spelled Dionisio)
> Dionisio et Eleutherio.
> Dionisio et Eleutherio
>   "the brace of 'em
> That Calvin never blacked out
>   en l'Isle.)
>   [95/647]

To Michael Alexander it is quite clear that this is "not . . . serious." And he remarks sharply:

> The suppositiousness here is pretty marked. Though it may well be true that free love is commoner in Paris than in Geneva, this is not a consequence of the etymology of the names of Saints Hilary and Denis; nor is it easy to see how Calvin could have been able to black it out . . . In this mood, Pound might have been just as happy to play with the names of Calvin and Charles le Chauve. The passage is a harmless example of playful free association yet suggests a weakness for seeing historical significance in convenient verbal coincidence. There is no reason to suppose St. Hilary of Poitiers was particularly cheerful or particularly sensitive to nature, pleasant though it is to think that he was.[1]

The bluff common sense of this is refreshing. Yet the difficulties it runs us into are surely obvious; the transition or glissade from Hilary to *hilaritas*, or from Denys to Dionysus (for which Pound has a premodern precedent, Walter Pater's "Apollo in Picardy") is not at first sight any different from the "convenient verbal coincidence" that has many times in earlier cantos linked Helen, or various Helens, with various Eleanors. If a difference is to be found, it can be found only by appealing in all these cases from *verbum* to *res*—and pointing out for instance that as a matter of historical record

Eleanor of Aquitaine did destroy men and ships and cities, just as did
Aeschylus's legendary Helen; whereas, as Alexander points out, the historical record concerning St. Hilaire is just not full enough for us to predicate
about him so certainly. And it's notable that Edgar Glenn, when he discusses Ovid's glissades among Coronis and *corvus* and *cornix,* seems in the
end to justify them by a similar appeal to *res:* "although this is word play,
the identifications are operative in the tale because all three are betrayers
and all three are punished" [p. 631]. The *res* here, however, is much more
dubious, for there is no question of appeal to any historical record other
than the fabulous history that Ovid chooses to tell, and so the *res* turns
out to be nothing other than the internal necessities and structural principles of Ovid's verbal artifact. The *res* in fact *is* structure: which is just
what structuralism claims. In precisely the same way the necessities and
principles of Pound's poem require that Denys and Hilary and Calvin be
given the significances that in this passage he demands for them. It seems,
therefore, that to be consistent Michael Alexander would have to deny the
plea that Edgar Glenn enters for Ovid.

Alexander says that this passage, though it "suggests a weakness," is all
the same "harmless." It is hard to see how this can be true; for anything
that diminishes a reader's confidence in his poet cannot help but be harm-
ful to that poet and his poem. And one need not go all the way with
Michael Shuldiner in his ambitiously schematic treatment of *hilaritas* in
relation to *sinceritas, caritas,* and *humanitas* [*Paideuma*, 4–1, 71–81] to feel uneasily
sure that from *The Pisan Cantos* onward hilarity, or *hilaritas,* is being asked to
carry a lot of weight, in a way that demonstrably irresponsible play with
St. Hilary cannot help but weaken. The point at issue is surely much more
crucial than Michael Alexander wants to admit, and it follows that if
Pound's wordplay in this passage *can* be vindicated, that vindication should
be spelled out.

To that end we may consider a passage from Canto 92 that is superficially dissimilar:

> But in the great love, bewildered
>   farfalla in tempesta
> under rain in the dark:
>   many wings fragile
> Nymphalidae, basilarch, and lycaena,
> Ausonides, euchloe, and erynnis
>
>   [92/619]

I dare say many readers have been content to suppose (hazardously however, for we should know by now that Pound is a tricky poet who for instance neologizes) that the six splendidly resonant nouns in the last two lines name species or families of butterflies; but there may have been others like me who only lately, after knowing the lines for many years, chose to check that hunch against Alexander B. Klots's *Field Guide to the Butterflies of North America, East of the Great Plains* (1951). Klots's index does indeed list five of these six names, along with others (e.g. "Dryas" and "Dione") which have cropped up in *The Cantos* in contexts where butterflies seemed not to be in question. Having thus linked these *verba* with the *res*, butterfly, one has perhaps achieved something; but certainly one has not achieved meaning, significance, where before there was none. On the contrary, a range of significance has been rather grievously contracted from the time when, in ignorance of Alexander Klots, one mused happily over etymologies, linking "euchloe" with the Greek *euchloos*, with its sense of "making fresh and green", or recognizing in "erynnis" one form of the Latin word for the furies, the Greek Eumenides; discovering too from the Latin dictionary that the one name missing from Klots, "Ausonides," is poetical for *Ausonii*, Italians. As for "basilarch," that thunderous compound of the Greek roots for "king" (basileus) and for "ruler" (arkhon), one feels positively let down by the discovery in Klots that it names the Viceroy butterfly, so named because for protective purposes it seems to mimic in colors and markings the inedible Monarch butterfly. Further, I can recall from rather long ago the almost mutinous disappointment with which I discovered that "farfalla" is common Italian for "butterfly," thus not ruling out, but certainly muting, a translingual pun that I thought I detected, between "farfalla" ("in tempesta") and an English expression: "far fallen." Do I stand convicted of having been a frivolous, an irresponsible reader? Or was it my poet who was frivolous when he exploited an apparently unearned resonance from the word "basilarch," applied to a *res* that seemed not to merit such a trumpet note? Or is it not the case, rather, that neither Pound nor I was being frivolous when we refused to let the multivalent potencies of the *verba* be channeled into the narrow duct of a single and highly specialized "meaning"? Supposing that, I am forced to suppose that structuralist criticism has indeed much to offer readers of *The Cantos*, being in this case the only way to let both Pound and me off the hook. "I suppose," says Pound in the passage from Canto 95, "I suppose St. Hilary looked at an oak-leaf." And Michael Alexander rejoins smartly: "The suppositiousness . . . is pretty marked." But surely "I suppose" functions quite precisely in poetic discourse just as does in discourse of another kind, "I propose" or "I postulate"; stated or unstated (and here it is stated), it reiterates what Philip Sidney declared when he said that as for the poet "he nothing affirmes, and therefore never lyeth." This declares that the business of the poet is serious play—play between signifiers, letting the signified for the nonce go hang.

Accordingly, as the first earnest attempt to read *The Cantos* from a structuralist standpoint, John Steven Childs's "Larvatus Prodeo: Semiotic Aspects of the Ideogram in Pound's *Cantos*" has considerable importance, though it is limited, as the title makes clear, from being focused on the special case of how the Chinese ideograms function. The structuralist authority that Childs most often cites is, not surprisingly, Roland Barthes. And some of the passages cited from Barthes are as usual vitiated by declaring or assuming an absolute discontinuity between the poetry that can be called "modern" and that to be called "classique." One of them, however, has peculiar pertinence in that it links up with what Barthes could not have known about and Childs does not notice: the work that has been done on how *forma*, a concept that originated apparently with Allen Upward, figures alike in Pound's theory and his practice:

> Dans la Poétique moderne . . . les mots produisent une sorte de continu formel dont émane peu à peu une densité intellectuelle ou sentimentale impossible sans eux; la parole est alors le temps épais d'une gestation plus spirituelle, pendant laquelle la 'pensée' est préparée, installée, peu et peu par le hasard des mots. [*Pai*, 92, 305]

What Barthes with characteristic incautiousness predicates of all modern poetry is certainly true of one body of that poetry, the *Rock-Drill* cantos; in those cantos at any rate (in others less insistently) the *res* to which Pound's *verba* point is ultimately not this or that *thing*, still less this or that proposition. What is pointed to, and earnestly invoked, is a disposition of mind and feeling, a disposition which *precedes* the framing of propositions or the making of distinctions, which precedes, and in the event of course may make unnecessary, the distinguishing between medieval Church history (St. Denys, St. Hilaire) on the one hand, and on the other pagan and perennial morality (*hilaritas*, the Dionysian); which refuses the demand to know whether "Druas" and "Dione" and "Erynnis" belong in entomology or in classical mythology. (The names belong in both realms; and it is just their dual belonging which, it may be argued, makes them sanative and harmonizing.) This realm of thought and feeling *before* the crystallizing out and the making of distinctions is precisely what Upward and Pound alike seem to have understood by the realm of "the *forma*"; and so that apparently so reasonable plea, "But come, distinguish," is just what they are vowed not to satisfy.

Nevertheless, Michael Alexander must have some right on his side. There must be some point at which we feel (and can vindicate the feeling) that Pound's wordplay ceases to be serious and becomes frivolous. For me, and I think for some others, the point comes by and large between the conclusion of *Rock-Drill* and the beginning of *Thrones*. From this point of view nothing is so disappointing in John Steven Childs's discussion as his assumption that *Rock-Drill* and *Thrones* are much of a muchness. I will return to the beginning of this article, and at the same time cite a case that I have used elsewhere, by recalling that in the *Rock-Drill* Canto 94, and thereafter in the *Thrones* cantos, we are required to extend the "Helen" identification to other Eleanors than Eleanor of Aquitaine; and that in the *Thrones* Canto 107 one of these other Eleanors appears, Eleanor of Provence, consort of Henry III of England:

> & this Helianor was of the daughters, heirs
> of Raymond Berengar
> and sister of Arch. Cantaur
> [107/759]

We must note that the case of this Eleanor is not on a par with that of St. Hilaire of Poitiers: the historical records tell us enough of this Eleanor, tell us in particular that she fiddled her kinsman into the see of Canterbury ("Arch. Cantaur"). What baffles and in the end exasperates us is not that we do not have this *res* to which to attach the *verba* about her, but that, the *res* thus established, we do not know what to do with it. Where does Eleanor's maneuvering her relative into Canterbury fit into the still developing structure of Pound's poem? Are we to applaud her for the maneuver, or deplore it? In neither of these ways, nor in any other, does this *res* rhyme with, or hook on to, anything else in the poem. In other words, the identifying of this Eleanor with the older and greater Eleanor, and through her with Helen of Troy, offends us because it has no *structural* significance, not because it has no meaning in terms of the historical record. This suggests—I may dare to say, it *shows*—that, whereas few structuralists care to stoop to value judgments, nevertheless their own procedures permit of such judgments being made. They would disarm the prejudices of some of us if they showed more interest in pursuing that possibility. There is *logopoeia* that is legitimate (St. Denys identified with Dionysus), and other *logopoeia* that is not (Eleanor of Provence identified with Helen of Troy); and the test of legitimacy is not any appeal to authorities outside the poem, but on the contrary appeal to the poem's own structural requirements.

I shall assume (for I have argued the case elsewhere) that what goes on in these lines about Eleanor of Provence is fairly typical of the *Thrones* sequence as a whole; that among the rather many things wrong with these cantos is wordplay of this tired and pointless sort, *logopoeia* pursued at the expense of *phanopoeia* and *melopoeia* (image-play and sound-play), and also of common sense. This is still a minority opinion, but one that I think is gaining ground—a great deal of *Thrones* is simply a bore. However, some *Thrones* cantos are better than others; and in the better ones one encounters *logopoeia* that is, to put it grudgingly, at least a borderline case. A rather crucial instance is Canto 106:

> Help me to neede
> By Circeo, the stone eyes looking seaward
> Nor could you enter her eyes by probing.
> The temple shook with Apollo
> As with leopards by mount's edge,
> light blazed behind her;
> trees open, their minds stand before them
> As in Carrara is whiteness:
> Xoroi. At Sulmona are lion heads.
> Gold light, in veined phylotaxis.
> By hundred blue-gray over their rock-pool,
> Or the king-wings in migration
> And in thy mind beauty, O Artemis
> Over asphodel, over broom-plant,
> faun's ear a-level that blossom.
> Yao and Shun ruled by jade.
> Whuder ich maei lidhan
> helpe me to neede
> the flowers are blessed against thunder bolt
> helpe me to neede.
> That great acorn of light bulging outward,
> Aquileia, caffaris, caltha palistris,
> ulex, that is gorse, herys arachnites;
> Scrub oak climbs against cloud-wall—

three years peace, they had to get rid of him,
 —violet, sea green, and no name.
Circe's were not, having fire behind them.
  Buck stands under ash grove,
   jasmine twines over capitols
    Selena Arsinoe
So late did queens rise into heaven.
   At Zephyrium, July that was, at Zephyrium
   The high admiral built there;
     Aedificavit
TO APHRODITE EUPLOIA
   "an Aeolian gave it, ex voto
   Arsinoe Kupris.
    At Miwo the moon's axe is renewed
     HREZEIN
Selena, foam on the wave-swirl
  Out of gold light flooding the peristyle
   Trees open in Paros,
    White feet as Carrara's whiteness
     [106/754–755]

This passage is a sort of tie-beam. Considered as a structural member, it carries much weight, resolves many stresses. On the one hand, it reaches far back into preceding cantos, picking up for instance ("violet, sea green, and no name") the three pairs of differently colored eyes which figured so hauntingly and repeatedly in *The Pisan Cantos*, picking up also from *Rock-Drill* Canto 91 ("Help me to neede . . . Whuder ich maei lidhan") Brutus's prayer to Diana in Layamon's *Brut*, beseeching her to lead him to a new realm, the third Troy that Layamon identified with Albion. On the other hand, the passage also reaches forward, for instance to "the great acorn of light" in Canto 116. Among the matters thus picked up from quite far back in the poem, and then conveyed forward, is the matter of butterflies. For "the king-wings in migration" clearly "rhymes" (structurally) with the "farfalla" passage that we have looked at in Canto 92, and carries that forward to what may well be the last lines of the entire poem, among the "Notes for Canto CXVII et seq.":

  Two mice and a moth my guides—
  To have heard the farfalla gasping
   as toward a bridge over worlds.

That the kings meet in their island,
          where no food is after flight from the pole.
Milkweed the sustenance
          as to enter arcanum.

To be men not destroyers.

                                              [*D&F*, 802]

For the Monarch butterfly (*Danaus plexippus*), which does indeed live on the poisonous milkweed, in mid-September migrates southward, if not from the pole at least from arctic Canada, along skyways that have been mapped; and there are known locations where large flocks of them can be found resting, at staging posts on the migration. (The northward migration in spring is less marked, because apparently less marshaled.)

Thus, what in this way binds Canto 92 through Canto 106 with Canto 117 is a "rhyme" of *res*, not of *verba*. The only wordplay involved is the easy substitution of "king" for "monarch." And so this transition can be (and should be, I think, for surely it is masterly) applauded as warmly by nonstructuralists as by structuralists.[2] The "borderline" cases come later in the passage when, if "king-wings in migration" have alerted us to the presence of butterflies, we ponder the lines:

                    Selena Arsinoe
          So late did queens rise into heaven.
                    At Zephyrium, July that was, at Zephyrium
                    The high admiral built there;

                                              [106/755]

For there is a butterfly called *Boloria selene* (the silver-bordered fritillary), and every one knows that there are butterflies called Admirals. One species of Admiral (the Viceroy) we have met already under the name *basilarch*; the other two species are named for or after a Greek goddess, whose name has resounded many times in the cantos and will resound even more loudly in the cantos that remain—they are *Limenitis arthemis* and *Limenitis arthemis astyanax*. So whoever the high admiral is in human terms (one thinks perhaps wrongly of Drake, for "Zephyrium" means "western promontory" and one promontory that might qualify is Circeo, with which Francis Drake was memorably connected in Canto 91), one cannot, and perhaps one should not, exclude the possibility that the admiral is as much insectile as human. If this is fanciful, a good deal less so is the nimbus or aura that hangs around "So late did queens rise into heaven." What this recalls first is a line from Canto 97, "Bernice, late for a constellation, mythopoeia persisting"; and another from Canto 102, "Berenice, a late constellation." A look into Lemprière will identify the Queen Berenice in question, and sketch the myth which transforms her, or rather the hair of her head, into a constellation. But what are we then to make of the perhaps unwelcome information from the invaluable Alexander Klots, that there is a Queen butterfly (*Danaus gilippus*), which in many ways corresponds in the Southern states to the Monarch in more northerly latitudes; and that one subspecies of the Queen is called *Danaus gilippus berenice*? Are the queens, like the admirals, insectile as much as they are human, or mythologically divine?

What strengthens this alarmed or alarming supposition is that a few lines earlier has occurred ("caltha palistris . . . herys arachnites") what we may take to be an allusion to Linnaean botany—an important foreshadowing, if so, of the otherwise unheralded veneration to be given to Linnaeus in the *Drafts and Fragments*. For of course the classification of butterflies is itself Linnaean, and some of the taxonomic namings (notably that of the Monarch) are credited to Linnaeus himself. When in the latest cantos Linnaeus is named for veneration along with Mozart and Ovid, is he in fact honored as "natural scientist" [JW, *Later*, 184]? Is he not rather, or equally, honored as a genius of language, a masterly inventor of, and source for, interlingual punning (*logopoeia*) between Greek and Latin on the one hand, English and presumably Swedish on the other? According to Harry Meacham, in *The Caged Panther*, Pound's interest in Linnaeus dated from the St. Elizabeths years, and may have been prompted by the devotion to Linnaeus of the then Secretary-General of the United Nations, Dag Hammarskjold. It would be interesting to know precisely the grounds on which Hammarskjold venerated his great compatriot.

One of the rather few commentators who can help us in difficult speculations like these is Guy Davenport. His essay "Persephone's Ezra" [EH, *Approaches*] is illuminating for instance on the relation between tree and marble pillar which accounts, in the passage we have been considering, for

> trees open, their minds stand before them
> As in Carrara is whiteness: . . .
>
> [106/754]

and

Trees open in Paros,
    White feet as Carrara's whiteness . . .
                    [106/755]

And plainly, what we have more particularly been looking at is glossed when Davenport says in the same essay: "Pound cancelled in his own mind the dissociations that had been isolating fact from fact for four centuries. To have closed the gap between mythology and botany" (or, we may add, lepidoptery) "is but one movement of the process; . . ." However, when we return these sentences to their context we cannot help but wonder if the commonsense objections of a Michael Alexander are being given what is after all their due. For Davenport is quite uncompromising:

> To say that *The Cantos* is "a voyage in time" is to be blind to the poem altogether. We miss immediately the achievement upon which the success of the poem depends, its rendering time transparent and negligible, its dismissing the supposed corridors and perspectives *down* which the historian invites us to look. Pound cancelled in his own mind the dissociations that had been isolating fact from fact for four centuries. To have closed the gap between mythology and botany is but one movement of the process; one way to read the cantos is to go through noting the restorations of relationships now thought to be discrete—the ideogrammatic method was invented for just this purpose. In Pound's spatial sense of time the past is here, now; its invisibility is our blindness, not its absence. The nineteenth century had put everything against the scale of time and discovered that all behaviour within time's monolinear progress was evolutionary. The past was a graveyard, a museum. It was Pound's determination to obliterate such a configuration of time and history, to treat what had become a world of ghosts as a world eternally present. [p. 157; also above, pp. 57–58]

This is wonderfully eloquent, and phrase after phrase in these sentences speaks justly to what we experience, and respond to, when we are reading *The Cantos* at their best. Yet is it not clear that in this passage Davenport, whether or not he intends it, is handing over the entire poem to the synchronic or synchronizing vision of the structuralist? He speaks of Pound as canceling "the dissociations that have been isolating fact from fact", but of course, as any structuralist will point out with glee, it's not clear that *facts* figure in any poetic discourse whatever. We can't any longer suppose, naively, that a fact gets into a poem as soon as it is named there. For a fact, and the name of that fact, are different; and it is only the name, not the thing named, that is at home in the verbal universe that is a poem. As John Steven Childs remarks with obvious satisfaction, "modern poetry" (in which clearly he includes *The Cantos*) "is based on the exploitation of non-referential discourse." If we do not share his satisfaction, if we want the discourse of *The Cantos* to be in some ways or in some degree referential, the *res* that we look for must be something different from what Guy Davenport means by "facts." It must be, I have suggested, what Upward meant by the *forma*; and I glossed this provisionally as a state of mind and feeling anterior to the making of distinctions. Thus where Davenport speaks of the canceling of dissociations (which a Michael Alexander would surely, and with much reason, rephrase as the blurring of distinctions), we might do better to speak of the postponement, or the "willing suspension," of distinctions. And I think this is more than nitpicking. For it permits of, and indeed requires, a *diachronic* vision, such as we might expect of a poet who told Grazia Livi in 1962: "The modern world doesn't exist because nothing exists which does not understand its past or its future." (Guy Davenport, who quotes this with approval, must be confident that it doesn't make against his reading of *The Cantos*, though to my mind it certainly does.)

These difficult matters are best dealt with in relation to some particular crux in our reading of the poem. Accordingly I will cite one more such crux, from Canto 110, the first of the *Drafts & Fragments*:

> The purifications
> > are snow, rain, artemisia,
> > also dew, oak and the juniper
>
> And in thy mind beauty, O Artemis,
> > of mountain lakes in the dawn, . . .
> > > [110/778]

The question is, very simply: Does it matter, for our reading of the poem aright, that we identify "artemisia" as wormwood? If it does not matter, then the link from "artemisia" to "Artemis" is a mere adventitious jingle of sound, and so obvious that we might justly call it "mechanical." Even if we take note of John of Trevisa in 1398 ("Artemisia is callyd moder of herbes and was somtyme hallowed . . . to the goddesse that hyght Arthemis"), we are still wholly in the realm of *verba* and moving from signifier to signifier by way of disputable etymology. If on the other hand we identify wormwood, and learn from *O.E.D.* that as early as 1535 wormwood was "an emblem or type of what is bitter and grievous to the soul," we have moved from *verbum* to *res*; and the link to Artemis accordingly takes on substance and specificity. For we are compelled to infer that the Artemis who is so markedly the presiding deity of these cantos is every inch the Artemis of Canto 30, she by whom we "maintain antisepsis," her special function the dispensing of what is, medicinally, "bitter and grievous to the soul." This means that the *forma* invoked and created in *Drafts & Fragments* is dark and tragically bitter in a way that, among the commentators, only Eva Hesse seems to have recognized. She must be right, I think, for if we move once more from *verbum* to *res*, we find the perception reinforced in those last lines where the Monarch butterflies "meet in their island":

> Milkweed the sustenance
> as to enter arcanum
> [*D&F*, p. 802]

It is only by ingesting that which is to all others bitter and poisonous that the kings can enter, or think to enter, arcanum.

I conclude therefore that, much as structuralist criticism can illuminate for us what is going on in many pages of *The Cantos*, and however much nonstructuralist criticism must refine its assumptions so as to allow for this, yet in the end Pound's claim to attend to *res* not *verba* can be, and must be, vindicated; and that a thoroughgoing or dogmatic structuralism milks this text, as presumably any other, of human pathos and human significance.

Notes

1. Michael Alexander, *The Poetic Achievement of Ezra Pound* (London & Boston, 1979), p. 215.
2. To take the full force of it one needs to consult the elegant and learned examination by Sieburth in *Paideuma*, 4-2 & 3, 329–332.

Bibliography

Ezra Pound, *The Cantos*. London: Faber, 1975.

Abbreviations

D&F: Ezra Pound, *Drafts and Fragments of Cantos CX–CXVII* (section of the above edition of *The Cantos*).

EH, *Approaches*: Eva Hesse, ed., *New Approaches to Ezra Pound*. London: Faber, 1969.

JW, *Later*: James J. Wilhelm, *The Later Cantos of Ezra Pound*. New York: Walker, 1977.

Pai: *Paideuma: A Journal Devoted to Ezra Pound Scholarship* (Orono, Maine).

"Unstill, Ever Turning"

The Composition of Ezra Pound's Drafts & Fragments

RONALD BUSH

◆ ◆ ◆

1

Textually and critically, the most interesting installment of Ezra Pound's *Cantos* may have been the last, *Drafts & Fragments*.[1] Even in the early stages of composition, Pound vacillated (as he had in the *Pisan Cantos*[2]) in his structural idiom between the openness of a diary and the shapeliness of a distinct thematic organization, as well as in the political coloring of the stories he told between authoritarianism and anarchy. Then, as Peter Stoicheff pointed out in 1986, the instabilities of the text were compounded by nonauthorial interventions. Donald Hall, the most significant intermediary, entered at a critical moment. In early 1960, with a proto-sequence fully drafted, Pound drifted into a severe depression. Interviewing him for *The Paris Review*, Hall had Pound read his drafts aloud and then responded so enthusiastically to the paradisal elements in the poetry that Pound felt impelled to renew work on the sequence. Ultimately, Pound resisted Hall's vision, but in the process he produced a radically different, truncated, and unfinished text, which he sent off to Hall for comment. Pound's work then stopped, but some seven years later Hall allowed his typescript of the new sequence to be copied, and inadvertently enabled the publication of a piracy of the unfinished material. In 1968/9 James Laughlin of New Directions, surmounting Pound's reluctance to publish, convinced him to proofread and authorize a "canonical" text that except for Hall might never have seen the light.[3]

The following discussion supplements Stoicheff's publication history with an augmented account of *Drafts & Fragments'* composition. My efforts involve elements of biography, textual history, and criticism, and draw on unpublished manuscripts at the Beinecke Library at Yale, the Humanities Research Center at Texas, the Houghton Library at Harvard, and the private collection of Marcella Spann Booth. I also refer to Donald Hall's unpublished letters to and from Pound and James Laughlin at Harvard and Yale and to Dorothy Pound's large and small diaries for 1958 and 1959 at the Lilly Library, Indiana University. Although her diaries consist mainly of shorthand notes of important movements and events, alongside available letters and memoirs they allow us to pin down Pound's movements during the last important journey of his life.[4]

Drafts & Fragments, first and foremost, is a poem about Pound's return after thirteen years of incarceration in St. Elizabeths Hospital in Washington, D.C., to the European sites of his strongest adult memories. Or rather, it is a poem about his return to what seemed a diminished Europe and a diminished self. The tone of these last cantos seems to have been set by September 1958, when Pound wrote Archibald MacLeish that it was "one thing to have Europe fall on one's head. Another to be set in the ruins of same."[5]

Some composition had, however, preceded Pound's return. And the way he altered these first jottings gives us a fix on how the poem found its course. The manuscript record indicates that Pound composed the first fragments of his final cantos during the last year of his enforced hospitalization. After he finalized *Thrones* in the summer of 1958, two typescripts, both drawn from Pound's handwritten poetic notebooks, remained: a short political typescript labeled "Canto 110 (or 111 or 112)" involving the Connecticut Charter, and drawing on a notebook dating from December 28, 1957; this was sent to Norman Holmes Pearson from St. Elizabeths on 22 January 1958 with the note "Juzza little one, before we git on to Linnaeus." And a much longer typescript drawn from a 1957 notebook; Pound internally dated this one (as if in a diary) "14 dec.[ember] '57" to "19th of june [1958]" and beyond.[6] Both typescripts are preserved in the Pound archives at the Beinecke Library at Yale,[7] and both echo *Thrones'* tone of political *assertion.* The first alludes to the historical importance of Pound's family history. The second announces "this part is for adults" and repeats the Dantesque insistence of *Thrones* that natural authority makes certain kinds of political arrangements "seats" for the gods.

Yet the second typescript also contained the seed of a different kind of poem and provides a bridge between the political preoccupations of Pound's St. Elizabeths years and the painful transit between St. Elizabeths and his final home in Italy. On April 18, 1958, a federal hearing ended Pound's confinement. And between then and July 1, when Pound and his wife, Dorothy, sailed for Genoa, he packed busily, visited, and paid farewells in Washington, D.C., and elsewhere. When he was not accompanied by Dorothy (who went with him, for example, to visit the journalist Harry Meacham in Charlottesville on the 31st of May) or by his friend Craig La Drière (then at Catholic University), he was with Marcella Spann, a young admirer who visited him frequently in St. Elizabeths. During that tumultuous spring he came to associate her with those young women represented in romances which Joseph Rock collected in studies of the Na Khi tribe of highland China—studies Pound had alluded to in *Thrones* and whose importance will soon be clear. In the long second typescript I have mentioned (but in a section that does not appear in Pound's notebook source and may have been composed at Brunnenburg) Marcella and the Na Khi are telescoped in one startling personal interjection—the cry of a "beach bird" on June 5 [1958] in Virginia, a day not recorded in Dorothy's diary. What followed, though still inhabiting the world of *Thrones,* introduced some of what were to become the inflections of *Drafts & Fragments:*

"four four four four

   tullup tullup tullup

June 5, beach bird's opinion

yellow iris alone..

   the mauve field

Oaks on Mt Sumeru

   and with eyes of coral and turquoise,

can you see with such eyes on Mt Sumeru

  had queen Ash
   such eyes of turquoise

and will you walk with the oak's root

    yellow iris rise in that river bed

> we have been here from the begining
>
> from her breath were the goddesses
>
>   ²La ²-mun ³-mi
>
> without ²Ndaw ¹bpo, nothing solid
>
> without ²Muan ¹bpo, no reality
>
> from the juniper is our agility
> botanic beauty of shoulders
>
> in fate's tray are winnowed [pictograph]
> ragion civile

The bird cry that opens this passage provides an occasion like the one T. S. Eliot records in *Burnt Norton,* and would eventually become the focus of a moment of genuine self-reflection. Here, in its first incarnation, it is a part of a self-assured mood associated with the brighter side of the Na Khi material. After a glance at yellow iris, taken from one of Pound's favorite Noh plays,[8] we become aware of the eyes of the heroine of a Na Khi Romance about the suicide of a girl forced to give up her lover and marry a man chosen by her parents. (The Na Khi were a non-Confucian tribe that countenanced easy sexuality and free marital choice. When they were forced to emigrate to Confucian China, the old customs were condemned, and many young people chose to commit suicide rather than submit to the new ways. Their tragedies were turned into romance, and the rituals that emerged from the poetry concern souls of the departed young women whose ghosts were said to inhabit the wind.)

What rings false in the fragment, at least from the perspective of what Pound eventually made of it, is how quickly it moves from the sombreness of the suicide romance ("will you walk with the earth's root") to another, more positive, ritual, the ²Muan ¹bpo, which the Na Khi believe connects man to earth and heaven. The point of the suicide, apparently, is its illumination. And having registered that illumination, Pound quickly (as he had in the mandarin *Thrones*) connects eros and ritual with an Italian phrase meaning roughly political sense. The rest of the typescript vacillates rather mechanically between eros and politics, first elaborating the Na Khi verses later revised for Canto CX and "From CXII," glancing at the farfalla which had appeared in Canto CIX, but concentrating on the political machinations of nineteenth-century America and Renaissance Florence. Fittingly then, the draft concludes with a gesture toward "Quemoy" (whose status was then a matter of controversy on the front pages of the Washington papers).

The scene now shifts to Italy. Having landed in Genoa, Pound arrived at his daughter's residence, a restored castle (Brunnenburg) in Tirolo on the 12th of July 1958. At the beginning of his Italian freedom, he said in a contemporary letter, he had a "bad break down" and was "not able to finish a paragraph."[9] But by the 5th of August, he began to find the "mountain air a pleasant change"[10] and was able to work and travel. Travel, in fact, became something of a necessity as the people around him got on each others' nerves. Dorothy's diary records that he went with Marcella to Venice on the 19th of September and that they returned on the 21st, and this accords with a typescript fragment at Yale in which we find the first record of lines near the beginning of the canonical Canto CX about the "gaiety" and the "exuberance" of the "waves" in Venice.[11] Marcella Spann Booth's manuscripts chronicle the growth of what surrounds them. On an envelope marked "Venice/ 12 Nov '58," Pound drafted lines beginning "To thy quiet house Torcello" and ending "what panache—." And by "December 10" he had made a typescript and carbon, on which he had among other things added the words "paw flap/ wave tap." Soon afterward, this opening was worked into an ur-Canto CX that exists in four copies at Yale and which adds a polished version of some of the Na Khi and most of the political material of the long St. Elizabeths draft to the Venice and Torcello lines. Finally, as the conclusion to ur-Canto CX, Pound annexed material from the little Connecticut Charter draft.[12]

Despite the "gaiety" of the Venice lines, though, the tone of the new beginning was hardly unrelieved exuberance. Even in his view of political history Pound painted a picture of human progress whose inevitable rhythm was one step forward, two steps back. Good people, though lionized, are beleaguered and foredoomed. Against history's power of dissolution the poem suggests that only moments of love matter. Here again, not only history but also culture resists. Remarkably, as Pound traveled with Marcella Spann, the difficulty of their situation recapitulated the autobiographical, bohemian themes of his earliest cantos. Sensing the fragility of their situation, Pound recoiled against decades of promoting neo-Confucian order and fashioned a tale like Canto VI of 1919, which in its unrevised form presented medieval lovers kept apart by powers of money, convention, and status, even as he and Dorothy had been separated before their marriage by the disapproval of Edwardian London.[13] Only this time, Dorothy had become one of the obstructors, and Marcella had no troubadour to save her.

As early as ur-Canto CX (late 1958), Pound was moved to darken the mood of the St. Elizabeths material, emphasizing the sadness and the ir-reparability of the Na Khi suicides. I quote from one set of the Yale drafts:

> che paion si al ven'
>
> har la llu k'o
>
> of the wind sway

the 9 fates and the 7

> and the black tree was born dumb
> the water is blue and not turquoise
> when the stag drinks at the salt spring
> and sheep come down with the gentian sprout
> Can you see with eyes of coral or turquoise,
> or walk with the oak's root

In this revision of the long St. Elizabeths typescript, Pound shifts with real reluctance from the eyes of the suicide to the ceremony of heaven. In the new draft the suicide, and not its illumination, takes center stage, and Pound's questions become anything but perfunctory. "Do you know," he asks the girl in the story, "that the black tree on which you will hang yourself is dumb, and that your courage will never be spoken?" "Are you aware of the darkness and silence to come?" What I have called ur-Canto CX neither smooths over death nor disconnects it from the forces of the surrounding wind.

By January 1959 relations at Brunnenburg continued to deteriorate, in ways Mary de Rachewiltz has recounted in her memoir, *Discretions.*[14] More than ever Pound needed to get out and about, and Dorothy's diaries record that starting from the 11th of January, she, Marcella, and Pound made extensive excursions. From the 11th to the 15th of January they traversed Lake Garda, stopping at Limone, Salò, Brescia (where they stopped at the Duomo, the Piazza, and the olive groves), as well as Sirmione. Then again from February 25 they toured Trento and Riva, Brescia and Cremona. On the first of these excursions and on stationery from the Albergo Le Palme in Limone, Pound drafted an ur-Canto CXI dated 11 and 12 January,[15] a text that roughly corresponds to the lines in the published text of Canto CX, running from "And in thy mind beauty, O Artemis" to the Chinese ideogram chih[3] (C110/792–4). The text was a poem of defiance associated with an erotic epiphany ("and the long suavity of her moving"), but broken by the theme of jealousy ("that love be the cause of hate, / something is twisted"). It incorporated the prophetic cry of the Virginia beach bird, only to telescope it with the cry of "the auzel here," lamenting destruction and restlessness.

Shortly after this January composition, in the early months of 1959, Pound reconceptualized his material, shuffling it to open up the sequence to come. For a Canto CXII that would anchor the sequence he was writing, he gutted what I have called ur-Canto CX, extracting both the political material and the ritual suicide Na Khi material. That left, for inclusion in a transitional typescript Canto CX now in Marcella Spann Booth's possession, the Venetian opening and an anticipation of the suicide, the Artemis portion of newly composed ur-Canto CXI and the Connecticut charter material from the little St. Elizabeths typescript. Experimenting later, between September 1959 and February 1960, Pound seems to have thought about calling the one-page Venetian opening Canto CX and trimming ur-Canto CXI to its first ["Artemis"] page. This is the configuration of a draft he sent to Craig La Drière and which is now among La Drière's papers at the Houghton Library, Harvard. The draft is especially notable because it is partly made out of early typescript leaves.

By moving his political material from CX to CXII, Pound cleared the way for an early typescript of Canto CXIII which begins with the jealousy theme from the Lake Garda ur-Canto CXI and bears the dates "5 Feb." [1959], "March 1959,"[16] and "19th May '59." After some further rearrangements (Pound would finally insert the lines about jealousy into Canto CX, shift "Thru the 12 houses of heaven" from the second to the first half of CXIII and remove the lines ending "To be men not destroyers" to a later canto), the substance of this early typescript would remain. Its roots in Pound's distress over the friction between Dorothy and Marcella can be confirmed by Dorothy's diaries, which record a "commotion" after an entry about Marcella on February 16th. (A bit later, on the first of May, Daniel Cory visited and noted Dorothy's apparently "frosty" feelings toward her.[17])

By then Brunnenburg had become impossible. One obvious alternative was Rapallo, where Pound and Dorothy had spent most of the years between the wars and where many of Pound's belongings still remained at Casa 60, Olga Rudge's little house in Sant' Ambrogio on the cliffs above the city. According to Dorothy's diaries, Pound, Dorothy, and Marcella first settled into Albergo Grande Italia & Lido in Rapallo on March 20th. The tension between them quieted some. It was still tangible enough for Pound to deplore human possessiveness in the next canto of the unfolding sequence ("114"): "These simple men who have fought against jealousy, / as the man of Oneida. Ownership! Ownership!" Besides remembering "good guys in [Pound's] family," this canto dwells on "kindness." Yet the themes of isolated and beleaguered excellence persist, both in the passing of Pound's good-guy relatives and in the fragility of the beauty which Pound notes Marcella observing. Canto CXIV would survive almost intact into *Drafts & Fragments*. A notebook containing a manuscript of the last half of it exists in Marcella Spann Booth's collection and bears the dates July 14th and 23rd. The first half can be dated from a reference to triangular spaces in Giordano Bruno, whose work Pound mentions in letters to Norman Holmes Pearson on June 2, 1959, and to Harry Meacham on 14 June 1959.[18]

Meanwhile, Pound had begun to go up the hill to Casa 60. Sorting out old papers would be one of his primary activities that summer. Even that, however, did not prove to be easy. Distressed by the experience of reencountering his wartime habitation, Pound, Dorothy's diary tells us, was constantly at the doctors or the hospital for x-rays and injections. On the 21st of June the proofs came for *Thrones*. Then Dorothy records a trip that reenacted Pound's 1945 relocation from Sant' Ambrogio to the site of his prison cage at Pisa. Pound, Dorothy, and Marcella left on June 29th, reached Pisa by noon, went on that afternoon to Florence, continued on July 1st to Perugia, then on July 3rd to Assisi and back, and on July 4th to Rome. In Rome they toured (Dorothy mentions Santa Maria in "Cosmedin" and "S. Sabina") and returned via La Spezia to Rapallo on the 7th. By that time Pound was up to finishing the *Thrones* proofs.

Then, in hopes of an easier arrangement, the three moved from the Albergo to an apartment, but the rhythm of their unhappiness did not change. There was, according to Dorothy, a "tempest in a teapot" on the 26th of July, and through August Pound continued to sort files and receive injections. Dorothy also writes in her diary that Pound found a file of Wyndham Lewis letters, a discovery which seems to have spurred a striking new canto, "115," which Pound wrote in a notebook now in Marcella Spann Booth's possession. I give the text of the typescript she later made from it (now at Yale):

> The scientists are in terror
>   and the european mind stops.
>   Su! coraggio.
>   do not accept it.
>   Tan [pictograph] the dawn
>   somewhere.
> Wyndham taking blindness, rather than risk having his mind stop.
> A bronze dawn, bright russet—but dawn of some sort
>   _____and some how.

There is so much beauty.
>How can we harden our hearts?
A beautiful night under wind mid Garofani.
>That wind wd be?
>>>Apeliota.
Do not move
>let the wind speak
>>That is Paradise
The petals are almost still.
[. . . .]
The beauty of my thought has not entered them.
>That is, it has as but a flash in far darkness—
I have tried to write Paradise—
>let the Gods forgive what I have made.
>Let those I love try to forgive what I have made.
Mozart, Linaeus—
>>Sulmona
>out of dust—
>>>out of dust,
>>The gold thread in dark pattern at Torcello.
The wall still stands.
>>There is a path by a field almost empty.
Ub. '43
>"God damn it,
>>it is your future utility
I am thinking of."
>'45:
>>"fa un affare,"
he said, "chi muore oggi."
>>>Since when has been action.
Poiché 'l superb' Ilion
>>and Europe crashed without Maud's assistance
(ref. Yeats on burning)
>and to get this into simple language,
and not transmit private discouragements.
>The gt inscription: @ Behistien
>>"They LIED."
which the arcivescovo thinks, as Ari. sd. about something
>>or other (monopoly,
>>>Thales)

common practice.
m'amour
          ma vie
m'amour
          ma vi'
for the blue flash and the moments,
          benedetta Marcella,
the young for the old
                    That is tragedy.
And for one beautiful day there was peace.
          Brancusi's bird
                              in the hollow of pine trunks
or when the snow was like sea foam,
                         Twilit sky leaded with elm boughs,
under the Rupe Tarpeia,
                    weep out your jealousies
To make a church
                    or an altar to Zagreus
          [. . .]
Son of Semele
     [. . .]
Two chicks without jealousy,
                              like the double arch of a window
or some great collonade.
Great trees over an avenue
When one's friends hate each other
                    how can there be peace in the world?
peccavi.
          Their asperities diverted me in my green time.
Their envies.
          Their paradise?
                    their best—
for an instant.
? to all men for an instant ?
                    Beati!
the sky leaded with elm boughs,
                    above the vision
                         the heart
"the flowers of the apricot blow from the East
                              to the West

I have tried to keep them from falling."
A blown husk that is finished

> but the light sings eternal

a pale flare over marshes

> where the salt hay whispers to tide's change

In this long and intensely personal prototype of the canonical "From Canto CXV" Pound gave new concreteness and poignancy to the themes of isolation and resistance that had been haunting him. In the background are Wyndham Lewis's 1951 decision to accept certain blindness rather than submit to an operation that might impair his mind, and his death in 1957.

Identifying with Lewis's fight against darkness and dissolution, Pound makes Lewis rhyme with his own resistance to history and to the jealousies of those around him. In this confessional text, his friends' "asperities" involve not only Lewis's early feuds, but the recent feud between Dorothy and Marcella; the image of Torcello, ruined and silent, rhymes with the aged Pound as well as the aged Lewis. Here Pound reaches out to moments of love and beauty in order to counter the darkness (as he had in Canto CX and earlier in *The Pisan Cantos*) and centers on a *cri de coeur,* "m'amour / ma vie." A great deal of the canto consists of private epiphanies of this kind, and their fragility shades the poem ever so slightly toward self-pity.

Very possibly Pound felt that the contrition which permeates "115" might facilitate a general reconciliation. In late summer 1959, however, there was no sympathetic magic in Pound's writing that could remedy the inevitable. As the situation between Dorothy and Marcella worsened, Pound composed a Canto CXVI (manuscript in the Marcella Spann Booth collection) which is very close to the one he finally published. He also composed a Canto CXVII (on one of the typescripts [in Marcella Spann Booth's collection labeled "117 (/? or whatever"]), which survives only in the typescript and which he later almost entirely discarded. Both are situated amid the tensions of seaside Rapallo and hillside Sant' Ambrogio; the latter a "nice quiet paradise— / over shambles" that required "some climbing / before the take off" (Canto CXVI). Never free from the depression Dorothy and other observers reported in Pound at the time, both advert to Pound's guilt over the unhappiness he had caused. Thus, in the manuscript and first typescript version, "Canto 116" declares "Charity is what I've got— / damn it / I cannot make it flow through / A little *love* [the word would later be changed to *light*] like a rush light / to lead back splendour." "Canto 117" was even more self-monitory: "I have been a pitiless stone— / stone making art work / and destroying affections." (Typescript at Yale.) Finally, Booth's typescripts include a version of a fragment Pound would finally insert into "Notes for CANTO CXVII et seq." It is marked "not cantos" (I quote from the published version):

> M'amour, m'amour
>> what do I love and
>>> where are you?
> That I lost my center
>> fighting the world.
> The dreams clash
>> and are shattered—
> and that I tried to make a paradiso—
>>> terrestre.[19]

Yet at the end of this sequence, Pound refused to succumb to the dark forces he portrayed. After Canto CXVII's bleak retrospective (later shifted into "From XCV")—"in meine Heimat / Kam ich wieder / where the dead walked & the living were / made of cardboard"—Pound drew a line underneath and inserted verses he said in a note could "be Finis if necessary":[20]

> Till suddenly the tower
>> blazed with the light of Astarte
> Genova the port lay below us.
> Miracolo di Dio
>> che amor riceve
>>> ne la calunnia
> ne l'invidia te toca.
>> Serena, neither pride nor pretentions to
>> ownership move thee.

In Dorothy's diary we find that on September 26, Pound was "in a fuss—re M[arce]lla" and that on the 27th Dorothy was "exhausted." By the next day, Dorothy's attorney Arthur V. Moore was relaying to James Laughlin that "Dorothy . . . is having a very worrying time indeed, and she feels that he is really too difficult for her alone, and that the young Texan Secretary [Marcella] says she is returning to the U.S.A. I gather E.P. changes his mind so often, and worries—and now says he wants to go back to Brunnenburg to die, and has suicidal spells."[21]

According to Dorothy's diary, the same day Moore wrote his letter, Pound set off for Brunnenburg. Dorothy would follow on the 4th of October.

II

To sum up: by September 28, 1959, Pound had composed a substantially polished typescript that included full Cantos CXII–CXVII and a long transitional "CX" fragment that included what would later become the first two sections of "Canto CX" and also "Notes for Canto CXI." This long typescript I will henceforth refer to as the protosequence version of *Drafts & Fragments*. But in September 1959, Pound could not will himself to finish his work. Relaying a letter from Dorothy on January 3rd, Arthur Moore wrote James Laughlin that Pound had allowed himself to be soaked to the skin and was complaining constantly that "his head is slow and hardly works at all—which worries him dreadfully."[22] His daughter Mary was so concerned she advised him to go south, and in January he went to stay in an apartment in Rome that belonged to his old friend Ugo Dadone, number 80, Via Angelo Poliziano. (Dorothy went back to Rapallo.) At the end of February, after two rocky months, he was visited in Rome by the young poet Donald Hall, who had come to interview him for *The Paris Review*. For four days, Hall treated him like a hero and eagerly sought out news of the continuation of *The Cantos*. The interview altered the history of *Drafts & Fragments*.

Though an admirer of *The Cantos*, Hall had been annoyed and perplexed by *Thrones* and was eager to see Pound break out of the style of their condensed political discourse. According to his memoir, he sympathized with Pound's intermittent interest in writing a Paradiso, and strongly registered Pound's moments of self-doubt. Pound read to him from the manuscripts he had so far composed. Hall enthused, and (as a back-door method of paying Pound for the interview) asked Pound to send fragments to *The Paris Review* for publication. Pound told him he would need to send his revisions to Mary to retype them, and Hall encouraged him to hurry.

Donald Hall has told this story in *Remembering Poets* (1978). However, we need not trust Hall's twenty-year old memories for the details of his appeal to Pound. He or his correspondents deposited letters at the Beinecke Library, Yale, and at the Houghton Library, Harvard (Hall also gave E.P. letters to the University of New Hampshire Library and still retains one post card). On March 22, 1960, for example, back in England where he was spending the year, Hall wrote Pound that "I have some of those lines from the next Cantos fixed in my head. I was terrifically impressed by them. . . . They are the paradiso, all right. They have the burst and power of the end." (Letter of March 22, 1960, at Yale. Hall's undated carbon at Harvard.) Then, several letters of reminders later, Pound sent Hall a first batch of seven pages of fragments and Hall responded on April 7th, "<u>Very</u> good to have the Cantos!!!!" "These are good examples . . . of the Paradiso. Is nothing of the vanity theme—or the personal passages yet printable?" (Letter at Yale.)

A month later, in the midst of an intermittent postal strike, Pound sent a second batch of thirteen more pages, following up with a letter and asking Hall to send him one set of retyped manuscript, and to send another to Laughlin at New Directions. Among the thirteen pages, he said, were "9 pages, numbered one to 9—the most finished, in fact quite a bit in final form." (Undated letter at Harvard.) I will return to those pages in a moment.

Hall was overjoyed that Pound (albeit reluctantly) had released his new poems, and in a long important letter of May 21st, told Pound "Reading these, and typing them, I have been continually impressed by them. The diction is very strong, and you are making it paradise. 115 I find extraordinarily moving. Perhaps 116 is the best <u>whole</u> long stream." (Letter at Yale, carbon at Harvard.)

The first batch of seven revised pages, which Hall received on April 7th, tells us something about what Pound was thinking, what themes Hall had promoted in his mind, and where the new sequence was going. Reconstructing from the letters and the typescripts, the package consisted of: the Na Khi materials slightly revised from the first two typescript leaves of "112" in the prototype sequence; a newly labeled "from 111,"[23] descended from the early "Connecticut Charter" draft and recently pulled from the second half of Pound's transitional "CX"; the two-page "116," only slightly revised; a page of fragments drawn from "114" and "115" with the heading "114;" and the middle page of the confessional proto-"115" containing "m'amour/ma vie." (See Appendix.)

Significantly, in what Hall received in April Pound had left out the "vanity" lines from "115" ("I have tried to write Paradise"), and Hall was disappointed. But—urged on by Hall's taste for paradisal landscape—Pound had omitted the political material in 112 and given prominence to the Na Khi materials well beyond what they had possessed. And, buoyed by Hall's praise, Pound had chosen to make public the self-questioning Canto 116, perhaps already deciding it would become the last finished Canto in the sequence.

In May Hall received a second batch of thirteen typescript leaves, and in his letter of May 21 ecstatically confirmed his receipt of what Pound had designated a nearly final sequence of nine pages carrying authorized page numberings. Again reconstructing from the letters and accompanying manuscripts (Hall's letter contains a long list of small editorial questions keyed to alphabetical characters he had inscribed on the pages of both sets of typescripts), Hall had received more than a single sequence, since some pages appeared in slightly different versions. (For a tabular account, see Appendix.) The thirteen typescript pages consisted of the following: *pages 1 & 2:* two leaves of a "CX" drawn from transitional "CX" and consisting of (*page 1*) Venice plus the Na Khi suicide, and (*page 2*) "And in thy mind beauty" (first composed for ur-Canto 111); *page 3:* and third section of Canto CX, containing the jealousy lines "That love be the cause of hate" originally composed for ur-Canto 111 and then placed in the proto-sequence 113; *page 4:* the second movement of the proto-sequence 113 ("Then a partridge shaped cloud"); *page 5:* the Na Khi suicide in its "112" form; *page 6:* the fifth typescript leaf of the proto-sequence 113, to become the first page of the canonical "CXIII"; *page 7:* the typescript leaf of the proto-sequence 112 ("owl and wagtail," labeled "CXII" and eventually to become "From Canto CXII"); *pages 8 & 9:* a revised version of the proto-sequence 116. Pound also included (*pages 10 & 11*) variants of pages 1 and 2; and he enclosed as *page 12* a variant of "from 111." Finally he included (*page 13*) the first appearance of a shortened and revised "115," ultimately to become the canonical "From CXV."

In short, to produce his authorized nine pages, Pound had torn his proto-sequence apart. Among other things, he had transformed Canto CX, splitting his transitional Canto CX by retaining the Venice and Na Khi material and transferring the Connecticut Charter lines to make a new "From CXI," then adding material to CX from the proto-sequence 113. When he finished, Canto CX had nearly attained its final form.

In tandem Pound made drastic cuts in Canto 112, removing the political material and leaving the ceremony-of-heaven Na Khi material he did not absorb into Canto CX. Hence the present lyrical but truncated "From CXII." He also reorganized what remained of CXIII, sending Hall only the lines from "Thru the 12 Houses of Heaven" to "does not mean one, oh, four, 104%." Later, much that remained of the longer interim draft (minus the lines about jealousy that were absorbed into CX) would return. And, in the thirteen new pages, Pound retained very little of Cantos CXIV and CXV. No part of them appears in the authorized nine pages. However, in the four pages that accompanied the authorized nine, we find the first draft of what would become "From CXV." This revised, smaller "115" tells a story in itself. I give the Harvard text:

> The scientists are in terror
>   and the European mind stops
> Wyndham Lewis accepted blindness

> rather than have his mind stop
> night under wind mid garofani
> > the petals are almost still
> Mozart, Linnaeus, Sulmona,
> When one[']s friends hate each other
> > how can there be peace in the world
> Their asperities diverted me in my green time.
>
> A blown husk that is finished
> > but the light sings eternal
> a pale flare over marshes
> > Where the salt hay whispers to tide's change
> Time, space,
> > neither life nor death is the answer.
> and of men seeking good,
> > doing evil.
> in meine Heimat
> > where the dead walked
> > > and the living were made of cardboard

Momentarily swayed by Hall's enthusiasm for self-questioning and paradisal landscape, Pound had finally resisted. Abandoning the paradisal landscape Hall so admired, this version of CXV is less personal and more pessimistic than its predecessor. True, it begins like the earlier text by celebrating Lewis's courage. But in the earlier, more sentimental poem Pound had moved from the beauty of Lewis's act and the natural beauty of the benevolent wind, Apeliota, to a "Paradise" he unhesitatingly affirmed, even as he was compelled to confess that his own attempts "to write Paradise" required forgiveness. In the new, shorter version, to quote Timothy Materer, the elegy "darkens."[24] That is, Pound causes Lewis's rebarbative resistance to align itself with the night wind against the peaceful petals of the carnation, and against the achieved serenity of the work of Mozart, Linnaeus and Ovid. What had started as Pound's affirmation of Lewis's energy turns into a questioning of Lewis's hate, and youth's diversions appear all the more wasteful from the perspective of "a blown husk that is finished." Lewis's disputations over time and space in *Time and Western Man* provided no answers, and here Pound suggests that his own categories were no more adequate ("and of men seeking good, / doing evil. / in meine Heimat / where the dead walked / and the living were made of cardboard"). Hauntingly, though, Lewis returns in the penultimate line, becoming one of the dead who continue to walk.

Thematically, Pound's revisions of CXV are of a piece with the way he had fashioned his nine-page sequence. He had, after all, relocated the Lake Garda "jealousy" material from proto-113 to the new Canto CX in order to further emphasize the sombreness of the opening. He had also omitted the family material from "114," rejecting its easy pride for the moment. And by making CXIV and CXV less personal and less sentimental, he underscored the confessional moments of Canto CXVI, which however, would end with a qualified assertion much like Canto LXXXI's "error is all in the not done, / all in the diffidence that faltered" (C81/536). I quote the revised Hall text at Harvard:

> To confess wrong without losing rightness?
> Charity I have had sometimes,
>   I cannot make it flow thru.
> A little light like a rush light
>   to lead back splendour.

III

What happened to the text of *Drafts & Fragments* after May 1960 was by any standard extraordinary. True to his word, Hall retyped the sequence, sending one copy to James Laughlin and another to Pound who answered a first set of editorial queries about the text and Hall's interview, then stopped responding. Hall was frantic. He wanted to finalize publication of the cantos and the interview for *The Paris Review*, but that now seemed impossible. He only proceeded after September 24, 1961, when Laughlin wrote Hall that Dorothy had sent him a corrected interview which Pound had started to edit but, in Dorothy's words, "about halfway through" his "concentration gave out."[25]

Hall then worked as quickly as he could. In Summer–Fall 1962 (vol 7, no. 28), the Pound issue of *The Paris Review* appeared, containing among other things Hall's smoothed over interview and two cantos—"*from* Canto 115" and one of the "Canto 116" variants.

Over the next five years and with some help from Pound, James Laughlin placed other fragments of cantos in periodicals. By 1967 parts of all the cantos between CX and CXVI had appeared. For the most part these were variants of the revisions Pound had made for Hall and Hall had copied for Laughlin. There were, however, two substantive exceptions, and both of these involved variants of lines from the confessional proto-115 (the core line was: "I have tried to write Paradise"). One of them, labeled "Fragment from Canto 115," appeared in a 1962 number of the Belfast, Ireland, magazine *Threshold.* The other was part of a selection of small fragments entitled "Mindscapes" that appeared in the 1963 *National Review.* Among the fragments were twenty-four lines taken from the body of proto-115 and now separated into two distinct groupings.[26]

One way of thinking about the persistence of these kernels of the earlier sequence is to see them as a sign of Pound's reluctance to give up the confessional and paradisal colors he excised when he made the Hall revisions. (Pound confirmed his reluctance late summer 1960, when he asked Marcella Spann to send him a new typescript of the proto-sequence because his own copies had become confused. Obviously he wanted to reconsider his changes, and the *Threshold* and "Mindscape" fragments were a product of that reconsideration.[27]) Another way of thinking about these developments, though, is to say that between 1960 and 1967 variants of two distinct sequences circulated freely in Pound's thoughts and among the reading public. At that point, it became impossible to speak of an authorized text. All texts became reader's texts, including those reassembled by the aging and increasingly uncertain Ezra Pound. Given the circumstances, it could hardly have been otherwise. Because of the confused state of the manuscripts and a breakdown of communication, Hall himself had arranged Pound's pages, deciding on which was an earlier or later state of individual canto and sorting out the status of unlabeled or inadequately labeled pages in preparing what was to become the base text for most periodical publications. (He never understood, for example, the status of a page of proto-115 ["g" in the Appendix].)

Moreover, the two sequences were distinct in that they moved in different emotional and ideological directions. Though brooding and sometimes self-pitying, the proto-sequence took its coloring from intimations of natural glory associated with the mystical (and mystified) Confucian moments of previous cantos. In comparison the Hall text, with its radical revision of proto-115, was more thoroughgoingly sombre (too sombre for Hall) and more genuinely skeptical. Featuring an opening movement concerned with jealousy and wreckage and an increased appreciation of the power of the "night wind," the Hall version packed significantly more power when it came to contemplate man's ability to "go wrong / thinking of rightness." (Canto CXVI, common to both sequences.) Though less explicitly confessional than the proto-sequence, the Hall text more genuinely mimes the twisting and turning of difficult thought. In sum, although it is possible to talk only in relative terms, it is clear that the Hall revisions had taken Pound a long way from the tone and material of

Thrones. Just as clearly, this development worried Pound, as can be deduced from his growing reluctance to authorize a final shape to the sequence and from the way he persistently returned to the "paradisal" bits he had excised. In Peter Stoicheff's words, the text's "own dynamics had eluded his control . . . the poem had ceased to remain compliant, and had instead become adversarial."[28]

These artistic and ideological conflicts came to a head in 1967, and once again Donald Hall bore responsibility. He had lent a student a copy of his retypings, and two borrowings later it had been retyped and mimeographed into a pirated text—"Cantos 110–116," "printed and published by [Ed Sanders at] the FUCK YOU/ press at a secret location in the lower east side."[29] As in the "originals" Pound had sent Hall, the piracy contained a confused truncation of proto-114, and unwittingly included the new "From CXV" (simply called "115") following a piece of the old proto-115 and the last typescript page of proto-115. (The latter—"Ub. '43. . . . Or some great collonade"—was tacked on to the end of 113.) At that point and apparently with little sense of the critical issues involved, James Laughlin decided to put out his own text "fast . . . to try to stop some more piracies." "It was on the basis of this piracy," Laughlin wrote in the same letter, "that I was able to persuade Ezra to do some work in putting these Drafts & Fragments into shape."[30] The fact remains, however, that when New Directions wanted to bring out a revised text of *Drafts & Fragments of Cantos CX–CXVII* in 1968/9, Pound at first withheld his authorization. According to his daughter, Mary de Rachewiltz, she and Laughlin struggled to get Pound's permission in order to remedy the situation caused by the piracy.[31] He finally acquiesced (perhaps because Laughlin forced his hand), and his signature ("23 Aug. 1968/ Venezia") as well as his corrections can be found in a set of New Directions galley proofs now at the Houghton Library.

Nor is the ambivalence shown in Pound's agreeing to revise the suite and then holding up its publication altogether absent from the New Directions text. Building on the Hall version, Pound's revision for Laughlin restored important features of the proto-sequence: the long pre-Hall 114, for example, and more interestingly a conclusion that contained two 1941 fragments and "Notes for CANTO CXVII et seq." made up of two fragments ("For the blue flash." "M'amour, m'amour") descended from proto-115 and another ("La faillite") which is derived from the long typescript of the first proto-113. Pound could not bear, it seems, to omit these affirmations of light, love, and natural order (however qualified).

Not even then was the textual and ideological shape of the sequence ultimately determined. In the same year (1969) that New Directions printed its version of *Drafts & Fragments,* a magazine entitled *The Anonym Quarterly* published "CANTO 120" which presumably followed the three fragments of "CXVII et seq." In fact "Canto 120" was a slightly revised version of the "I have tried to write Paradise" lines from proto-115:

> I have tried to write Paradise
>
> Do no move.
>> Let the wind speak.
>> that is paradise.
>
> Let the Gods forgive what I
>> have made
> Let those I love try to forgive
>> what I have made.

The *Anonym* publication raised several portentous questions.[32] If these lines were intended to conclude *The Cantos,* they make a major difference. Though a recantation of sorts, they represent more of an affirmation. Out of the dialectic—out of the search—they announce a natural site of wisdom. In this light, Pound's decision to publish "Canto 120" reinforced the resurgence of the three "CXVII et seq." fragments. All four passages reconfirm the mystical portions of earlier parts of the poem and resist the skepticism of the 1960 revisions—exactly as Pound had resisted pressure to publish those revisions.

There remains the further problem that we do not know for sure that it was Pound who authorized or titled the *Anonym* publication. The magazine's acknowledgments page assigns the copyright to "Ezra Pound," but William Cookson, the editor of *Agenda,* wrote James Laughlin in 1973 that the *Anonym* poem was pirated.[33] If the latter is true (and a letter from Pound to Cookson exists in Cookson's collection that seems to verify it), it was not Pound but one of Pound's readers who had insisted on emphasizing paradise at the end of *The Cantos.* Yet, after the eight-year interplay between Pound as author, Pound as belated reader, and mediators like Hall, to say as much might be to enforce a distinction without a difference.

What happened next made things more vexing still. Three weeks after Pound's death in November 1972, James Laughlin inserted "Canto 120" into an obituary notice which New Directions placed in *The New York Times Book Review.*[34] Then in a 1972 reprinting of the 1970 collected *Cantos,* New Directions placed "Canto CXX" at the conclusion of the poem, capping the mysterious but apparently inevitable return of Pound's excised material which had originated in his letter to Marcella Spann in the summer of

1960. Peter Stoicheff, whose insightful account of the history and signifi-cance of Canto CXX I have been following, notes that Laughlin justified his decision on the basis of copyright alone, because no copyright had been recorded in the Library of Congress for either of the poem's serial appear-ances. Stoicheff, however, quite rightly goes on to speculate that this, like so many of the other interventions that altered *Drafts & Fragments,* repre-sents more than an accidental event. The decision to end the 1972 text with "Canto CXX" was a substantive editorial act which involved inter-pretative and aesthetic matters and corresponded "in its own way to what its editor(s) vainly hoped Pound intended, or to what they thought *The Cantos* requested in the absence of its author."[35]

Nor did the story end in 1972. As circulated in the collected edition, "Canto CXX" was greeted by some as a small miracle. While Pound re-leased his grip on the poem, his readers—including not only the friends who thought they were helping to complete the poem as he would have wished, but also his detractors who were glad to have *The Cantos* end as they expected—instinctively supplied a reflex Pound himself had (for a while) outgrown. At the same time, another group of readers, including editors at Pound's English publishers, Faber and Faber,[36] rejected the new conclusion. The result was that New Directions was forced to rethink its 1972 decision and to experiment with an alternate one, so that, in Sto-icheff's words, "we have been given, over twenty-two years, at least six" significantly different versions of both *Drafts & Fragments* and the conclusion to *The Cantos.*[37]

THE HISTORY OF *DRAFTS & FRAGMENTS* provides a powerful example of the complex nature of literary authority and authorship in the twentieth century. Not only, as Peter Stoicheff has argued, is authority in such a case "interwoven" between author and mediator, but our common notion of authorship ill suits a situation in which conflicting author-formations fash-ion genuinely distinct texts. Nor, as I attempt to show in a longer work on Pound of which this essay forms a part, is the case of *Drafts & Fragments* unique, either in Pound's career or in the annals of modernist literature. The writing of Pound, Eliot, Joyce, Yeats, H.D., and Wallace Stevens took place in a contested aesthetic and political arena whose vicissitudes peri-odically reshaped the way these authors conceived and framed their writ-ing. Practically, this means that as critics responding to internally divided and/or remade texts such as *Drafts & Fragments,* we might want to entertain the heuristic fiction that there was more than one "Ezra Pound," self-constructed or constructed by readers over time, and that different versions of "Ezra Pound" are associated with variants of a single text.

Appendix

Designations Donald Hall Applied to Typescript & Used in Letter to Pound 5/21/60	Pound's Numbered Sequence (Numbers Inked on Typescript Pages)	Identification
First Package		
a		Proto-112, p. 2 (revised)
b		Proto-112, p. 1
c		"from 111"
d		116, p. 1
e		116, p. 2
f		"114" fragments (from Proto-114 & -115)
g		Proto-115, p. 2
Second Package		
h	version of 1, below	CX, p. 1 (from Transitional CX)
i	version of 2, below	CX, p. 2
j	3	CX, p. 3 (material once located in ur-111 & Proto-113, p. 1)
k	4	Proto-113, p. 2
l	5	Proto-112, p. 1
m	6	CXIII Proto-113, p. 5
n	7	CXII Proto-112, p. 2 (revised)
o	8	116, p. 1 (revised)
p	9	116, p. 2 (revised)
q	2	CX, p. 2
r	1	CX, p. 1
s		"from 111" (revised)
t	on one page	"115" (Later, "From CXV")
u		"Ambracia" (Extracted from Proto-114)

Notes

1. *Drafts & Fragments of Cantos CX–CXVII* (New Directions: New York, 1968. [Actually printed 1969.] Faber and Faber: London, 1970). Unless otherwise indicated, references will be to the eleventh printing of the 1970 text of the collected *Cantos of Ezra Pound* (New Directions: New York, 1989) in the form of canto and page number (e.g., C114/805). An earlier version of this paper was published in *Text,* 6 (1993).

2. On the difficulties of the text of *The Pisan Cantos,* see my " 'Quiet, Not Scornful'?: The Composition of *The Pisan Cantos*" in Lawrence S. Rainey (ed.), *A Poem Including History: The Cantos of Ezra Pound* (Ann Arbor: University of Michigan Press, 1997), 169–211.

3. For Peter Stoicheff's groundbreaking work on *Drafts & Fragments,* see "The Composition and Publication History of Ezra Pound's *Drafts and Fragments,*" *Twentieth-Century Literature,* 32, 1 (Spring, 1986): 78–94. Although my essay augments and silently corrects Stoicheff's account of Pound's composition, in general I follow the contours of his publishing history, especially as it has been revised and theorized for "The Interwoven Authority of a *Drafts & Fragments* Text," in Rainey, ed., *A Poem Including History,* 213–231. Professor Stoicheff generously sent me an advanced copy of the latter, and my indebtedness to him is apparent in my notes.

For Donald Hall's memory of the events recounted here, see his *Remembering Poets: Reminiscences and Opinions* (New York: Harper and Row, 1978). On Pound's failure to authorize the publication of *Drafts & Fragments,* see note 30.

4. Use of Dorothy Pound's diaries by permission of Omar Pound. Thanks to Richard Taylor for sharing copies of manuscripts Marcella Spann Booth made available to him for his research.

5. Cited in Humphrey Carpenter, *A Serious Character: The Life of Ezra Pound* (London: Faber, 1988), p. 859.

6. The notebooks, in order of mention, are 59 and 58 as Pound numbered the covers. Both are in the Beinecke. Stoicheff (1986) refers to the first but not the second.

7. Box 71. Folders 2754 and 2757.

8. The play is *Kakitsubata* as (very roughly) translated by Pound, whose introduction explains that the Iris represents "thoughts of the body of [a lady's] spirit." See Ezra Pound, *Translations* (New York: New Directions, 1954), p. 332.

9. To Huntington Cairns, quoted in Carpenter, p. 853.

10. To George Yeats, quoted in Carpenter, p. 853.

11. Beinecke. Box 71. Folder 2741.

12. Beinecke. Box 71. Folder 2756.

13. For the full context of Canto VI as first published, see my "Excavating the

Ideological Faultines of Modernism: Editing Pound's *Cantos*" in George Bornstein (ed.), *Representing Modernist Texts: Editing as Interpretation* (Ann Arbor: University of Michigan Press, 1991), especially pp. 71–6.

14. Mary de Rachewiltz, *Discretions* (Boston: Little, Brown, 1971), pp. 305–7.

15. Manuscript notes in the Booth collection, typescript in the Beinecke: Box 71. Folder 2751.

16. The latter only in a variant of the typescript proto-sequence that once belonged to Agnes Bedford, now at the Humanities Research Center, University of Texas.

17. Quoted in Carpenter, p. 857.

18. In the letter to Pearson (at the Beinecke), Pound writes, "[I] have just hit another treasure, i.e. Guzzo's 'Dialoghi del Bruno' with some very clear pencil notes by Santayana." The Meacham letter is quoted in Harry M. Meacham, *The Caged Panther: Ezra Pound at St. Elizabeths* (New York: Twayne, 1967), p. 167), p. 175. Pound there calls his friend's attention to "I Dialoghi del Bruno (i.e. Giordano Bruno) by A. Gozzi, with very interesting pencil notes by Santayana, who gave me the book."

19. *The Cantos of Ezra Pound* (New York: New Directions, 1989), p. 816.

20. On the back of Agnes Bedford's copy, now at the Humanities Research Center at the University of Texas. See note 16.

21. Letter of 28 September, quoted in Carpenter, p. 860.

22. Letter of 16 January 1960, cited in Carpenter, p. 862–3.

23. The *from* in the title is an autograph addition on the typescript.

24. See Timothy Materer, "A Reading of 'From CXV,' " *Paideuma*, 2, 2 (Fall 1973): 205.

25. Dorothy's words as quoted by Laughlin in a letter to Hall, 27 September 1961. (Letter in the Houghton Library at Harvard.) See also Hall, *Remembering Poets*, p. 181.

26. The penultimate "Mindscape" (with one line from the second) would become the "For the blue flash" passage of "Notes for Canto CXVII et seq." In the final "Mindscape" lines from proto-115 are joined with some of the "Ambracia" lines that had come from and would return to Canto 114/CXIV. A full publication history of these cantos can be constructed from Donald Gallup's *Ezra Pound:A Bibliography* (Charlottesville: University Press of Virginia, 1983). The first attempt to make sense of Gallup's evidence was Stoicheff, 1986.

27. A carbon of this typescript was ultimately deposited in the Beinecke Library with the rest of the Pound papers. The original, a second carbon, and some of the *Drafts & Fragments* notebooks are still in Marcella Spann Booth's possession.

28. Stoicheff, "Interwoven Authority," 224.

29. Stoicheff (1986), p. 88.

30. To Robert Gales, 9 September 1968, cited in Stoicheff, "Interwoven Authority," 215.

31. In conversation, 16 July 1991.

32. Stoicheff, "Interwoven Authority," 218.

33. Letter cited in Barbara Eastman, *Building the Temple* (Ph.D. diss., Oxford University, 1977), p. 210.

34. *New York Times* (26 November 1972), p. 42.

35. Stoicheff, "Interwoven Authority," 221.

36. Cf. a letter that appeared in the *TLS* for August 20, 1976, in which Peter du Sautoy of Faber and Faber wrote that Faber in its edition of *The Cantos* chose not to reproduce "the 'Canto 120' that appears in the New Direction edition as we did not feel certain that these lines were what Pound intended to come at the end of the long poem" (p. 1032).

37. Stoicheff, "Interwoven Authority," 221.

An Interview with Ezra Pound

D. G. BRIDSON

◆ ◆ ◆

D. G. BRIDSON OF BRITISH BROADCASTING Corporation first interviewed Pound at St. Elizabeths Hospital in Washington in 1956. Three years later he visited Pound in Italy for further conversations and recordings of the poet reading his poems. Bridson presented his edited tapes on three BBC Third Programme broadcasts in July 1959 . . .

BRIDSON: In many ways, Ezra Pound *is The Cantos.* No work of its time has been more hotly debated—praised, attacked, enjoyed, deplored, imitated—and avoided. Students of *The Cantos* probably remember the description of their structural form that W. B. Yeats once gave—when he drew parallels with the formal pattern of the Schifanoia Frescoes at Ferrara, and the structure of the fugue.

POUND: Well I thought that he'd caused a good deal of confusion by talking about a "fugue," and as he wouldn't have known the difference between a fugue and . . . what shall we say? . . . I mean to say, his idea of fugue was very vague so he can't have known what the hell I was talking about. And the Schifanoia Frescoes I discovered after I had done something similar. The Schifanoia does give—there is an analogy there. That is to say, you've got the contemporary life, you've got the seasons, you've got the Zodiac and you have the *Triumphs* of Petrarch in different belts—I mean, that's the only sort of map or suggestion of a map. No, the Schifanoia, that might give a clue, but I don't think Yeats knew what a fugue was . . . the analogy there would create more confusion than light.

BRIDSON: One of the carps sometimes leveled at *The Cantos* is that the "Chinese history" and "American history" sections make pretty heavy reading for most people. But whatever one makes of Pound's intense interest in Adams, Benton, and the other American figures that bulk so large in the later *Cantos,* there can be no doubt as to the magnificent poetry which he has made out of his attack on usury in *Canto 45.*

POUND: There is a turning point in the poem toward the middle. Up to that point it is a sort of detective story, and one is looking for the crime. The *Usura Cantos* would be more comprehensible if people would understand the meaning of the term "usury." It is not to be confused with legitimate interest which is due, teleologically, as Del Mar says, to the increase in domestic animals and plants. Consider the difference between a fixed charge and a share from a proportion of an increase. Now *usura* is a charge for the use of purchasing power levied without regard to production, often without regard even to the possibilities of production. The famous Medici Bank went bust when they started taking more deposits than they could invest in legitimate commerce and started making loans to princes—which were nonproductive loans.

BRIDSON: One of Pound's perennial insistencies is the need for accurate and established terminology. There is much in *The Cantos* on this theme, and he turned to the subject during our conversations.

POUND: There's the question of terminology, or the right words—using a word to mean what it has been generally considered that it ought to mean. Daniel Cory comes along and tells me there's a boy named Wittgenstein who's getting them all flummoxed in what he calls philosophy by twisting the meaning of words to something else. But there's a buzzard in the theology racket in America and someone says to him that the terminology is rotten and he says, "Oh, I can't bother about that, it's not in my field." "Not in his field!" And one of the most painful strains on old friendship is when the Reverend Possum Eliot comes along and defends this son of a gun. Well, I don't know what he is defending him for—maybe he knows some extenuating circumstance but he hasn't brought it out. And I would point out that this is the furthest possible remove from St. Anselm.

BRIDSON: For the record, I gather that "the buzzard in the theology racket" was Reinhold Niebuhr. As for Anselm, Pound had considerably more to say in his favor:

POUND: He was an interesting little cuss, he was, with a weak stomach. But he came pretty near to saying that theology is a grammatical exercise, and you can be damn well thankful to St. Anselm, because all your liberties back before "Maggie Carter," as they used to call her in the law schools in America—I mean the fight between him and William Rufus, the dirty bandit—all your liberties come out of that . . . and the mortgaging of Normandy and the swindles of the First Crusade and right on down to the murder of Becket. Well, I point out that this is where you got started.

On to Magna Carta, or on down to Cook, or Coke, who wrote the *Institutes* (I hope my friend Horton will get the chapter on Magna Carta reprinted before long). And why your Conservatives don't reprint Blackstone. . . . There was one of the noble lords of your country who thought about doing it and they found him stiff on the floor of his club. But there is a new edition of Blackstone and you'd think the Conservatives would go look at it if they wanted to conserve anything decent. Huntington Cairns did an article fifteen years ago in the *Michigan Law Review* and he said Blackstone was of interest and if you read Blackstone you'd get an idea that the real aim of law is "to prevent coercion either by force or by fraud." Now I won't swear Blackstone said that, but you might at least look at him and find out. And even the Reverend Eliot was admitting that Blackstone might be studied for his style—you might sneak him into the literature courses to show people how to write the noble English language when it *was* noble.

BRIDSON: Pound's attitude to life and living really adds up to the better part of *The Cantos.* In a very simple form, his attitude toward writing can be summed up in the next statement that he made to me.

POUND: You cannot have literature without curiosity, and when a writer's curiosity dies out he is finished—he can do all the tricks you like, but without curiosity you get no literature with any life in it.

BRIDSON: Pound's interpretations of history are often made in terms of semantic analysis.

POUND: Confusion is caused by package words. You call a man a Manichaean or a Bolshevik, or something or other, and never find out what he is driving at. The technique of infamy is to start two lies at once and get people arguing which is the truth. That is, somebody says two and two make three, and somebody else says two and two make six, and nobody gets a chance to give the correct answer. Now as I see it, billions of money are being spent to hide about seventeen historic facts which the copyists in the Middle Ages, or more recently, have been too stupid to cross out. Alexander of Macedon is too hot for a lot of the press. There's a kid named Carrega in Genoa who has done an intelligent review of General Fuller's book on Alexander, but some of the details of Alexander's life are unwelcome. Fuller wrote me that he'd seen the *Kuan-tzu* three years ago and that it was the best book on economics he'd ever read. A man named Maverick—symbolic name if you like—brought out an edition at his own expense and that is the absolute start of the history of economic thought. When Mencius and a few highbrows were objecting to Kuan Chung because he wasn't a saint, Confucius said, "You cannot judge a man like that as you would any bum who could die in the gutter and nobody know it." If it weren't for Kuan Chung, we'd still be dressing ourselves like barbarians.

BRIDSON: After reading *Canto 101,* Pound had some interesting comments on some of the economic theory which is included in it.

POUND: Now there are things there that I don't expect anyone to get if they come on them for the first time in that canto. What Rossoni said was *"cosí lo stato . . ."* that's where the state gets its cut, because Gesell, as a merchant, was thinking about nothing but quick turnover. Rossoni saw the stamp on the stampscript as a tax. Douglas said it was an oppressive tax because he'd probably heard only about the hooey out in Alberta, where the damn fools put a two-cent stamp on per week. And there are still people like Paul Peters who can't see that a 104% tax on money would be of no benefit to humanity. All those Gesellites who have gone off on that weekly stamp are all hooey. And another thing . . . I mean Delcroix, who was the head of the Italian Veterans—he was blinded and lost both arms in the other war—when he first heard of stampscript, he beat on his head with his little wooden artificial arms and said *"che magnifica idea"*— what a magnificent idea. He saw where it led to and he grabbed a telephone and telephoned to somebody to come over and hear about it. Most of these things I do get into *The Cantos* somewhere, and if they are calling me obscure, they had oughtta go back and look at the *Divina Commedia.* Dante'll give you a string of three names; when I give you a string of two names even, I at least give some hint as to why I'm talking about 'em. . . .

Ezra Pound

An Interview

DONALD HALL

✦ ✦ ✦

S INCE HIS RETURN TO ITALY, Ezra Pound has spent most of his time in the Tirol, staying at Castle Brunnenburg with his wife, his daughter Mary, his son-in-law Prince Boris de Rachewiltz, and his grandchildren. However, the mountains in this resort country near Merano are cold in the winter, and Mr. Pound likes the sun. The interviewer was about to leave England for Merano, at the end of February, when a telegram stopped him at the door: "Merano icebound. Come to Rome."

Pound was alone in Rome, occupying a room in the apartment of an old friend named Ugo Dadone. It was the beginning of March and exceptionally warm. The windows and shutters of Pound's corner room swung open to the noises of the Via Angelo Poliziano. The interviewer sat in a large chair while Pound shifted restlessly from another chair to a sofa and back to the chair. Pound's impression on the room consisted of two suitcases and three books: the Faber *Cantos,* a Confucius, and Robinson's edition of Chaucer, which he was reading again.

In the social hours of the evening—dinner at Crispi's, a tour among the scenes of his past, ice cream at a café—Pound walked with the swaggering vigor of a young man. With his great hat, his sturdy stick, his tossed yellow scarf, and his coat which he trailed like a cape, he was the lion of the Latin Quarter again. Then his talent for mimicry came forward, and laughter shook his gray beard.

During the daytime hours of the interview, which took three days, he spoke carefully and the questions sometimes tired him out. In the morning when the interviewer returned, Mr. Pound was eager to revise the failures of the day before.

INTERVIEWER: You are nearly through *The Cantos* now, and this sets me to wondering about their beginning. In 1916 you wrote a letter in which you talked about trying to write a version of Andreas Divus in Seafarer rhythms. This sounds like a reference to *Canto 1.* Did you begin *The Cantos* in 1916?

POUND: I began *The Cantos* about 1904, I suppose. I had various schemes, starting in 1904 or 1905. The problem was to get a form—something elastic enough to take the necessary material. It had to be a form that wouldn't exclude something merely because it didn't fit. In the first sketches, a draft of the present first *Canto* was the third.

Obviously you haven't got a nice little road map such as the middle ages possessed of Heaven. Only a musical form would take the material, and the Confucian universe as I see it is a universe of interacting strains and tensions.

INTERVIEWER: Had your interest in Confucius begun in 1904?

POUND: No, the first thing was this: you had six centuries that hadn't been packaged. It was a question of dealing with material that wasn't in the *Divina Commedia.* Hugo did a *Légende des Siècles* that wasn't an evaluative affair but just bits of history strung together. The problem was to build up a circle of reference—taking the modern mind to be the medieval mind with wash after wash of classical culture poured over it since the Renaissance. That was the psyche, if you like. One had to deal with one's own subject.

INTERVIEWER: It must be thirty or thirty-five years since you have written any poetry outside *The Cantos,* except for the Alfred Venison poems. Why is this?

POUND: I got to the point where apart from an occasional lighter impulse, what I had to say fitted the general scheme. There has been a good deal of work thrown away because one is attracted to an historic character and then finds that he doesn't function within my form, doesn't embody a value needed. I have tried to make *The Cantos* historic (vid. G. Giovannini, re-relation history to tragedy. Two articles ten years apart in some philological periodical, not source material but relevant) but not fiction. The material one wants to fit in doesn't always work. If the stone isn't hard enough to maintain the form, it has to go out.

INTERVIEWER: When you write a *Canto* now, how do you plan it? Do you follow a special course of reading for each one?

POUND: One isn't necessarily reading. One is working on the life vouchsafed, I should think. I don't know about method. The *what* is so much more important than how.

INTERVIEWER: Yet when you were a young man, your interest in poetry concentrated on form. Your professionalism, and your devotion to technique, became proverbial. In the last thirty years, you have traded your interest in form for an interest in content. Was the change on principle?

POUND: I think I've covered that. Technique is the test of sincerity. If a thing isn't worth getting the technique to say, it is of inferior value. All that must be regarded as exercise. Richter in his *Treatise on Harmony,* you see, says, "These are the principles of harmony and counterpoint; they have nothing whatever to do with composition, which is quite a separate activity." The statement, which somebody made, that you couldn't write Provençal canzoni forms in English, is false. The question of whether it was advisable or not was another matter. When there wasn't the criterion of natural language without inversion, those forms were natural, and they realized them with music. In English the music is of a limited nature. You've got Chaucer's French perfection, you've got Shakespeare's Italian perfection, you've got Campion and Lawes. I don't think I got around to this kind of form until I got to the choruses in the *Trachiniae.* I don't know that I got to anything at all, really, but I thought it was an extension of the gamut. It may be a delusion. One was always interested in the implication of change of pitch in the union of *motz e son,* of the word and melody.

INTERVIEWER: Does writing *The Cantos,* now, exhaust all of your technical interest, or does the writing of translations, like the *Trachiniae* you just mentioned, satisfy you by giving you more fingerwork?

POUND: One sees a job to be done and goes at it. The *Trachiniae* came from reading the Fenollosa Noh plays for the new edition, and from wanting to see what would happen to a Greek play, given that same medium and the hope of its being performed by the Minorou company. The sight of *Cathay* in Greek, looking like poetry, stimulated crosscurrents.

INTERVIEWER: Do you think that free verse is particularly an American form? I imagine that William Carlos Williams probably does, and thinks of the iambic as English.

POUND: I like Eliot's sentence: "No verse is *libre* for the man who wants to do a good job." I think the best free verse comes from an attempt to get back to quantitative meter.

I suppose it may be *un-English* without being specifically *American.* I remember Cocteau playing drums in a jazz band as if it were a very difficult mathematical problem.

I'll tell you a thing that I think *is* an American form, and that is the Jamesian parenthesis. You realize that the person you are talking to hasn't got the different steps, and you go back over them. In fact the Jamesian Parenthesis has immensely increased now. That I think is something that is definitely American. The struggle that one has when one meets another man who has had a lot of experience to find the point where the two experiences touch, so that he really knows what you are talking about.

INTERVIEWER: Your work includes a great range of experience, as well as of form. What do you think is the greatest quality a poet can have? Is it formal, or is it a quality of thinking?

POUND: I don't know that you can put the needed qualities in hierarchic order, but he must have a continuous curiosity, which of course does not make him a writer, but if he hasn't got that he will wither. And the question of doing anything about it depends on a persistent energy. A man like Agassiz is never bored, never tired. The transit from the reception of stimuli to the recording, to the correlation, that is what takes the whole energy of a lifetime.

INTERVIEWER: Do you think that the modern world has changed the ways in which poetry can be written?

POUND: There is a lot of competition that never was there before. Take the serious side of Disney, the Confucian side of Disney. It's in having taken an ethos, as he does in *Perri,* that squirrel film, where you have the values of courage and tenderness asserted in a way that everybody can understand. You have got an absolute genius there. You have got a greater correlation of nature than you have had since the time of Alexander the Great. Alexander gave orders to the fishermen that if they found out anything about fish that was interesting, a specific thing, they were to tell Aristotle. And with that correlation you got ichthyology to the scientific point where it stayed for two thousand years. And now one has got with the camera an *enormous* correlation of particulars. That capacity for making contact is a tremendous challenge to literature. It throws up the question of what needs to be done and what is superfluous.

INTERVIEWER: Maybe it's an opportunity, too. When you were a young man in particular, and even through *The Cantos,* you changed your poetic style again and again. You have never been content to stick anywhere. Were you consciously looking to extend your style? Does the artist *need* to keep moving?

POUND: I think the artist *has* to keep moving. You are trying to render life in a way that won't bore people and you are trying to put down what you see . . .

INTERVIEWER: The political action of yours that everybody remembers is your broadcasts from Italy during the war. When you gave these talks, were you conscious of breaking the American law?

POUND: No, I was completely surprised. You see I had that promise. I was given the freedom of the microphone twice a week. "He will not be asked to say anything contrary to his conscience or contrary to his duty as an American citizen." I thought that covered it.

INTERVIEWER: Doesn't the law of treason talk about "giving aid and comfort to the enemy," and isn't the enemy the country with whom we are at war?

POUND: I thought I was fighting for a Constitutional point. I mean to say, I may have been completely nuts, but I certainly *felt* that it wasn't committing treason.

Wodehouse went on the air and the British asked him not to. Nobody asked me not to. There was no announcement until the collapse that the people who had spoken on the radio would be prosecuted.

Having worked for years to prevent war, and seeing the folly of Italy and America being at war—! I certainly wasn't telling the troops to revolt. I thought I was fighting an internal question of constitutional government. And if any man, any individual man, can say he has had a bad deal from me because of race, creed, or color, let him come out and state it with particulars. The *Guide to Kulchur* was dedicated to Basil Bunting and Louis Zukofsky, a Quaker and a Jew.

I don't know whether you think the Russians ought to be in Berlin or not. I don't know whether I was doing any good or not, whether I was doing any harm. Oh, I was probably offside. But the ruling in Boston was that there is no treason without treasonable intention.

What I was right about was the conservation of individual rights. If when the executive, or any other branch, exceeds its legitimate powers, no one protests, you will lose all your liberties. My method of opposing tyranny was wrong over thirty-year period; it had nothing to do with the Second World War in particular. If the individual, or heretic, gets hold of some essential truth, or sees some error in the system being practiced, he commits so many marginal errors himself that he is worn out before he can establish his point.

The world in twenty years has piled up hysteria—anxiety over a third war, bureaucratic tyranny, and hysteria from paper forms. The immense and undeniable loss of freedoms, as they were in 1900, is undeniable. We have seen the acceleration in efficiency of the tyrannizing factors. It's enough to keep a man worried. Wars are made to make debt. I suppose there's a possible out in space satellites and other ways of making debt.

INTERVIEWER: When you were arrested by the Americans, did you then expect to be convicted? To be hanged?

POUND: At first I puzzled over having missed a cog somewhere. I expected to turn myself in and to be asked about what I learned. I did and I wasn't. I know that I checked myself, on several occasions during the broadcasts, on reflecting that it was not up to me to do certain things, or to take service with a foreign country. Oh, it was paranoia to think one could argue against the usurpations, against the folks who got the war started to get America into it. Yet I hate the idea of obedience to something which is wrong.

Then later I was driven in to the courtyard at Chiavari. They had been shooting them, and I thought I was finished then and there. Then finally a guy came in and said he was damned if he would hand me over to the Americans unless I wanted to be handed over to them.

INTERVIEWER: In 1942, when the war started for America, I understand you tried to leave Italy and come back to the United States. What were the circumstances of the refusal?

POUND: Those circumstances were by hearsay. I am a bit hazy in my head about a considerable period, and I think that . . . I know that I had a chance to get as far as Lisbon, and be cooped up there for the rest of the war.

INTERVIEWER: Why did you want to get back to the States at that time?

POUND: I wanted to get back during the election, before the election.

INTERVIEWER: The election was in 1940, wasn't it?

POUND: That would be 1940. I don't honestly remember what happened. My parents were too old to travel. They would have had to stay there in Rapallo. Dad retired there on his pension.

INTERVIEWER: During those years in the war in Italy did you write poetry? The *Pisan Cantos* were written when you were interned. What did you write during those years?

POUND: Arguments, arguments, and arguments. Oh, I did some of the Confucius translation.

INTERVIEWER: How was it that you began to write poetry again only after you were interned? You didn't write any cantos at all during the war, did you?

POUND: Let's see—The Adams stuff came out just before the war shut off. No. There was *Oro e lavoro.* I was writing economic stuff in Italian.

INTERVIEWER: Since your internment, you've published three collections of Cantos, *Thrones* just recently. You must be near the end. Can you say what you are going to do in the remaining *Cantos?*

POUND: It is difficult to write a paradiso when all the superficial indications are that you ought to write an apocalypse. It is obviously much easier to find inhabitants for an inferno or even a purgatorio. I am trying to collect the record of the top flights of the mind. I might have done better to put Agassiz on top instead of Confucius.

INTERVIEWER: Are you more or less stuck?

POUND: Okay, I am stuck. The question is, am I dead, as Messrs. A.B.C. might wish? In case I conk out, this is provisionally what I have to do: I must clarify obscurities; I must make clearer definite ideas or dissociations. I must find a verbal formula to combat the rise of brutality—the principle of order versus the split atom. There was a man in the bughouse, by the way, who insisted that the atom had never been split.

An epic is a poem containing history. The modern mind contains heteroclite elements. The past epos has succeeded when all or a great many
of the answers were assumed, at least between author and audience, or a
great mass of audience. The attempt in an experimental age is therefore
rash. Do you know the story: "What are you drawing, Johnny?"

"God!"

"But nobody knows what He looks like."

"They will when I get through!"

That confidence is no longer obtainable.

There *are* epic subjects. The struggle for individual rights is an epic
subject, consecutive from jury trial in Athens to Anselm versus William
Rufus, to the murder of Becket and to Coke and through John Adams.

Then the struggle appears to come up against a block. The nature of
sovereignty is epic matter, though it may be a bit obscured by circumstance.
Some of this *can* be traced, pointed; obviously it has to be condensed to
get into the form. The nature of the individual, the heteroclite contents
of contemporary consciousness. It's the fight for light versus subconscious-
ness; it demands obscurities and penumbras. A lot of contemporary writing
avoids inconvenient areas of the subject.

I am writing to resist the view that Europe and civilization is going to
Hell. If I am being "crucified for an idea"—that is, the coherent idea
around which my muddles accumulated—it is probably the idea that European culture ought to survive, that the best qualities of it ought to
survive along with whatever other cultures, in whatever universality.
Against the propaganda of terror and the propaganda of luxury, have you
a nice simple answer? One has worked on certain materials trying to establish bases and axes of reference. In writing so as to be understood, there
is always the problem of rectification without giving up what is correct.
There is the struggle not to sign on the dotted line for the opposition.

INTERVIEWER: Do the separate sections of *The Cantos,* now—the last three
sections have appeared under separate names—mean that you are attacking particular problems in particular sections?

POUND: No. *Rock Drill* was intended to imply the necessary resistance in
getting a certain main thesis across—hammering. I was not following the
three divisions of the *Divine Comedy* exactly. One can't follow the Dantes-
quan cosmos in an age of experiment. But I have made the division between people dominated by emotion, people struggling upward, and those
who have some part of the divine vision. The thrones in Dante's *Paradiso*
are for the spirits of the people who have been responsible for good gov-

ernment. The thrones in *The Cantos* are an attempt to move out from egoism and to establish some definition of an order possible or at any rate conceivable on earth. One is held up by the low percentage of reason which seems to operate in human affairs. *Thrones* concerns the states of mind of people responsible for something more than their personal conduct.

INTERVIEWER: Now that you come near the end, have you made any plans for revising *The Cantos,* after you've finished?

POUND: I don't know. There's need of elaboration, of clarification, but I don't know that a comprehensive revision is in order. There is no doubt that the writing is too obscure as it stands, but I hope that the order of ascension in the Paradiso will be toward a greater limpidity. Of course there ought to be a corrected edition because of errors that have crept in.

INTERVIEWER: Let me change the subject again, if I may. In all those years in St. Elizabeths, did you get a sense of contemporary America from your visitors?

POUND: The trouble with visitors is that you don't get enough of the opposition. I suffer from the cumulative isolation of not having had enough contact—fifteen years living more with ideas than with persons.

INTERVIEWER: Do you have any plans for going back to the States? Do you want to?

POUND: I undoubtedly want to. But whether it is nostalgia for America that isn't there any more or not I don't know. This is a difference between an abstract Adams-Jefferson-Adams-Jackson America, and whatever is really going on. I undoubtedly have moments when I should like very much to live in America. There are these concrete difficulties against the general desire. Richmond is a beautiful city but you can't live in it unless you drive an automobile. I'd like at least to spend a month or two a year in the U.S.

INTERVIEWER: You said the other day that as you grew older you felt more American all the time. How does this work?

POUND: It works. Exotics were necessary as an attempt at a foundation. One is transplanted and grows, and one is pulled up and taken back to what one has been transplanted from and it is no longer there. The contacts aren't there and I suppose one reverts to one's organic nature and finds it merciful. Have you ever read Andy White's memoirs? He's the fellow who founded Cornell University. That was the period of euphoria, when everybody thought that all the good things in America were going to function, before the decline, about 1900. White covers a period of history that goes back to Buchanan on one side. He alternated between being ambassador to Russia and head of Cornell.

INTERVIEWER: Your return to Italy has been a disappointment then?

POUND: Undoubtedly. Europe was a shock. The shock of no longer feeling oneself in the center of something is probably part of it. Then there is the incomprehension, Europe's incomprehension, of organic America. There are so many things which I, as an American, cannot say to a European with any hope of being understood. Somebody said that I am the last American living the tragedy of Europe.

Note

Mr. Pound's health has made it impossible for him to finish proof-reading this interview.

Selected Further Readings

Ezra Pound's Writings

Fenollosa, Ernest. *The Chinese Written Character as a Medium for Poetry*, edited by Ezra Pound. San Francisco: City Lights, n.d.

Pound, Ezra. *ABC of Reading*. London: Faber, 1961.

————. *The Cantos of Ezra Pound*. New York: New Directions, 1998. (See Preface, p. xxx.)

————. *Collected Early Poems of Ezra Pound*, edited by Michael John King. New York: New Directions, 1976.

————. *The Confucian Odes: The Classic Anthology Defined by Confucius*. New York: New Directions, 1959.

————. *Confucius: The Great Digest; The Unwobbling Pivot; The Analects*. New York: New Directions, 1969.

————. *Guide to Kulchur*. London: Peter Owen, 1966.

————. *Literary Essays of Ezra Pound*, edited by T. S. Eliot. London: Faber, 1960.

————. *Personae: The Shorter Poems of Ezra Pound*, edited by Lea Baechler and A. Walton Litz. New York: New Directions, 1990.

————. *Poems and Translations*, edited by Richard Sieburth. New York: Library of America, 2003.

————. *Selected Cantos of Ezra Pound.* London: Faber, 1967. (Pound's selection)

————. *The Selected Letters of Ezra Pound 1907–1941,* edited by D. D. Paige. New York: New Directions, 1971.

————. *Selected Prose 1909–1965,* edited by William Cookson. New York: New Directions, 1973.

————. *The Spirit of Romance.* New York: New Directions, 1968.

————. *Translations.* New York: New Directions, 1963.

Pound, Ezra, and Dorothy Pound. *Letters in Captivity, 1945–1946,* edited by Omar Pound and Robert Spoo. New York: Oxford University Press, 1999. This is one of many volumes of Pound's correspondence with individuals that have been edited, with annotations, in recent years.

Biography

Carpenter, Humphrey. *A Serious Character: The Life of Ezra Pound.* London: Faber, 1988.

Heymann, C. David. *Ezra Pound: The Last Rower: A Political Profile.* London: Faber, 1976.

Rachewiltz, Mary de. *Ezra Pound, Father and Teacher: Discretions.* New York: New Directions, 1975.

Stock, Noel. *The Life of Ezra Pound.* Harmondsworth, England: Penguin, 1974.

Passage-by-Passage Commentary

Kearns, George. *Guide to Ezra Pound's "Selected Cantos."* New Brunswick, New Jersey: Rutgers University Press, 1980.

Pound, Ezra. *Letzte Texte (Cantos CX-CXX): Entwürfe und Fragmente,* edited by Eva Hesse. Zurich: Die Arche, 1975.

Terrell, Carroll F. *A Companion to the Cantos of Ezra Pound.* Berkeley: University of California Press, 1980.

————. Volume II (Cantos 74–117). Berkeley: University of California Press, 1984.

Bibliography

Gallup, Donald. *Ezra Pound: A Bibliography.* Charlottesville: University Press of Virginia, 1983.

Criticism

Bacigalupo, Massimo. *The Forméd Trace: The Later Poetry of Ezra Pound.* New York: Columbia University Press, 1980.

Baumann, Walter. *Roses from the Steel Dust: Collected Essays on Ezra Pound.* Orono, Maine: National Poetry Foundation, 2000.

Bush, Ronald. *The Genesis of Ezra Pound's Cantos.* Princeton, New Jersey: Princeton University Press, 1976.

Casillo, Robert. *The Genealogy of Demons: Anti-Semitism, Fascism, and the Myths of Ezra Pound.* Evanston, Illinois: Northwestern University Press, 1988.

Dasenbrock, Reed Way. *The Literary Vorticism of Ezra Pound and Wyndham Lewis: Towards the Condition of Painting.* Baltimore: Johns Hopkins University Press, 1985.

Davie, Donald. *Pound.* London: Fontana/Collins, 1975.

Davis, Kay. *Fugue and Fresco: Structures in Pound's* Cantos. Orono, Maine: National Poetry Foundation, 1984.

Eliot, T. S. "Ezra Pound." In Walter Sutton, ed., *Ezra Pound.* Englewood Cliffs, New Jersey: Prentice Hall, 1963.

Flory, Wendy Stallard.*The American Ezra Pound.* New Haven, Connecticut: Yale University Press, 1989.

Froula, Christine. *To Write Paradise: Style and Error in Pound's* Cantos. New Haven, Connecticut: Yale University Press, 1984.

Hesse, Eva, ed. *New Approaches to Ezra Pound.* London: Faber, 1969.

Kenner, Hugh. *The Poetry of Ezra Pound.* London: Faber, 1951.

————. *The Pound Era.* Berkeley: University of California Press, 1971.

Liebregts, Peter. *Ezra Pound and Neoplatonism.* Madison, New Jersey: Fairleigh Dickinson University Press, 2004.

Makin, Peter. *Pound's Cantos.* Baltimore: Johns Hopkins University Press, 1992.

————. *Provence and Pound.* Berkeley: University of California Press, 1978.

Mancuso, Girolamo. *Pound e la Cina.* Milan: Feltrinelli, 1974.

Marsh, Alec. *Money and Modernity: Pound, Williams, and the Spirit of Jefferson.* Tuscaloosa, Alabama: University of Tuscaloosa Press, 1998.

Nadel, Ira, ed. *The Cambridge Companion to Ezra Pound.* Cambridge: Cambridge University Press, 1999.

Nicholls, Peter. *Ezra Pound: Politics, Economics and Writing.* London: Macmillan, 1984.

Rabaté, Jean-Michel. *Language, Sexuality and Ideology in Ezra Pound's Cantos.* Albany: State University of New York Press, 1986.

Rainey, Lawrence S., ed. *A Poem Containing History: Textual Studies in* The Cantos. Ann Arbor: University of Michigan Press, 1997.

————. *Ezra Pound and the Monument of Culture: Text, History, and the Malatesta Cantos.* Chicago: University of Chicago Press, 1991.

Stoicheff, Peter. *The Hall of Mirrors:* Drafts & Fragments *and the End of Ezra Pound's* Cantos. Ann Arbor: University of Michigan Press, 1995.

Surette, Leon. *A Light from Eleusis: A Study of Ezra Pound's "Cantos."* Oxford: Oxford University Press, 1979.

————. *Pound in Purgatory: From Economic Radicalism to Anti-Semitism.* Urbana: University of Illinois Press, 1999.

Tryphonopoulos, Demetres P. *The Celestial Tradition: A Study of Ezra Pound's* The Cantos. Waterloo, Ontario: Wilfrid Laurier University Press, 1992.

Wilhelm, James J. *The Later Cantos of Ezra Pound.* New York: Walker, 1977.

Wilson, Peter. *A Preface to Ezra Pound.* London: Longman, 1997.